W9-BBV-634

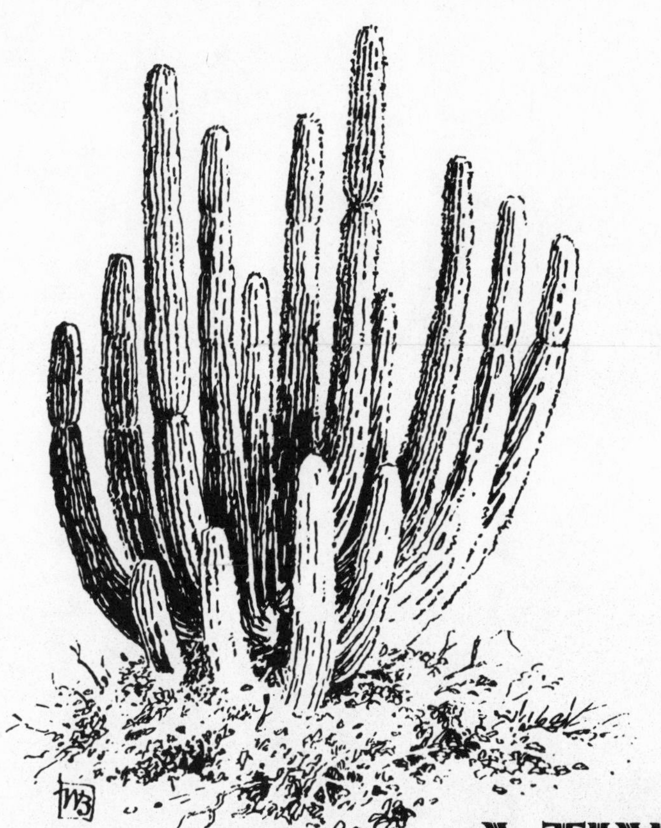

A TIME FOR HEROES

Books by Will Bryant

For young people:
Kit Carson and the Mountain Men

Nonfiction:
Great American Guns & Frontier Fighters

Novels:
The Big Lonesome
Escape from Sonora
Blue Russell
A Time for Heroes

A TIME

FOR HEROES

A Novel by

WILL BRYANT

Drawings by the Author

St. Martin's Press / *New York*

Grateful acknowledgment is made for permission to reprint material from the following source:

Webster's Collegiate Dictionary © 1916 by Merriam-Webster Inc., publisher of the Merriam-Webster ® Dictionaries.

 For information, address St. Martin's Press, 175 Fifth Avenue, New York, N.Y. 10010.

Design by Will Bryant

Library of Congress Cataloging-in-Publication Data

Bryant, Will.
A time for heroes.

I. Title.
PS3552.R898T5 1987 813'.54 87-4377
ISBN 0-312-00694-2

First Edition

10 9 8 7 6 5 4 3 2 1

Heroes All

Lawrence Tohill
Pal of my youth, born Alamosa, Colorado, 1922
Commander, Battery B, 90th Field Artillery Battalion
whose spirit left his body in the storm of battle
near the village of Kong Dong, Korea, 1952
Adiós, muchacho

Harrison Bryant
Once Sergeant, 7th Illinois Volunteer Cavalry
"Grierson's Raiders"
Soldier, pioneer homesteader in Oregon and Arizona
born 1833, died 1921

Charley Shattuck
California pioneer, 89 years old in 1940,
who went to his grave believing he had bested
the second law of thermodynamics in a fair fight

John David "Jack" Peggs
1860–1919
Cattleman, concert musician, prospector—
In these pages are the ashes of his campfires

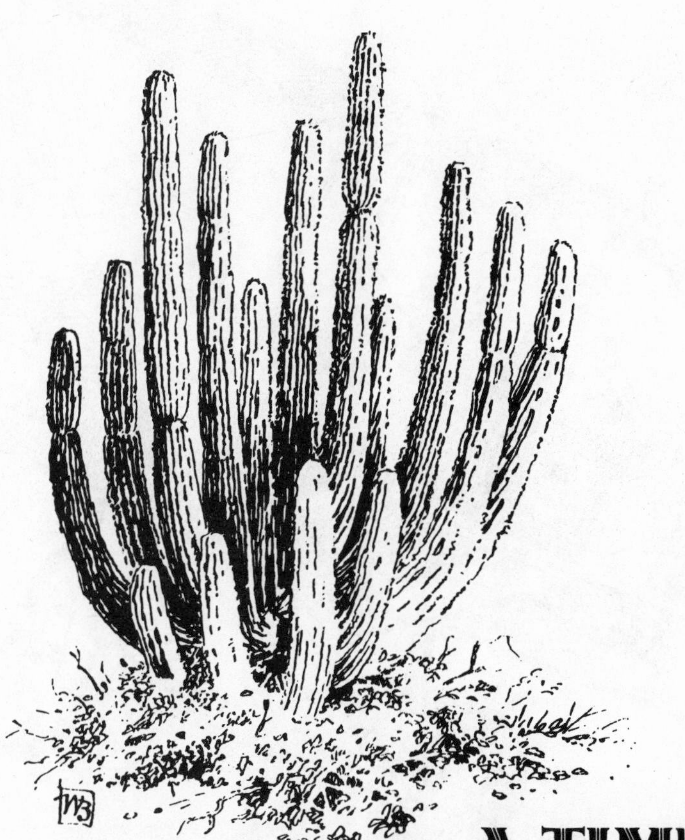

A TIME FOR HEROES

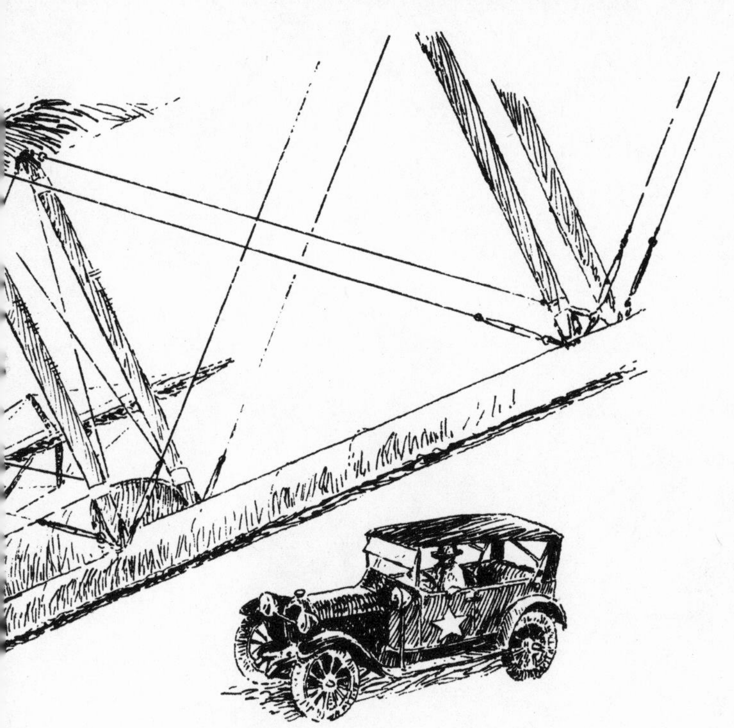

II

Chronique scandaleuse
[F.] A history, etc., that stresses scandalous details.

Enfants perdus
[F.] Lit., lost children; soldiers sent to a dangerous post; a forlorn hope.

—(From the *Foreign Words and Phrases* section, Webster's Dictionary, edition of 1916, the well-thumbed and annotated copy in possession of Othello Biggers, Master Sergeant, U.S. Army, Ret.)

1

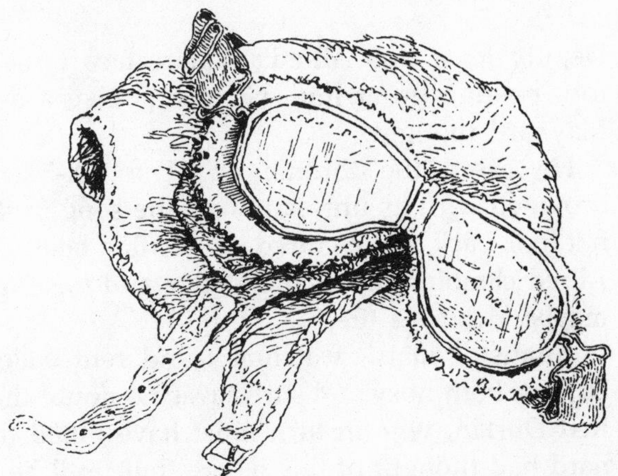

THE JENNY'S ENGINE coughed and missed all the way north from Hermosillo. Maynard Gaylen crossed the border not far from the brooding purple mass of the mountain called Baboquivari, staying well clear of the town of Nogales. He saw San Xavier Mission, gleaming white in the desert, when he was still twenty miles away. He stayed west of the mission and of Tucson itself until he picked up the Southern Pacific tracks and followed them in to the airport. The wind was from the southwest. He banked across the highway and made his letdown over the cemetery, the big OX-5 engine missing raggedly as he throttled back.

It was some kind of saint's day, for the graves were banked with flowers and fluttering streamers of brightly colored ribbon. Maynard lined the JN-4 up on the dirt runway ahead, amused to read the wind for his landing from ribbons on the graves of departed faithful.

Slight crosswind from the south—he throttled back, disregarding now the coughing of the engine. He could hear the wailing of wind in the rigging wires. Crabbing a little into the wind, he eased the heavily burdened Jenny down over the mesquite and tamarisk trees bordering the cemetery. Then he saw the Dodge touring car nosing out between two trees off the end of the runway. A star was painted on its door. He saw

Deputy Jesse Bob Allred's square face under the car's black top, peering up at him. Grinning? Like a dog sucking eggs, Maynard thought.

He eased the throttle on. The OX-5 coughed, caught, drowned with its unsteady roar the song in the wires. He did not look back, but pictured in his mind beefy Deputy Jesse Bob Allred climbing out of the Dodge and looking after him, then maybe kicking a tire.

August Willard, watchman and rent collector around the airport, both nosy and surly, was no doubt the one who called Red Durkin, who in turn must have called the deputy. Maynard had thought of this before, but until he actually saw the car with the sheriff's star on the door, it had seemed perfectly reasonable and safe to fly in and out of the airport, especially when the loads were, more often, such things as dynamite, fuse, caps, drill bits and canned goods for mining outfits here and there in the desert—the Tennessee Rebel, say, or the Silver Bell, or Zopilote.

The Jenny *felt* heavy, sluggish, especially with the engine cutting out. His load weighed about as much, he was thinking, as a couple of wing-walkers. No wing-walkers now, but lockers of thin plywood riding just outboard of the cockpit, their bottoms and covers curved to follow the airfoil of the wings. How deep? As deep as a case of dynamite or, in this case, three bottles deep, bottles of Napoleon brandy, Courvoisier, lying neck to neck and padded with cotton quilt batting. And the front seat was gone, the space occupied by a wicker laundry hamper holding another thirty-six bottles of cognac. All taken aboard shortly after daybreak this November morning in 1923, in a field outside of Hermosillo, Sonora.

The round eye of the fuel gauge stared at him, dancing with the rough beat of the engine. Maynard needed a place to land. Someplace with a road nearby, so he could get back to the Jenny with his Ford. And not find the lockers on the Jenny's wings ripped open, emptied.

The red mass of Picacho Peak jutted against the sky, miles ahead, one side of the peak smudged by smoke coughed from the stack of a Southern Pacific locomotive headed his way, pulling a seventy-car freight. Closer, he saw the big water tank at Rillito, a plowed field across the tracks from it. Tempting. Could land there, take the train to town, like a banker going to work. Meanwhile a railroad bull, bored with rousting bums out of freight cars, would poke into the Jenny's lockers.

Maynard nudged the stuttering Jenny into a gentle sweep north. The land, brush-stippled, scored by dry watercourses, swept up from the valley in a vast, broad slope to fetch up against the red battlements of the Catalinas like foam-capped surf, only the foam here was pale, shattered rock at the foot of the cliffs. A broad dry riverbed opened before him. Across the riverbed lay a long patch of once-plowed ground. It made a rectangular scar through thick brush and tall saguaros. An old homestead, he thought—a failed homestead, from the look of it. Adobe hut and rickety cow shed at one end, dilapidated house and windmill a half-mile away at the other, close to bluffs along the riverbed. And a narrow dirt road coming from the highway, winding through the thick pelt of brush and cactus, dipping into the riverbed and ending there at the house.

Maynard cut the throttle, dropped into a shallow glide, held her off the ground just above the tops of the tall saguaros, scanning the cleared ground passing beneath his left wing. Not so clear anymore, for low clumps of greasewood had grown back. But nothing else in the way, no wires, poles or trees.

He went on around, climbed a little, banked gently, lined her up—a touch of throttle, nose up. And she was down, rumbling, big tires crunching through scrubby greasewood. Ahead, the old cow shed, the ground clear of brush around it, horse-drawn plow and cultivator sitting there, sinking slowly into red earth. An old buggy sagged under a mesquite, two wheels collapsed, the other two going.

Maynard switched off the engine. The prop kicked through and quit. He pulled off his helmet and goggles and hung them on the stick and then climbed out of the cockpit and jumped down, a tall young man with sun-streaked hair, about thirty, wearing a worn leather jacket with ratty cuffs, high laced boots and an old pair of blue military breeches with a patched knee. Hot metal ticked behind the Jenny's brass radiator shell. The sun was warm on his shoulders and he smelled the sharp tang of greasewood and creosote.

He had that feeling he always had after a flight, of being a little unsteady on his feet, of relief, glad he was down again. He opened the turtleback locker and pulled out three picket pins, once cavalry issue, serving now to picket the Jenny instead of a trooper's horse. They were twisted like big iron corkscrews. He screwed one into the ground off each wingtip, one off the tailskid, and tied her down with short lengths of rope. The time a wind would start blowing was when an airman failed to tie down his machine.

He opened the laundry hamper and took out a bottle of cognac. He grinned to himself, thinking of the time a year ago when he had made a forced landing on a farm in Texas, offered the farmer a drink from the pint he carried with him—no load like the one today—and got himself roundly scorched with promised hellfire and brimstone, for the farmer was an unreconstructed hard-shell Baptist who forgave him not his trespasses. Maynard slept that night under the wing of the airplane, without supper and without a blanket. And next morning cleaned out a grit-loaded fuel filter and went on his way hungry.

Maynard tucked the bottle inside his jacket and set out toward the house, a half-mile away.

Gravel crunched beneath his boots. A big hawk with a banded tail glared at him from a mesquite branch. Suddenly, the hawk looked toward the house, then lurched, startled, into the air and banked away just as a shotgun blasted, *blamm-m*, and a charge of shot whistled through the brush a scant six feet from Maynard, if that. He froze. Mesquite leaves spun to the ground and a plume of sulphurous smoke drifted away.

"Now, goddammit, who goes there?" a cracked voice screeched. An old man in faded blue overalls, with white spiky hair and whiskers like cactus stubble, stepped out of the brush, breaking the action on a big old 12-gauge with Damascus-twist barrels. The empty shell kicked out with a *tonk!* sound. The old man thumbed another shell in and snapped the breech closed. Yellow smoke still curled from the muzzle. Maynard's bowels squirmed. The old man was *scary*.

"Move an eyelash, mister, and I'll blow your belly out."

"I'm too scared to move," Maynard said.

"Don't git smart with me. I want to see them hands in the air. Both of em."

One of Maynard's hands went up. The other held the bottle of cognac next to his body. He lifted the arm gingerly, the bottle rolling against his ribs under the leather jacket, slipping down. Seeing the bulge made by the bottle, the old man eared back a hammer.

"Son of a bitch. Heeled, are ye? All right, goddammit, take the piece out real easy and drop it."

Maynard carefully retrieved the neck of the bottle with two fingers and pulled it into sight, then held it out for the old man to see.

"It's a bottle of cognac, French brandy. For you, if you'll take it." Maynard's mouth was dry. "I had to land my airplane. The engine was cutting out."

The old man regarded him balefully. "By god, that's just the kind of simpleminded excuse I expected. You take me for some kind of idjit?"

"No, sir, I take you for a gentleman whose privacy has been disturbed, and I'd like to offer you a sip of brandy by way of a peace offering." Maynard twisted the cork. It came out with a squeal. He sniffed the bottle, caught the scent of cognac. Held it out, offering it to the old man. "It would be easier if we had glasses," he suggested.

The old man hesitated, then grunted and stepped back, but did not uncock the shotgun. "Mebbe so. Git out of the sun, anyway. But no tricks, git me? Bear this in mind—I know what to expect from you people."

You people? thought Maynard. What people? He walked slowly, carefully, toward the house. Out of the corner of his eye he could see the rippling shadow of the shotgun trained on his spine.

They came upon the house from the rear. It looked, Maynard thought, as if once there might have been fifty people busy doing different things—most carrying trash, though—and then something suddenly happened and they all threw down their loads and departed, leaving sticks, strewn scraps of wood, broken crates, buckets, paint cans, tangles of wire, broken-handled tools, collapsed barrels, scraps of harness, unmatched shoes and broken crockery.

The house was of adobe, the bricks showing through gaps in the cracked, stained plaster, scrofulous whitewash flaking away, sun-crisped shingles curling on the broad-eaved roof. Near it sat a weathered pump house and windmill, and an old T-model Ford flatbed with a piece of corrugated sheet iron for a roof. Near the pump house sat a sagging open-faced shed—a forge, Maynard saw, complete with a huge bellows and anvil.

The old man made him stand at the back door, holding it open while he, the old man, stepped through a littered screened porch, backing all the way, training the 12-gauge on Maynard. Glass chinked. The old man came back into the light carrying two glasses, motioned Maynard over under the shade of a big old mesquite. There were two chairs, a wicker armchair with a piece of canvas thrown over the torn cushion, and a broken-backed kitchen chair with a torn-out cane seat.

Wicker squealed as, with a grunt, the old man collapsed onto the canvas. A tarantula dropped out beneath him and Maynard flinched as it scuttled away. The old man motioned Maynard to the other chair and then kicked a weathered crate between them for a table. Faded stenciling on the wood read DU PONT EXPLOSIVES, RED CROSS EXTRA DYNAMITE, 60% STRENGTH.

The glasses were unwashed and dusty. Maynard blew at them without effect, shrugged and poured a half-inch of cognac into each, placed one on the crate. The old man leaned across and took it with a big bony hand.

"Your health, sir." Maynard raised his glass and sipped. Without acknowledgment, the old man took a drink, swished the brandy in his mouth reflectively and then, apparently satisfied, swallowed. His Adam's apple lunged up and down the ropy column of his neck. Disturbed whiskers bristled like the quills on a porcupine.

"By god, that cuts the dust, don't it?" he wheezed. He put the glass down with a thump and Maynard refilled it. The shotgun remained at the ready.

"Parlous times for a citizen, goddammit!" the old man announced suddenly. His eyes roved under deep frown wrinkles as he drank again. "Sons of bitches, there is nothing the bastards won't do! Lie, cheat, steal, or kill—it don't matter a damn."

Unsure yet of the identity of the "bastards," Maynard could only purse his lips sympathetically and hope he was not included among them.

Blue eyes suddenly riveted on Maynard. "So, it's your engine, is it? *Pah!*" He spat in the dirt. "Let's just keep the cards on the table, shall we? It may interest you to know that I know why you was sent here."

"I wasn't *sent* here, sir," Maynard said gently. "I was low on fuel and my engine was cutting out. I needed a place to land."

Ignoring him, the old man went on. "It aint enough they've got their heels on the necks of the people. Now spose you tell me who you are, or claim to be."

Name, rank and serial number, Maynard thought, and before he could catch himself he blurted, "Captain Maynard Gaylen"—and then stopped short of giving the old man his serial number.

"A soldier, you say?"

"Ex-soldier, anyway. Air Service."

"I done some soldiering myself. Seventh Illinois Cavalry, you want to talk soldiering. Never used to matter, Yank or grayback, goddammit, a man could talk soldiering." The old man took another pull at his glass. "Yes, by god, and know he was talking to a *man,* not a puppet bought and paid for, with them sons of bitches workin the strings."

"No one is working my strings, if that's what you mean." Maynard leaned forward and poured brandy into the old man's glass.

"Or so you claim. Money talks, a man listens. That's how the bastards operate."

"*Whose* money?" Maynard said. "Who are they?"

"Well you might ask." The old man cackled explosively. "Down the line, from the top, they're bought and don't even know whose money it is, but by god they do what they're told. Don't they?" He grinned suggestively and tapped his nose. His eyes were watery—whether from the brandy or laughter, Maynard didn't know.

"If that's the way it works," Maynard said, "it's a damned long time between paydays. I'm on no one's errand but my own, and if I make a dollar everyone's lined up to get a piece of it." Maynard wanted suddenly to laugh. He was sounding just like the old man. And he was thinking that having this kind of place to put the airplane down occasionally might not be a bad thing at all. "Look, can't we make a deal? I don't want anything you have except a place to put my airplane now and then, and I'm willing to pay you. Call it rent, say for the use of the shed and maybe the old adobe cabin out there near it, if I have to sleep over."

"Ha! You could keep your eye on me then, all right."

"That's half a mile from here," Maynard said, "and clear out of sight, with all this brush. I wouldn't have to come a foot closer if you want it that way. You'd have the airplane for security, too, so the way it works you'd be keeping an eye on *me*. Ten dollars a month, how would that be? And a bottle of this stuff now and then." He poured into the old man's glass again, gave himself a touch more.

The old man sipped slowly, eyeing Maynard over the rim of the glass. "Tell you the truth," Maynard said, "they're after me, too."

"Who?"

"You know." Maynard was fumbling a little. *"Them."*

"Them." The old man exhaled slowly. "Or their agents, right?"

"Sure, their agents."

"Sons of bitches!" the old man said savagely and slapped his skinny thigh. Wicker squalled under him. The shotgun wagged at Maynard.

"We could help each other," Maynard said. "A man gets tired of watching his back all the time."

"What do they want from you?" the old man said.

"I . . . I'm going to be strictly truthful about this," Maynard said. "I think I've found a man I can trust"—putting a little question on it so that the old man nodded, intent now, even eager, leaning forward a little.

"Go on," he breathed.

"A man might talk just because he's got a shotgun in his belly," Maynard said. "Would you believe him?"

The old man looked down at the 12-gauge as if surprised to find it there. He shook his head. "No, goddammit. I wouldn't." He put the gun aside, leaning it against the chair so the barrel slid against the crook of the chair arm. As if to confirm it, he drank again from his glass. "Go on," he said hoarsely.

"I've designed an airplane," Maynard said. "It's like nothing ever done before. That's why the bastards want it." He was beginning to enjoy the idea, working up a little outrage. "They're trying to get at me in the pocketbook. It takes money to build this thing, every dime I can scratch together, see? So I've been flying some of this stuff across the border to help me pay for it." He tapped the bottle. "Sure, it's illegal, but, the way I have to look at it, if the money doesn't go for . . . *power*, say, or high living, a man has to ask himself if the cause isn't worth it. Can you go along with that?"

"Damn right," the old man said, "if it's for the *people*."

"There you are. I went to land at the airport near town, and a deputy was waiting. My guess is, he's an *agent*, right?"

"Or the agents are just using the mizzerble bastard."

"So I had to land someplace else, and I can't tell you how grateful I am to find a man who understands what it's like. Can we make a deal?"

"Sow confusion in their ranks! By god, that's what we'll do!" the old man exulted. He tossed off an ounce of brandy at a gulp and tears ran down his cheeks.

They heard the car then, laboring up out of the riverbed. Stopping. A car door slammed. The old man scrambled to his feet. He snatched up the 12-gauge and trained it on Maynard's belly. His bristly face was mottled with sudden rage. "You've led em here, have you? Sons of bitches! I should've knowed!"

2

ALEXANDRA CLARK stepped out of her dusty blue Durant Star coupe beneath a big, sprawling palo verde. Carrying an orange crate full of groceries, she ducked low-hanging branches, walked toward the house. Skirting the sagging steps up to the front porch, she went on around toward the back of the house. She could have driven in the back gate, but last time she tried that she picked up a nail in one of her tires. She heard the old man's voice but thought nothing of it, knowing that he often talked to himself. But then she came around the rear corner of the house, and there under the big mesquite tree she saw him with a shotgun trained on a young man with sun-streaked hair whose face was chalky pale beneath its tan.

"Uncle Hector!" she burst out. "What—*is* this?"

The old man swung toward her, his mouth open, his eyes red and watery in his bristling buzzard's countenance. "Lexie!" he croaked. "Goddammit, Lexie, what a start you give me!"

"I suppose," she said tartly, "you expected the Confederate army."

Suddenly aware of the shotgun in his hands, he wavered, then raised the muzzle and leaned the gun against the wicker chair. The young man's hands came down slowly.

The box was heavy and her shoulders sagged suddenly. She stepped between them and put the box on the seat of the wicker chair. And saw the bottle of cognac, the two dirty glasses. When she stood, she could see that the old man was swaying on his feet.

"I thought you . . . I—" He stopped, clamped his lips in a stubborn line, hanging on to the back of the chair.

"We haven't met, have we?" she said to the young man. It was like an accusation.

"Maynard Gaylen," he said, still shaken at the old man's outburst, but beginning to take in the effect of her presence, sunlight darting through mesquite leaves striking coppery glints in her hair and dappling her face and slim shoulders, the navy middie blouse falling straight to a belted waistline somehow charmingly if ridiculously misplaced about her hips, the skirt falling then almost to her ankles, gathered so as to hobble her walk absurdly.

"*Captain* Gaylen?" Not very military now, she thought, his hair rank, wearing a cracked and dusty leather jacket, scuffed laced boots. His nose was slightly misaligned. "You're the aviator?"

He nodded. "I had to land out there"—a flick of his hand—"and I came here looking for a ride into town. This gentleman"—he paused and licked his lips—"mistook me . . . mistook my intentions. But we were working it out."

She looked at the bottle and glasses, and then at the shotgun. "I see you were." A smile tugged at her lips. "You've got the ride to town then, but first help me put away these groceries. And then I think Uncle Hector needs something to eat." The old man glared and looked away, offended, but not ready to argue about it. She put the cork in the bottle and handed it to Maynard, who spread his hands, not wanting to take it. She frowned. "All right, then, supposing I put it inside, on the sideboard. For another time?" It carried less a question than a stern reproof.

* * *

Lexie's Durant Star coupe fishtailed in the soft sand of the riverbed. She shifted down and gunned it, climbing out. A big mule-ear buck stared at them and then bounded away, spraying sand.

"You may as well know," she was saying, "I was absolutely furious to see him *drunk*. He could hurt himself."

"Or someone else," Maynard said. "I didn't mean to get him drunk, but after he touched off that shotgun I needed to . . . ease his mind, let's say."

Her frown smoothed and she laughed suddenly, shaking her head. "I'm sorry, but I can just *see* it, like something in a Charlie Chaplin movie."

"Terrifying is more like it. He took me for some kind of spy, wanted to know who sent me. I was just getting him to believe they were after me, too, that I was on *his* side, when you got there. That . . . set him off again. Is he always like that?"

"Not with me, no."

"Is he some kind of hermit?"

"Maybe he is. I hadn't thought of him that way. He's something like a great grand-uncle, or maybe it's great-great, on my father's side," she said. "We used to see him every year or so when I was little. And Aunt Hattie was still alive. He . . . it was all different in those days. Then she died, and my father died when I was fourteen and . . . I don't know, I guess we just *lost* Uncle Hector. One day last year, I had to go to Florence, and driving past that big riverbed made me think of him, so I turned off and—found him. He wasn't really starving, but close to it. He was catching quail and cottontails—in a figure-four trap, he called it." She brushed a curl of auburn hair back from her cheek. "So I've been coming out once a week with a few things. He eats a lot of beans, biscuits, potatoes cut up and fried in lard, things like that."

"Soldier grub," Maynard said.

"I suppose so. He was in the Civil War. He's close to ninety years old. I want to try to get him into an old soldiers' home or pioneers' home, something like the one in Prescott." The narrow track wound over toward the red and purple battlements of the Catalinas, then joined the highway. An open touring car sped toward town, a dust plume boiling in its wake. She turned the Durant after it. The town was visible then below them in the valley, still miles away and looking compact from this height, blocks of low buildings merging like brush strokes of ocher and white clustered close to the channel of the Santa Cruz in the broad sweep of the valley, with a veil of dusty haze hanging above it. And that plume of pulsing smoke from the locomotive he had seen out by Picacho was just now stitching its way into town.

"Where do you want to go?" she said after a pause.

"My car's at the airport. Anywhere near there would be fine."

"I've been meaning to look you up," she said.

Startled, he blurted, "Me? Why?"

"Because you run a flying service. I work for the *Courier* and I've been doing some historical things, maybe you've seen them."

"You're Alexandra Clark then. He called you—"

"Lexie, yes, for short. Anyway, I want to do one on the old Butterfield Stage that used to run through Tucson back in the eighteen-sixties, and I think it would be possible to see the old stage route from the air and follow it."

"Lots of roads out there. How would you know which was which?"

"Pick it up, say, at Dragoon. The old stage station is still standing. So is the one at Camp Grant on the San Pedro. We could follow it on through Tucson to Maricopa Wells where there was a terrible massacre once. What do you think? How much would it cost?"

"Depends on how far we go—how long in the air, that is—and how much fuel we burn. If it takes half a day, it might run fifty dollars." He wished he had said twenty-five—he didn't want to scare her away.

"That's a lot of money. We could talk to Woodie Craddock.

He's my editor. He might let me do it, but I warn you, he's pretty tightfisted." She laughed. "Anyway, how about stopping in at the office after you get your car?"

Five minutes later he was walking through the cemetery, smelling the fragrance from all those flowers on the graves, cutting across from the highway to the airport and to his own car. Deputy Jesse Bob Allred was parked over under the cottonwood trees a quarter of a mile away and didn't see him.

3

LEXIE CLARK was typing at her desk in the newsroom when she looked up over the tall carriage of her Remington and saw a man stop at the counter in the front office.

He wore a gray soft hat, and his suit—though it appeared to be expensive—was a disagreeable shade of greenish tan with a chalk stripe. The coat was too tight and was dark with sweat under the arms. He had an elbow on the counter and waved a beefy hand as he talked. She couldn't quite see his face at that angle, but his jowls were *engorged*—that was the word—clear back under his ears so that these meaty pads of violet-hued flesh actually bent his earlobes outward.

Something about him triggered a small icy avalanche somewhere under her heart. "You ever get really nasty first impressions?" she asked Woodie Craddock, whose desk was separated from hers by three feet.

"Starts inside, does it? Like an adder curled up next to your gizzard?" He went on typing, smoke curling past his freckled beak.

"How did you know?"

"Only kind to trust. . . . *And* the mayor extended his personal felicitations to the retiring chief"—Craddock's typing became rhythmic as he recited, ash dribbling onto his tie—"and now the old son of a bitch has to break in a new crony and thrash out the terms of the take."

"Take? As in on the take?"

"Did I say take?" Craddock's eyebrows elevated. "The bastard would take a red-hot stove."

"Which bastard, Woodie? I was talking about a hasty first impression." She looked again. The man was no longer visible.

"Either, actually. Both adept. Equally venal." His cigaret waggled on his lip. He darted a look at her. Woodie Craddock was thirty-seven years old, six-foot-two, 127 pounds, scholarly newspaperman of the old school who learned his trade on the Baltimore *Sun*, a lunger, gassed and shredded with shrapnel all in one day in France, the marks slick white, blending now unobtrusively into freckles, head, face, neck, one hand, the fingers hooked and curling. "But, what was this impression?"

"Bad news. A man out there at the counter. One of those people, you know, who looks like trouble just walking in the door."

"Now we're getting there. Trouble for whom?"

There he was—he had walked the length of the counter out of her sight and come through the gate, was entering the newsroom. And now she saw his face. The adder coiled next to her gizzard stirred. Struck. She heard herself gasp.

"For me. Oh-h, no! It *is* him!"

The man's eyes, roving, settled on her. He grinned, showing large yellow teeth, a big man, solid, pushing a paunch along beneath a striped tie.

"Tell me who, Lexie," Craddock said quickly, but the man was already there, reaching out, collecting her slim hand from the carriage of the Remington, holding it.

"Lexie, my dear girl. It's been jus' way too long." He moved as if to embrace her, but she stiffened her arm and that made him start to pull her in, hand over hand, like a fish. She braced herself against the desk, snatched her hand loose.

"No, it hasn't. It could never be too long, J. W." She flashed an icy-bright smile at Craddock. "My colleague, Mr. Craddock. J. W. Whitlock. Mr. Whitlock is—*was* my brother-in-law."

"Pleasure, Mr. Craddock." Whitlock took Craddock's skinny hand, squeezed it too hard, dropped it, grinning his affection for her. "Lexie, cain't we—I mean, where can we talk?"

"There's nothing to talk about, J. W."

"Cup of coffee? There's so much to catch up on. My son, and all. His mama. And you too, Lexie." He had a habit of peeling his lips back, baring those big yellow teeth in what he may have confidently felt was a warm and disarming smile.

"You're not going to see Jason. Not if I can prevent it." She moved papers on her desk, straightening them.

"My own boy? Got to see him, all there is to it. Pay my 'spects to his mama, too, visit the grave, see? Bygones with you too, y'know. Come on, hon, let me get you a cup a coffee, a Coke maybe."

Craddock stood up. "Look here, Mr. Whitlock, it's pretty clear, Lexie doesn't want to talk to you."

The lips peeled back. "Who ast you, pal? Lexie? Cup a coffee? Little family chat?"

"Whitlock," Craddock said, "we get, off the street from time to time, some mean bastard, mad we printed something, wants to straighten us out"—he hesitated, moved the big pair of scissors sitting next to the paste pot on his desk, thumped them down next to his right hand, his watery blue eyes icy through curling smoke—"and *most of the time* he's willing to drop it before he gets opened up and it all runs down his leg, if you know what I mean. Lexie, I apologize. Soldier talk."

"Woodie, don't—" Lexie started to say.

"Soldier, hunh," Whitlock said. The lips peeled back. "I knew it. I mean, I could tell. I done some soldiering myself. Rainbow Division. We could cut up some touches, I bet. The Argonne? Sure thing. Like to hoist a few with you. Matter fact, I been with two armies. Two *flags,* that is. *Three* wars. Believe it?" He chuckled, wagging his head. "Now, Lexie, bout my son. Couldn't we?—"

"All right," she said suddenly. "No, it's okay, Woodie. We'll go down to the drugstore for a few minutes. J. W.?"

Maynard Gaylen was coming in the door to the front office as Lexie and J. W. Whitlock approached it on the way out. Her icy smile surprised him.

"Captain Gaylen, I'll be with you in a few minutes. Go on in and say hello to Mr. Craddock, will you?" And swept past him. Maynard hesitated, then did as he was told.

She walked serenely ahead of him, chin up, a cold little smile on her lips. J. W. Whitlock, examining his ex–sister-in-law as he followed her out onto Congress Street, found much to admire in the way her hips moved beneath the low waistline, the way her navy skirt inhibited her slender ankles. Her auburn hair was bobbed in the new fashion, with a V showing on the nape of her neck. Her stockings were navy, too. There were little red, white and blue ribbons on her patent-leather pumps.

"No need of that, J. W.," she said, removing her elbow from his grasp at the street crossing. She led him into Noriega's drugstore on the corner. *Hablamos Inglés y Español aquí* was lettered on the glass door. Inside, a shoe clerk from Penney's on his coffee break was leafing through a copy of *Black Mask* at the magazine rack. There were four tiny round-topped tables with twisted wire legs opposite the marble-topped soda fountain. She sat in one wire-backed chair—the wire twisted in double loops like a carpet beater. The other one splayed alarmingly when Whitlock let his bulk sag onto it. As soon as he moved a knee close to her own, she swung sideways, crossed her legs and smoothed her skirt.

"Two coffees, Alvino," she said to the young man. The coffee came in thick china mugs. She watched Whitlock pour two teaspoons of sugar and a big shot of cream into his. He stirred noisily, left the spoon handle sticking out, tucked behind his forefinger. He wore a diamond in a gold setting on his pinkie finger and, she now noted, another diamond in a stickpin. Outside, a big hard-tired dray truck rumbled by, drive-chains clicking on sprockets.

"Now, then," she said.

"Town looks about the same." His affable grin was there again. "Good to me, is what it was. Had a wife, a little family. Prospects. Now all I got is prospects. Good ones, though. Gone take a little working out."

"I'm sure you'll work it out, the way you did before. Or should I say excuse me? That slipped out."

"I did, uh, kind of leave in a hurry. Too much of a hurry. Way it worked out, it didn't hardly pay. I had it set up a whole lot better, only the cards commenced to run sour. But, anymore, that's all under the bridge. Never look back with tears in your eyes when a smile says it so much better. My motto."

"Touching, but I have a story to get out. An afternoon's worth of them, in fact. So—"

"Little newslady, right? I always knew you had it upstairs. Not like your sis, and no offense, don't misunderstand me, but she was more fun and games. Brains?—Okay, she was a whiz with crossword puzzles. Who swam the Hellespont? she would ask me. What do I know?"

"Leander," Lexie said.

"What?" His brow crinkled in puzzlement. Spidery capillaries crept about his nose and cheeks.

"Leander swam it, to see his girlfriend. Anyway, look—she's gone. And you weren't with her or even in touch with her. And maybe you can guess how I found out she was sick—Jason wrote me a letter. You ought to read it. A ten-year-old child, watching his mother die and no one to turn to."

Lexie sipped her coffee, looked away. He stared at her.

"I'm just awful sorry to hear about this, Lexie." He toyed with his coffee mug. "My idea, I need a base of operations, figured I would come back home—"

"*Come back home*? You're not serious!" She could feel the adder lashing, whipping its tail. Golly, more like an alligator, she thought.

"As a boarder, is all. To be near my son. Got a perfect legal right, that part of it. Get to know him, see, and then later cut him in on my deal. I mean, spose something happens to me down the line—he's my *heir*." He beamed.

"That's purely an accident and you know it—like something that happened . . . in a *field*! The miracle of procreation." She stopped herself. "Look, I didn't come here intending to argue. Jason is . . . he's only eleven years old. He's not some smelly crony of yours. All you'll leave him is heartaches."

"I sure didn't come here to lock horns with you, hon. Fact, I had only the warmest sentiments all this time."

"Nothing embarrasses you, does it? I had to leave home because of . . . your warm sentiments." She felt her face flush.

"A lovin hug is what it was. You misunderstood, is all."

"I see things like that come out in court, J. W., and there it's called molestation."

"Pains me, your thinkin that." He shifted his weight suddenly and the chair legs squealed. "But the thing now is, I want to get to know the boy again. It's been almost a year."

Lexie stood up. "Since you abandoned him? Left him and Sis stranded in Fort Worth? You'll run smack into a court order."

"The boy's *mine*, Lexie. And I guess, bein it aint convenient for me to come back home, then soon's I find a place, Jason can move in with me. I want to take care of that boy and I mean to do it." That beaming grin again.

The alligator rolled completely over inside her. She pressed a hand to the front of her middie blouse, felt it shuddering in there. She took fifteen cents from her purse, put the coins on the counter. "Give the gentleman another cup of coffee, Alvino. My treat." And left.

* * *

Maynard had described briefly the flight Lexie wanted to make. He had decided, to be on the safe side, to ask for forty dollars for a half-day, not fifty.

"This kind of story," Craddock was saying to Maynard, "is just a feature. It's not what I call solid news, which is what we're in business to deliver, and I can't justify that much expense for it." He sat back with an air of finality as Lexie entered the front office and came around the counter toward them.

Her expression was still chilly-bright and her face was noticeably pale. She walked between them and took her seat. "I'm glad you gentlemen had a chance to talk. But before you say anything, Mr. Craddock, I want to point out that over half the letters to the editor in the Sunday edition were in praise of the historical series, and *six* businesses in town are already tying in advertising to these articles, so we're *generating* income. That's why I think this flight is cheap at only fifty dollars. Don't you agree?"

Craddock took a deep drag on his cigarette, blew smoke toward the ceiling, laced his fingers together and cracked his knuckles. Maynard looked out the window. "Um, taken in that light, Lexie, I'm inclined to agree with you," Craddock said. "Why don't you go ahead with it?"

"Good." She turned to Maynard, who was trying to keep a straight face. "If you'll give me just another minute, Captain, we can decide when to make the flight. I just need a word with Mr. Craddock."

Maynard nodded, shook hands with Craddock and went out into the front office. Lexie quickly told Craddock the substance of her talk with J. W. Whitlock. "I'm going to have myself declared Jason's legal guardian," she said.

"The law," Craddock said, "acts with a speed that can only be described as glacial, matters like this. I mean, you can try for a court order—I'll go over to the courthouse with you—and maybe you can get it, but your only complaint is that the man is a son of a bitch. He hasn't *done* anything. What he will or might do is a matter of sheer speculation. And supposing he fights your application for guardianship?"

"The man's a felon."

"Not convicted—not in this state, anyway. He flew the coop, all right, coincidentally with the sudden disappearance of a considerable sum of invested funds. A warrant was issued but never served, and now the statute of limitations has run out on it, if I'm not mistaken."

"It was nineteen fifteen when he got into trouble and left," Lexie said. "My mother was still alive. I was in high school. Sis and J. W. had moved in with us after they got married. I moved out the year before, because of him, and lived with my friend Jessica Clawson and her family. He ran off to Mexico, we heard, got mixed up in the revolution—he was a soldier before we ever knew him, you know. Was in the Philippines, if you could believe him. And then he was in the AEF in France. In nineteen-nineteen, he came back, sent Sis a wire, and before I could do anything or even talk with her, she took Jason and went to live with J. W. again. It was all pillar-to-post after that."

"You want to try to get a court order right now?"

"I called the courthouse. The judge is in Phoenix, won't be back for two days. No, the first thing I'll do is get Jason out of the house."

"You want to take him to my place?"

"You're a dear, but—it ought to be someplace out of town, and where someone will be there to look after him. I'll have to take him out of school, too, see? Otherwise, J. W. could—" She stopped, in her mind a picture of J. W. waylaying Jason after school and walking off with him, hand-in-hand. "I don't even want to think about it. There's one place I can think of that J. W. wouldn't know about. I've got an old uncle, lives way out in the sticks. He's kind of a crank"—she sighed and held her hands up—"but it would only be for a few days." She was gathering up her things. "If I start now, I can pick up Jason when he gets home from school, before . . ." Her voice trailed off.

"Go on, Lexie, do it. If the bastard comes back here again, I'll brain him with the fire ax."

"I'm sorry to keep you waiting," she told Maynard, who thought she looked edgy. "We can make that flight tomorrow morning, I think—something's come up and I was afraid I'd have to put it off a day."

"Anything I can help with?"

"No. I've just got to get back out to my uncle's place in a hurry."

Maynard's thoughts raced. "Well, then, maybe you'll let me go along—I got a part for the magneto, and I could put it in and fly the airplane back to town this evening. That will simplify things." He was thinking he would unload the airplane out there, leave the stuff in the adobe shack until he could get back again later with his Ford.

"Let's hurry, then. I've got to pick up my little brother at home. Not my brother, really, but—anyway, let's hurry."

4

MULBERRY TREES overhung the dirt sidewalk for a distance of thirty yards. Purple fruit fallen from the trees lay thickly scattered the whole way. A trap, Jason Whitlock decided. In places, the mulberries had been squashed by heedless feet, the stains like splashes of blood. He thought of what had happened to the careless ones—tracked down by those devils, the Riffs, and turned over to their women for torture. Jason shuddered. He had vowed never to be taken alive.

He knelt, tied his shoe, considered. Heat waves shimmered above the street. Madness to go that way. A man's brains would broil in his skull, out there without a *kepi*. His fingers strayed to his sandy hair—Jason had no *kepi*. He would die raving, *le cafard*, desert madness. He carried a long whisk of pampas grass taken from a yard near the fort—Sidi Bel Abbes, headquarters of the French Foreign Legion, as he thought of his school—and he had carefully brushed out his tracks all the way from the fort. Had gone blocks out of his way to throw them off. A plan sprang to mind. He turned and walked backwards, careless now of the mulberries that squirted beneath his shoes. At the end of the mulberries, he knelt and carefully cleaned his shoes of the crushed fruit, getting a good deal of it on his hands and pants in the process. It would never do for the ground to show stains *before* his tracks reached the mulberries. Satisfied, he set out again, walking backwards, of course—let the devils pick up his tracks where they would, the tracks would lead them back to this patch of mulberries and then disappear! A laugh of defiance, deep and resonant, rumbled in Jason's chest. He eased the sling of the 8mm. Lebel service rifle, Legion issue, on his shoulder and marched on, looking back over his shoulder.

Lexie leaned against the front fender of her Durant Star and looked at the front of her house. She was nervous because Jason was late getting home from school. Her nervousness made her want to talk. No, chatter.

"Our house is the oldest one on the street, and absolutely without doubt the ugliest," she said. "Those walls are adobe, eighteen inches thick. It was built in seventy-three, I think, when they still expected the Apaches to come swooping down. It had shutters on it when I was little—thick enough to turn arrows, my father used to say. But bats and scorpions took up residence behind them and Mama complained until he took them down. What was your house like, where you grew up?" she asked him.

"Two stories, Georgian colonial, built 1784. Sat back from the street, big oaks and maples on the grounds. Carriage house in back. Montclair, New Jersey, that was."

"Sounds lovely. Do you miss it?"

"Not anymore. I left to start learning to fly, over on Long Island, . . . let's see, it was 1913, so that's ten years ago. After that, I never really lived at home again. My folks moved to Cape Cod when my dad retired from his law practice."

She was looking down the street, east. Jason would have to come that way. There was a little frown line between her brows. She moistened her lips with her tongue. The wind, dry as always, had picked up and sand skittered before it in little wavelets. She stepped away from the car.

"There he is. At least I think it's Jason. He's coming from the wrong direction for some reason. What on earth is he doing?"

The small figure had rounded the corner, marching resolutely backwards. "I can tell you exactly what he's doing," Maynard said. "He's laying down a false trail to throw them off the track."

"Throw who off?"

"Hard to say. Apaches, possibly. Maybe Sioux. They're deadly enemies, I know that."

Jason, intent on his navigating, was well down the block before he realized he was under scrutiny. His step faltered, he shuffled, kicked once and turned face front, looking back at the open book of betrayal his tracks had become, regret for a damaged subterfuge implicit in his frown. As he approached, Maynard saw a slight boy, about a seventy-pounder, sun-streaked hair, scarlet-purple stains on his hands, corduroys and the edges of his shoe soles, his right thumb hooked under a suspender—to ease, Maynard realized, the weight of his service rifle, if he was reading it properly. The boy's eyes swept the two of them, but the thumb stayed hooked where it was.

"This is Captain Gaylen, Jason." The boy nodded, his eyes widening a trifle. He shook hands, replaced the thumb.

Maynard pointed. "Is that a Springfield?" Jason shook his head, his lips compressed. "Uh, Remington?" Shook his head again, eyes flicking warily at Lexie. Could be Kipling he's reading, Maynard thought. "Martini? No? More recent then—Lee-Enfield?" The head shook again, very slightly. That pretty well took care of the Anglo-Saxons, Maynard thought. One certainly doesn't carry a Winchester on a sling. "Lebel, then?" Jason nodded, ever so slightly. Giving away nothing, Maynard thought. Aloud, he said, "Model 1868, eight-millimeter bolt action, eight-shot, length fifty-one inches, weight nine pounds. So"—Maynard's gaze wandered grimly back the way Jason had come—"it's those scoundrels the Riffs out there. . . ."

* * *

"All that stuff about the rifle—where did that come from?" Lexie said. Jason was inside. Lexie had gone in with him, told him to pack a bag and have a quick wash. She started to help him pack, but he stiffened and said, "I can do it myself," so she went back out to wait by the car with Maynard.

He grinned and started to reply, but Jason came out carrying a warped wicker suitcase that squeaked like a live thing when Maynard stowed it in the trunk. The front of Jason's face was washed clean. A muddy line separated the clean part from the rest, which still bore a grayish film of playground dirt. Several muddy water tracks ran down his neck and disappeared into his collar. A wet comb had made a single pass through his hair on top, leaving it slicked down and damp, the sides and back rank as a fistful of hay. Sitting between them on the seat, his small body emitted a slight doggy odor. His brow was furrowed in a manner that suggested worry, even dread, to Maynard. Why not? The kid is being hauled away without warning, headed where? He thought of the big ugly guy she had left the office with—her suddenly changed manner suggested he had something to do with this. Gravel sprayed under the car's wheels. She was in a hurry, he could tell that much.

They turned west and crossed through the old part of town, Lexie—purposely, it seemed to Maynard—driving on back streets. They stopped at a small and shabby restaurant near the railroad yards. Jason merely glanced at the menu. "Hot roast beef sandwich with mashed potatoes and gravy, glass of milk," he said.

"My favorite, too," Maynard said. "That's one thing you can order, anyplace you go, and they hardly ever ruin it, right?" Jason nodded. Lexie ordered split-pea soup and a salad. Jason ate soberly, resisting Lexie's questions about school, his eyes roving restlessly. Looking for a way out, Maynard thought. They were seated next to the window. Jason studied their reflections in the window.

"How did you know it was a Lebel?" Jason asked suddenly.

"That's Legion issue." Maynard said.

Jason nodded. "But its length and weight and model year, that's what I mean."

"When a soldier is issued his rifle, those are the first things he learns. It's drilled into him."

Jason stared. "You were in the Foreign Legion?"

Maynard felt Lexie's eyes fasten on him, her fork poised in midair.

"That's right. When the war started in 1914, the only way an American could get into it without losing his citizenship was to join the Legion—the Legion's oath was to the Legion only, and not to France, see? Lots of Americans joined that way."

"Did you have a *kepi*?"

"Sure. I've still got mine, in fact."

"How long did it take for you to be a captain?"

Maynard laughed. "A long time, but that wasn't in the Legion. I transferred into the flying corps in 1915, and then after the U.S. got into it, most of us switched over to the American air service."

"So you were in the Lafayette Escadrille, too."

"No, the Lafayette Flying Corps. There's a difference—same army, different squadron. I was in Spad 58, and then later in the U.S. 103rd Pursuit Squadron."

Jason went on eating, but kept looking up at Maynard.

"My problem," Lexie said after a long pause, making swirl patterns appear in her soup, "is what and how much to tell Jason."

Jason steadfastly attended to his eating. Learned to handle these things like a soldier, Maynard thought. Keeps his head down, looks busy, waits.

"It's because of your father," she suddenly said directly to the boy. "It's hard to tell you anything without maybe stepping on feelings you may have stored up for him, but let me put it to you this way—if you had the chance right now, would you go back to J. W.?"

Maynard felt a tremor run through Jason. The eyes flicked warily. Looking for a way out, thought Maynard, if that's in the cards. Jason shook his head.

"Jason is in the sixth grade," Lexie said. "He's been in twenty schools in nine states. J. W. is something of a . . . drifter. Sales deals, various kinds. Quick in, quick out, before the gendarmes arrive. Oops, that was a mistake—no use my trying to hide my meaning behind obscure words. Jason's scholarship would shame us both. What I'm getting at, anyway, is to tell you, my little brother"—she faltered, reached for Jason's hand—"that J. W. Whitlock is in town, wants to see you, maybe take you with him, which possibly is his legal right, but won't happen, not if I can help it, understand? So we're taking you out to Uncle Hector's place for a few days—we're not yet sure how long. You'll be out of school and we're not telling anyone where you'll be. We're not certain how much effort J. W. will put out to find you. Uncle Hector is a little . . . strange, but he's all we've got. . . ." Her voice trailed off, stopped.

They each had a piece of apple pie. When they went back to the car, the sun was low and the sky was turning amber, streaked with blowing dust. Lexie headed north on the road to Papago Junction and Florence, the red cliffs of the Catalinas soaring to the right. Every few hundred yards, the gravel road dipped into a sandy wash, the car swooping smoothly with it. Lexie turned off left on a narrow, rutted track through thick cactus—saguaro, ocotillo, frosty glistening cholla, buckhorn, prickly pear. They passed a single house, a stuccoed adobe with oleanders in the front yard, and then the track dropped suddenly into a broad riverbed. There were feathery gold-green palo verde trees on the banks. Seven or eight javelinas scampered away in front of them, their short legs churning up sprays of sand. Jason sat bolt upright, staring after them.

"Wild pigs," Maynard said. "Peccaries, actually. A man doesn't want to get caught afoot in a bunch of javelinas. Tusks like that—" He held up two curved fingers. "Tear you to pieces. Even a six-shooter wouldn't save you, twenty, thirty of them after you."

Jason's eyes widened. Lexie said, "All the times I've seen those little pigs, no one ever told me that."

Ahead, the sky was turning red. The Durant climbed out of the wash, swung up a grade that angled up between eroded sandy pillars onto a mesa, a long finger of high ground pointing south and west down the vast slope of the desert valley. A thick haze of windblown dust in the valley glowed like a molten sea. Mountains thrusting up through it caught the sun, burned red.

"Holy Moses," Jason said, "look at that!" And Lexie almost passed the house. Would have, but there was no more road. Lexie switched off the engine.

Maynard was thinking how the house might have looked to the kid. From this side, with broken plaster revealing the adobe bricks beneath, it was *spooky,* that was it, despite the weathered frivolity of gingerbread skirting the porch eaves, paint long since scoured from sun-bleached wood. It sat back behind wind-tossed palo verde and mesquite trees. A curtained bay window on the side caught the red light of the sky and stared at them like a blind, inflamed eye.

"You mean," Jason said in a hoarse small voice to Lexie, "I've gotta stay *there*?"

"Not long, Jason," Lexie said. "A few days. Let me go speak to Uncle Hector." She slipped out of the car, mounted steps to the porch, knocked and waited, her back to them. Maynard felt the boy's helplessness—dread sat between them, heavy-bodied. Poor little devil, he thought, what can I tell him?

"Think of it," he said, "as a mission. Your uncle is all alone.

He's old and he needs help. There are agents trying to infiltrate the place. Your orders are to mingle with them, find out where their strength is, but don't tip your hand. Learn all you can about the operation. You're the only man we could send to do this. They won't know that you know about them, see?"

"Infiltrate." Jason savored the word carefully. "Then will I come back through their lines?"

"No. We'll have to get in touch with you. The waiting may seem hard, but we won't forget you're here. Remember that."

"Will I need a password? Our men might not know me if I'm not in uniform."

"I'm glad you pointed that out. Let's say the password is . . ." His eye caught a wind-thrashed mesquite. "Mesquite, how's that? The response can be . . . javelina, okay?"

"Mesquite. Javelina." Jason whispered it. "Be sure everybody knows it. Stonewall Jackson was shot by his own men."

Lexie came off the porch, the wind whipping her skirt. She started to go around the side of the house, but the front door suddenly swung open with a crash. The old man stood there glaring at them, bathed in hellish red light, his white hair standing in wild spikes—like an enraged eagle, Maynard thought. He heard Jason's breath suck in. Jesus, that old boy is scary, Maynard thought.

"Who's yonder?" the old man cried.

"It's Lexie, Uncle Hector." She ran back up the stairs. The sound of their voices was garbled in the wind. Both gesturing.

Lexie was back suddenly. She lifted Jason's bag off the rear seat. "Let's go, Jason. Uncle Hector is a little confused. Let's not keep him waiting."

Jason got out and turned to Maynard. He was chewing his lip. Seemed to be waiting for something. Jason whipped his hand up to his forehead in a salute.

Maynard returned the salute, a smile tugging at his lips. "In the Legion, we salute with the palm out, like this, got it?"

"Yes, sir," Jason said gravely. "Got it." Still he waited.

Damn, Maynard thought, does she really have to send him in there? Then he remembered. "Mesquite, right?"

"Javelina," Jason said, relief in his voice. Leaning into the wind, he followed Lexie up onto the porch and through the door of the old house. Less than a minute later, she came out. Maynard got out of the car.

"I've got to run on," he told her, "and get that airplane into the air and back to town before it's dark."

"Damn! I feel like a traitor!" A tear spilled onto her cheek. She brushed it away.

"He'll be all right. He's on a mission. There wasn't anyone else we could send—he knows that agents are trying to infiltrate and he's going to learn all he can about their operation."

She stared at him through brimming eyes and then began to laugh shakily. She jumped into the Durant, started it, wheeled it around and gunned it back toward town.

5

JASON HEARD the snarl of the departing car. He swallowed, trying to hold down the dread that spread beneath his ribs. The old man glared down at him, chin stubble glinting little sparks in the yellow light of an oil lamp.

"There is no accounting, young sir, for the liberties people will take, is there?" His voice was like the sound of a rusty spike being pulled from wet wood. He was wearing faded bib overalls over a union suit. The stringy column of his neck, like a plucked turkey's, thrust up out of his long underwear. His feet wore shapeless carpet slippers. "I repeat the question, for we must be of one mind on this."

"No, sir," Jason said hastily. "No accounting."

The old man snatched up the lamp and led him through a dark hallway to the kitchen. Sand gritted underfoot on the linoleum. The old man pushed a plate of half-eaten food aside and set the lamp down on an oilcloth-covered table with a thud that nearly toppled the lamp chimney. Jason saw a wooden drainboard piled high with dirty dishes. A nickel-trimmed wood stove stood in one corner. Both the stove and the iron cooking pots sitting on it were thickly encrusted with burned grease. Two rickety chairs with torn cane seats sat next to the table. A wood box sat next to the stove, and along the wall was a litter of boots, piles of paper, empty bottles and boxes.

"It's a mess, sure enough," the old man said. "But what is a body to do? Maybe you'll tell me that."

Jason realized that the old man was not talking about the filthy kitchen, but about his own arrival.

Not waiting for an answer, the old man said, "If a man is drove to it, a call to the sheriff will set things right."

Jason's bowels churned. Lexie had said that J. W. Whitlock had a legal right to take him away. The law must be kept out of this.

"All in good time," the old man said. "Now it's my understanding that you've had your supper. That being the case, you may watch me eat mine, which is what I was embarked upon when so rudely interrupted. Praps you'd like a biscuit."

Jason shook his head, but the old man, heedless, thrust a biscuit into his hand. It was hot, and butter was about to drip from it. Jason caught the butter with his tongue and then took a bite. It was fragrant and tasty. The old man spooned some red beans from an iron kettle into a bowl and thumped it down before Jason.

"Beans will put taller on your ribs," he declared.

Jason began to eat, dipping the biscuit into the bean soup.

Maynard quickly replaced the rotor in the magneto and buttoned up the cowling. He walked over to the adobe shack, swung back the plank door and peered in. Dirt floor, piled trash, gunnysacks, enough harness he thought for a twenty-mule team. A gopher scuttled beneath the harness. Maynard took some gunnysacks back to the Jenny and opened a wing locker. He began putting bottles of cognac into grain sacks, carrying them to the shack.

While he worked, he thought of the kid, seeing again the misery etched into the poor little devil's features when Lexie led him into the old man's house. The misery caught in his own throat—he was putting down a gunnysack with half a dozen bottles in it and his nose was tingling with dust, and there in the murky shack he felt the ghost of that same bone-deep hollow dread that he remembered from his first night in the Legion, in the hideous barracks in Rouen. Nine years back it was, August of 1914. He remembered his helpless agony of spirit when he cried out to himself, *What the hell am I doing here?*

He looked around at piled trash, the awkward looming shape of the Jenny, suddenly aware of himself diligently making a cache of bootleg liquor in an adobe shack in the desert, driven helplessly there like a leaf caught in swirling water. The old feeling swept over him. *What the hell am I doing here?* He had to laugh at himself then. He put his hand on the rough planked door and stood there for a moment, then shook his head and went back to work. In a few minutes, he finished. He pulled the Jenny's prop through to prime the engine, then he set the throttle and switched on the ignition, went back around and propped her again. She fired on the first pull, straining at the tiedowns. He walked around to the cockpit, reached in and throttled back, and while she sat there ticking over, smoothly now, with the different rotor, he untied her. Then he climbed in, feeling the aircraft quiver with the gusting wind. The sun was gone, the purpling sky somber as light fled. He would be landing in dusk. Maynard pulled his goggles down and fed in throttle. The Jenny crunched through blurring scrub, bounced, bounced again, and then she was flying. He caught just a glimpse of a dim yellow light in a window as he swept past the house, a quarter-mile away, and he thought of the kid. Poor little bastard.

Jason ate two more biscuits and most of the beans while the old man gnawed on the carcass of a small bird, making appreciative grunting and sucking sounds as he tore it apart and cleaned the bones. Jason uncovered a piece of slick fat in the bottom of his bowl. Hesitantly, he pointed to a wrinkled protuberance on the surface of the fat. "What's that?" he said.

The old man looked into the bowl and laughed. "Sow belly. That there nubbin is a tit." He cackled again. Jason dropped his spoon and recoiled in horror.

At that moment, he heard the sound of a distant engine firing. It coughed once and settled into a smooth murmur. Shortly, the sound swelled in volume. A windowpane over the sink began to buzz from the vibration of the engine, and a glass that was touching it rattled noisily. Jason saw the airplane speed past, climbing against the streaked purple darkening sky. Then it was gone, the sound fading. The old man was listening, too, a quail wing poised in his gnarled fingers, a look of puzzled alarm on his face.

"That's Captain Gaylen," Jason said. "Now we're really alone, aren't we?"

"Damn right we are," the old man said.

"Do we stand guard?"

"Guard?" The old man barked a sharp laugh. "You're thinking there's Apaches out there, are you?"

"No." Jason wasn't sure he should be talking about this, but he didn't want to go to sleep if he was supposed to be standing guard duty. "Captain Gaylen told me that . . . the agents might try to infiltrate."

The old man clamped his jaw fiercely. "Chicken-livered bastards! Oh, they would infilterate quick enough if they could, but they don't dare interrupt my work before it's done. They could never figger it out by theirselves."

"Figure what out?" Jason said. A yawn was pulling at his jaw and he was having trouble concentrating.

"Never you mind, sonny. The less you know, the better off you are. Sleep is what you want now, I spect. Sleep is your great restorer. You'll bunk yonder—" He heaved himself to his feet and flung open a door. Jason stumbled into a cluttered screened porch. Wind sighed noisily through the screens. Rolled-down canvas blinds sucked in and out. A sagging cot was almost hidden under a pile of what appeared to be equal parts of rags and kindling wood. The old man heaved at one corner of a patchwork quilt and dumped everything onto the floor. Dust eddied. "Now, b'god, tell me that aint dandy!" Without another word he turned and left, slamming the door behind him.

Subdued light seeped past a flour-sack curtain over the door's single pane of glass. Jason brushed away sand and insect carcasses and spread the quilt. He pulled off his shoes, pants and shirt, rolled the pants into a pillow and started to crawl under the quilt. A pressing need stopped him. The old man had not told him where the bathroom was. And the one thing he did not intend to do now was disturb him, in view of his threat to call the sheriff.

Jason picked his way to a back door at the far end of the porch, creeping past unidentifiable piles of trash. He eased the door outward. Wind tugged at it. Holding it tightly, he slipped out onto teetering wooden steps. The door chunked closed behind him. Under the black tent of the thrashing tree above, it was quite dark. Three steps to the ground. He stepped off. Piercing pain shot through both feet. He realized he had stepped into a patch of bullhead stickers, but his bursting bladder would allow him to wait no longer. His toes clenched with pain, he turned his back to the buffeting wind and relieved himself, exhaling a long, shuddering sigh. He eased himself down and sat on a step, then felt for the bullheads embedded in his feet and plucked them out.

Jason stood and fumbled for a door handle. There wasn't one. He clawed at the door, but there was no purchase for his fingers. Panic stabbed through him. Was he to spend the night trapped on the back steps in a storm? Wind hooted, and the tall mesquite thrashed against the sky. He moaned softly. After a moment, he pulled himself together and methodically felt both sides of the door. No knob or handle. It had a screen over its top half. Feeling high on the door, he found a hole torn in the screen. Through the hole was a wooden cross-brace. He grabbed it and jerked with all his might. The door swung outward, caught the wind like a sail, swept him off the step and flailed him against the side of the house so hard he bit his tongue.

Knowing the ground beneath him was liberally salted with the devilish bullhead stickers, Jason dared not let go the door. The torn screen sawed into his right hand. He got a foot against the house behind him and shoved off—the door swung in an arc, caught the wind again and pounded him once more savagely against the plaster. His arms felt as if they would be ripped from their sockets. Jason's strength was going.

To add to his miseries, the aged elastic waistband of his underpants surrendered. The garment hung for a moment on his small buttocks, then fell. He kicked to impede their fall and managed to knot them around his ankles, secure and snug as rawhide horse hobbles.

Jason's wind sawed in his throat. He tucked both feet up as high as he could on the wall behind him, fighting the pain of cramped stomach muscles, took a deep breath and launched himself. Unaccountably, at that moment, the gusty wind subsided. His body hurtled, driving the door before it so that it slammed shut into the casing and very nearly flung him off. His manacled ankles rattled painfully against the top step. A sob of exhaustion and frustration was wrung from him. He got his hobbled feet under him, which eased the burden on his arms. Still holding the cross-piece, he rested, his chest heaving. Carefully as a surgeon, he eased the door open, clutching the inside handle against the mischievous tugs of the wind as he hopped around the door and into the room.

Jason bent down to untangle his knotted underpants, lost his balance and toppled with a crash onto a washtub full of bottles and tin cans. Inside the kitchen, the old man snarled, "Son of a bitch!" His chair scraped noisily on the floor. His shadow loomed on the flour-sack curtain. Jason squirmed to cover his nakedness, certain of discovery, his entrails shriveling. But at that moment a piece of windblown metal roofing, or a garbage-can lid—*something*—clashed noisily, close to the house. Muttering, the old man resumed his seat.

Jason crept to his cot, his heart pounding, and slipped gratefully beneath the quilt. Dust stung his nostrils. His skin was grainy with it. He thought he had never been so tired. Even so, he began to worry about tomorrow. Jason had learned, in his short, chaotic life, to dread the dawn of every day. He saw nothing in the old man or his present situation to give him comfort. He shivered like a wet pup, so hard his teeth chattered.

If the old man would not share information with him, he was truly alone on his mission. He lay for some time considering this. It suddenly occurred to him that he didn't even know where headquarters was.

Movement caught his eye—a stray sliver of light fell upon a train of large cockroaches scuttling along the floor. Their shiny backs glinted reddish lights. As he fell asleep, he was certain he could hear the scuffling of their spiked legs and the clicking of their brown horny plates.

WIND PUMMELED Lexie's light car. The red light smearing the sky faded to dusty purple. A sprinkling of lights appeared in the valley. There were stretches of highway that were severely corduroyed. The little Durant bucked and chattered, so she kept her speed down. She was near the cemetery when she heard the roar of an aircraft engine above. Startled, she pulled over. The airplane swept low overhead as it banked, crossing the road. It looked huge. Its wings wobbled unsteadily. The engine sound faded and she heard the shrill whistle of wind in its rigging. It dropped into the darkness beyond the cemetery. For a moment she wondered why the airplane was so late getting there—she had driven all the way in to town, and surely the airplane was much faster than her car; then she remembered that the captain had said he had to do something to the engine. That took, what, a half-hour?

On impulse, she turned off the highway and drove to the airport. A single floodlight in front of one of the hangars illuminated two tied-down airplanes. She saw canvas covers over their cockpits, drove on past them, out of the ring of light. Her headlights picked up the last hangar—there were only three. A big biplane she recognized as a Jenny was sitting in front of it and the captain was kneeling, tying a wingtip to a ring in a concrete block on the ground. A heavyset man in khaki was standing there, hands on hips, a truculent stance, waiting. Beyond was a Dodge touring car with the familiar county star painted on its door. Lexie left her lights on. The heavyset man glared at her. She recognized him. Deputy Jesse Bob Allred. She stepped out of the car and heard him say, "Who's that? Somebody meeting you, right?"

Lexie saw Maynard shake his head. She stepped forward and said, "I saw you land, Captain Gaylen, and thought you might need a ride to town. Hello, Jesse."

Maynard smiled quickly, finished tying the knot and stood up. "Any objections?" he said to the deputy. "My car's in town."

"Spose I look in the boxes. You got nothing to hide, so you don't mind, right?" The deputy jerked a thumb at the airplane, smirked at her.

"I mind a little, but go ahead if you want," Maynard said. He flipped a latch open and lifted the cover.

The deputy peered in. "All right, so it's gone. How come you didn't land before?"

"I remembered I was supposed to stop at the Papago Queen," Maynard said.

"That's easy enough to check," the deputy growled.

"I never got that far," Maynard said. "I had engine trouble and had to land in a field."

"Where?"

Maynard shrugged. "Out there, west somewhere."

"And it took all day to fix, is that it?" the deputy said belligerantly.

Maynard shrugged again, saying nothing. The deputy rocked on his heels, started to speak, thought better of it and strode to the county car. He glared back at Maynard for a moment and then climbed into the car and wheeled away.

"I could have backed you up," Lexie said. "Why didn't you tell him I gave you a ride to town earlier?"

Maynard looked at her. "Why tell him everything?"

* * *

"What was that all about?" Lexie said when Maynard got into the car. She turned and drove back toward the highway.

"He didn't say what he was looking for," Maynard said. He studied her face, outlined in the faint glow of light from the dashboard. "Never mind him—it's that little kid I'm thinking about."

She nodded. "It will only be for a few days—as long as it takes for me to be declared his guardian."

"A few days can be an eternity to a kid."

"I couldn't see any other way to handle it." He heard exasperation in her voice.

"Maybe not. He could have stayed with me."

"I didn't *know* you."

They rode in silence for half a minute. Maynard said, "You called him your little brother—he's your nephew, though. Why was that?"

She glanced at him, frowning. "That was just a slip, sort of. When this all started, I wasn't . . . prepared for it, I guess you'd say. I mean, I wasn't ready for the responsibility of taking on my sister's child. It was . . . you could call it an attack of selfishness. I hadn't seen Jason since he was little. I didn't know him. I was just beginning to get my own life sorted out the way I wanted it. Why *me*? I thought. So I asked myself a question—would I feel different about it if he were my own brother?"

"Would you?"

"I think so. It seemed to help—I began thinking of him as my little brother. I think he liked it, too, although that's hard to say. He is so secretive. I can't seem to get close to him. I certainly don't understand him. Not the way you did."

He smiled. "You were never in the Foreign Legion, that's all."

"That may be some of it, but it isn't *all*." She laughed. "Maybe I could understand him better if he'd been mine for the last ten years—I would've had some practice. Why am I telling you this?"

"Because I asked, maybe."

"Should I tell you then how *exasperating* it can be? I bought him new clothes. He won't wear them! He finally wore the shoes I bought him, but the first thing he did was scuff up the toes, and I know he did it deliberately."

"That's easy," Maynard said. "He doesn't want to be noticed. To draw attention to himself is to ask for trouble. Any soldier knows that." He laughed. "But what did you mean, you were getting your own life sorted out?"

She drove on in silence for a while. "Sorted out," he persisted, "from what?"

"Don't rush me," she said. "I've said too much already. Don't you just hate blabbing?" They turned again, onto pavement now, bumped across the railroad tracks. There were a few street lights now as they neared Congress Street. She suddenly spoke again. "From what it was . . . had been. My husband . . . that is, I was married in nineteen-seventeen. We were just kids, but war was declared and it was like an epidemic—it seemed like everyone was doing it. We had three days together. My husband got to France and then got sick, in camp. He went to the hospital."

Seeing her expression, Maynard said, "Don't—you don't have to say any of this."

She shook her head slightly. "They thought it was meningitis. Maybe they never really knew. Anyway, they shipped him back to the States. Someplace, during that time in the hospital, he caught TB. Finally they sent him to California to the vets' hospital. He died there, two years ago, about. I came back here and got a job at the paper, taking classified ads, but I kept writing stories until Mr. Warren moved me into the newsroom. And I was doing all right, just fine in fact, until my sister died, and Jason . . ." Her voice trailed off. She turned onto Congress and swung into a parking place. Switched off the ignition and lights, sat looking straight ahead. "You did ask, didn't you? I'm not just blabbing."

He nodded. "I guess I did."

She turned to look at him suddenly. "What should I wear to go flying? Riding things?"

"Perfect," he said. "Can you be there about five-thirty? We'll get an early start on it." She nodded as they got out of her car. He watched her go into the *Courier* building. He started toward his own car, a T-model Ford van parked down the block, but the lighted doorway of Kee's Tea Room across the street caught his eye. You could get a cup of tea in Kee's if you wanted. You could also get a beer or a drink in the back room, or shoot some pool. And Maynard thought he'd better tell Jimmy Kee when to expect his shipment of cognac.

Woody Craddock was at his desk, going over a galley proof of his editorial. How did it go? he wanted to know when Lexie sat down at her desk.

She shook her head. "Poor kid. He didn't want to go there. I felt terrible, doing that to him—for the first time, I realized how Uncle Hector must look to someone else. And that house! It belongs in a nightmare. I don't think I could have gone through with it without Captain Gaylen."

"Gaylen! What was he doing there?"

She rolled copy paper into her tall Remington. "He made a forced landing out there earlier today—that's how I met him. So I was able to give him a ride back to get his airplane, and he helped me with Jason."

"How could he help?"

She didn't answer directly. "Did you know he'd been in the Foreign Legion?"

Craddock nodded. "The Americans who flew for the French had to join the Foreign Legion first."

"Jason has been reading Foreign Legion stories, so he was very impressed. Captain, I mean, uh, Maynard . . . he made it seem like a . . . mission, I guess. Jason is pretending he is working undercover." She turned suddenly and stared at Craddock. "At least I think he's pretending! You don't suppose he's serious about it, do you?"

"So much the better if he is." Craddock grinned. "It helps a soldier to believe. So you left Gaylen out there, did you?"

"Yes. He had to do something to the airplane and then fly it back. I picked him up at the airport and gave him a ride to town, just now. That deputy, Jesse Allred, was out there asking him questions, wanting to know where he'd been."

"So they're onto him, are they? I wonder who complained."

"Why do you say that?"

"Some of the things he's into—he would want to have a runway out in the sticks someplace."

"What things? He takes people for rides at fair time. Barnstorming, isn't that it? And he flies charters—he took Emma Dillon's father to the hospital in Phoenix."

Craddock laughed. "He also runs a load of booze now and then. The guy's a bootlegger, didn't you know that?"

"Captain Gaylen? Are you serious?" Light from her desk lamp sharply etched the frown line between her eyes as she turned toward him.

"Look, if you keep on calling him Captain Gaylen, you'll have to start calling me Corporal Craddock. It's only fair. Sure I'm serious. I know he was an ace and all that, but there's no real money in the kind of flying he does. Booze pays the bills. I don't know exactly how deep he is in it, but he does fly down to Mexico now and then."

"That would account for the bottle he was sharing with Uncle Hector." She told him how she came upon them, the old man holding a shotgun on the white-faced captain.

Craddock laughed again. "The whole thing is a laugh anyway, but there's money in it."

"What's a laugh?"

"Prohibition. Speaking of which, it's still early. Will you have a drink with me at Jimmy Kee's?"

"Woodie, I'd love to, but I've got all these pieces to get done by eleven and then I have to get home. We're making that flight at daybreak."

"I'm beginning to regret giving you the go-ahead." He swung around in his chair, and then he said, abruptly, "I wonder if a man like J. W. will have much trouble finding Jason. That is, assuming he really does want to find him and isn't doing this merely out of mischief."

"Why do you say 'a man like J.W.'?"

"We're reporters. It's our business to find out things, often when someone has made an effort to hide what we want to know. I think we could find him without too much trouble if we tried, and I wonder if J. W. is much different."

"Where would you start if you wanted to find him?"

"School first. Then, say Jason is gone, he'll probably try to get a line on who his relatives are. Ask around at stores. Your family has been here a long time. Someone along the line will remember old Uncle Whosis. Maybe J. W. remembers him anyway."

"I don't think so. When J. W. was here, Uncle Hector was spending most of his time at a mining claim he had out in the desert, in Yuma County. We didn't see him for a year or two at a time, even when my father was living. My sister thought he was a crazy old coot, anyway. He embarrassed her. She wouldn't have been anxious to show him off to her men friends, and I'm betting J. W. doesn't even know of his existence."

"Okay, but don't count on it for long. This is something like a panic move for you, isn't it? Even the truant officer will be checking on it soon. And supposing J. W. is back in town to stay?"

Lexie bit her lip. "A few days will give us some answers, I hope."

She put a notebook next to her typewriter and began to type. Craddock fussed with papers on his desk, made an unnecessary change in his editorial and stood up. Lexie continued typing. Craddock touched her shoulder and left, dropping the galley off at the composing room downstairs on the way out.

He was restless. Seeing Lexie always made him restless. When Craddock left Baltimore in 1920 for Tucson, it was his understanding that he had less than a year to live. He had a letter of introduction to the editor of the Tucson *Courier*, but he left it tucked into a book he was reading on the train. He spent his first six months in Arizona doing some serious drinking and trying to write a book about his experiences in France. But that was an experience he had shared with a couple of million other Americans at the time, and one he really wanted to put behind him.

His body stubbornly refused to die on schedule. He tapered off on drinking. Instead of hastening his end or clouding it in blissful oblivion, it made him too sick to enjoy the drinking, but not sick enough to die. Once he went to Chinatown, not half a block from Kee's Tea Room, and smoked opium in a basement room that was like a cavern, walked there through a tunnel, his elbow held by a Chinaman. But the dreams frightened him. He began to look around the dusty little Arizona town he had settled in. He was startled to discover that it had been inhabited far longer than Baltimore. He poked around in the nearly undisturbed ash heap of its antiquity and shortly found himself writing some articles about what he saw there.

The letter of introduction fell out of the book one day when he was rearranging shelves. Craddock absolutely did not want to lose his freedom to an ill-paying newspaper job, but some tattered remnant of professional pride drove him to call on the editor of the *Courier*, Orville Warren, who read the pieces and said he was either going to hire him or kidnap him into captivity, take your pick, but wouldn't let a man with ink in his veins croak in the desert before he typed out those good stories. Two years later, it was Orville who died peacefully in his sleep, but not before he arranged with the Davidson family, who owned the *Courier*, to be succeeded in the editor's chair by Woodfin Craddock.

No, Craddock decided, it wasn't seeing Lexie that made him restless. It was not seeing her. At the moment he left her at the office, he wanted to swarm all over her. What stopped him was his sense of the ugliness, the decrepit decaying ugliness, of his own wrecked body, the shambling rack of bones he walked around in. He had the feeling that if he were to kiss her, he would *infect* her, and it seemed to him impossible that she could ever feel passion—blistering, unbridled, abandoned, totally reckless passion was what he wanted—for the raddled scarecrow that he was now.

"Damn!" he said aloud. He was about to climb into his Buick. He heard laughter down the block and saw two men walk into the spray of yellow light that was the entrance to Kee's Tea Room. He recognized both men. One was said to have figured in a story Craddock had been looking into during the last year or two, a story about an obscure incident in the Mexican Revolution. Damned good story, if there was anything to it. Craddock ambled toward Kee's Tea Room.

7

KEE'S TEA ROOM was neutral territory, where citizens of various stamps, persuasions and loyalties mingled easily. The tea room offered Chinese and Mexican dishes, family style. The teapots might contain gin if the customer ordered it, or hot Japanese *sake.* The waiters were all Kees, brothers, cousins, nephews, who spoke English with Mexican-Cantonese accents. A door in the hall next to the Gents led through a passageway to the Billiard Room, which was actually another old adobe building, presided over by Jimmy's brother Emilio. The plastered adobe walls were calcimined a sickly mauve, decorated with posters for Mexican beer. The stuffed heads of two longhorn steers stared outward with dusty eyes. There were two pool tables opposite an ancient and ornate bar, a few small tables where a man could have a steak and watch the pool shooters, and farther back beaded curtains screened alcoves where a good deal of business was conducted, as well as card games, dominoes and mah-jongg. Periodically, Jimmy Kee would appear in court and pay a fine for violation of the Eighteenth Amendment, having spiritous liquors on the premises. He always insisted the offending spirits were carried there by ignorant customers.

J. W. Whitlock was in Kee's billiard room having a steak with onions and fried potatoes and his fourth bottle of Mexican beer when Red Durkin came in the door from the alley and saw him. Maynard Gaylen was standing at the bar sipping a beer and Woodie Craddock came in through the door from the tea room at almost the same moment. Both saw Durkin staring at J. W. openmouthed and round-eyed with his lantern jaw hanging down, saw him walk stiffly to J. W.'s table where he leaned forward to plant both hands on a chair back, and heard him croak: "Jesus H. Christ, do I believe this?"

J. W. grinned messily around a big bite of steak. "Believe it, Red. It's old J. W. How's the como whacko, amigo?" He kicked the chair leg. "Take the load off." He signaled to Emilio's boy Carlos for more beer, and in the same motion reached out and gripped Durkin's hand. Durkin sank into the chair, still staring, wagging his head.

"Last I seen you—"

"Hell of a lot noisier," J. W. finished for him. "Man had a warsh tub, he could've held it up and filled it with lead. Goddam *federales*. I had a hunch the bastards would be on that train."

"What I seen," Durkin said, "you stuck your elbow in the kid's gut and jerked the lead rope of Vega's packhorse out of his hands, you had a holt of it and you were flogging the bastard up a little draw."

J. W. looked puzzled. "Well, I'll tell you, I was sure looking for cover—fucking *machine guns* in them ore cars for Chrissake!—but I don't remember nothing about a packhorse."

Durkin grinned sourly. "Hell you don't. Every man in the outfit knew Vega's packhorse. Five years of revolution riding on that horse, Vega's personal take."

"Vega *slept* with his packs. Wasn't nobody going to mess with that crazy Cuban. Not yours truly."

"Don't shit me, J. W. I *seen* you leading the packhorse. I would've give my left nut to do the same, get the hell out of there with that horse, but that crazy Vega is right there screamin at me, spit all over his chin, and I'm watchin *you* flog that horse's butt out of there with a cartridge belt." Durkin reached out, tapped the diamond ring on J. W.'s left-hand ring finger, pointed at the diamond stickpin glittering in J. W.'s necktie. "There hadda be a fuckin *bushel* of ice just like that in the goddam packs, just like what you're wearin. Don't tell me different, J. W., goddammit, we all knew it. And you got it."

J. W. sucked his teeth and studied his diamond ring appreciatively. "Honest toil, amigo. I'm in real estate now. All that soldiering, it's a hell of a long time ago, right? Another whole war since then, too." He poured half a bottle of beer down his throat. "No shit, Red. You want to know what happened, when the machine guns opened up, I skinned out of there like a scared lizard—deserted, hell yes, you want to call it that. That goddam crazy Vega! Five, six days crawling on my belly through the brush, I got to Guaymas, caught a boat out of there. I left the boat in Panama. Talk about down and out—try three months in Panama. I went over to the Zone and enlisted in the U.S. Army, that's the shape I was in! My third fucking hitch! They shipped a bunch of us to New York, and Red, so help me, I'm on the first goddam troop ship to land in France! How d'you like that one?"

Woodie Craddock nodded and grinned at Maynard, took a beer from Carlos Kee. One of the players bent forward over the green table, stroked through smoothly with his cue and a rack of balls burst apart with a noisy clatter. The voices of Red Durkin and J. W. Whitlock were muffled by the click of balls on the table and the laughing banter of the players.

"Looks like a big reunion," Maynard said, looking toward Durkin and J. W., who was examining his diamond ring just then.

"Two sharks sniffing for blood, is what it is," Craddock said. "And do you realize that Shark One over there, the big guy with the teeth, is the daddy of the kid you and Lexie bundled off to old Uncle Whosis's place today?"

Maynard's smile disappeared. So that's J. W., he thought.

"Enter third shark, stage right," Craddock said.

The man who had entered with Durkin stood now just inside the alley door. He was not tall, but was exceptionally broad-shouldered, the well-cut dark suit and vest snug across his chest. He was smooth-featured, his face white-skinned under a dark hat, with a deeply cleft chin, narrow eyes sweeping the room, settling then on Durkin, who looked up, beckoned him over.

"Shark Three," Craddock went on. "Othello Biggers, ex–master sergeant, AEF, Silver Star, Croix de Guerre, a bucketful of Purple Hearts. The one-man platoon, he was called. Know him?"

"He's been pointed out to me. Along with Shark Two, the guy talking to J. W." Maynard was thinking that Durkin was probably the one who had alerted Deputy Allred to wait for him at the airport that morning, but he didn't want to tell that to Craddock.

"Shark Two, right," Craddock said, "Peter Durkin, known as Red, pal, or call it flunky of Biggers in France and now here. Did two years in the old Yuma pen before it closed in 1909, finished his term at Florence, 1912, crossed the border in great haste in 1913. Became a trusted lieutenant of the infamous Colonel Rodrigo Vega of the legendary Gringo Legion, cesspool of Pancho Villa's armies. It appears that J. W. Whitlock was in the same outfit, and from what I just now accidentally overheard, Durkin is claiming that J. W. bugged out with something of great value that Durkin coveted. Vega's thirst for loot and gore would shame Attila the Hun. Rumors of the nature of what Vega's packhorse was carrying attracted me to this story when I first hit town. I'm a sucker for treasure stories."

"Vega was killed, is that right?"

"He was killed later. In fact, Durkin claims to have shot Vega to protect some Americans a few weeks later—this was all in 1916—and Pershing rewarded the virtuous Durkin by enlisting him as a scout. At present Durkin and Biggers are peddling booze from Mexico in defiance of the Eighteenth Amendment. How is that for a dossier?"

"Impressive," Maynard said. "Where did you get all that?"

"A couple of years of patient digging. First thing a newspaper type does upon hitting a new town is sit down with the back issues in the morgue. Then you go talk to people. Funny how some names keep popping up."

"Red Durkin's?"

"I'm also thinking of Captain Gaylen, war ace." Craddock blew smoke at the ceiling with a smug smile.

"I've only read one piece about him," Maynard said, "a couple of paragraphs when he started a flying service."

"His fame will spread. He's generally regarded as being into a little piece of Durkin's illicit booze trade. Biggers and Durkin have been quick to suppress competition. No doubt they will squash the ace."

Maynard hesitated. "Are you interviewing him?"

"Not yet. It isn't news till it happens."

"Maybe you're . . . warning him, then."

"I dunno. I haven't thought it all the way through yet. If there's a chance any of it could, say, rub off on someone else, then maybe it's a warning. Speaking of somebody else, did you get to talk to Uncle Hector?"

Maynard laughed. "I sure did. Had to talk fast, too, with my hands up—the old gent held a shotgun on me."

"I'm thinking how Lexie had to take her kid nephew out there. Is the old geezer a nut, or what?"

"He comes close, but I'm not sure I'd call him a real nut," Maynard said. "He's very touchy and suspicious. Unforgiving. Giving it some thought, now you ask, I'd say he's something like a walking repository of the sum total of grievances of all our citizens over the last half-century or so of exploitation by the industrial robber barons."

"Maybe he's just a sorehead."

"Maybe, but I wanted to be on the same side with him—had to convince him I was, too. He thinks people are after him, so in that way, he's a nut, I guess."

"Well, is the kid safe with him?"

"Probably, if the old gent doesn't scare him to death."

Craddock said, "Tell me, how did the ace get into this, you know, transporting spirits?"

"Not an interview, right? Okay, Emilio Kee got him into it. You know the stuff they serve?—the gin in the teapots out front in the tea room, the so-called rye whiskey?"

Craddock made a grimace of agreement. "Courtesy Durkin and Biggers Imports."

"Emilio overhears him agree to fly a load of detonators to a mine down at Cananea. That was right here, where we're standing. Emilio says how about making a stop in Hermosillo on the way back, get some genuine French cognac. So, I—the guy we're talking about, that is, who's trying to make this flying service pay wages, points out there is a certain risk involved. Emilio says make a good price—and Emilio helps the guy come up with a price. It was about twice what the guy would have asked if he had worked it out without Emilio's help. Two or three other people—proprietors, like Emilio—hear about this. They're tired of having to depend on Durkin and Biggers for service, so they want in, too. It begins to look like the flying service might pay after all."

"Naturally the guy can use the money," Craddock said.

"Well, sure. He pours it all into a . . . project, call it."

Craddock laughed. "Does the project wear skirts?"

"No. That at least might make sense. Get some kicks out of it, anyway. No, it's something the guy dreamed up when he was behind bars—it helped keep him from going nuts."

Craddock stiffened and turned to Maynard, frowning. "You mean he was in the pen?"

Maynard laughed. "Landshut, in Bavaria, about forty miles from Munich. I spent five months there after I was shot down in May 1918. It was the longest hundred years of my life. You had to do *something*. Some of the guys worked on escapes. I did that, too, but mostly I worked on an airplane—not a real one, but one I was trying to design. The more I got into it, the more I could . . . forget where I was. After I got out of there, I kept at it. Here we are, five years later, and I'm still working on it. It's not the same—it's changed a lot—but the real difference now is, I'm building it instead of just drawing it."

"A real airplane?"

"That's right. Very advanced, I like to think."

"Will you show it to me?"

"It's still all in pieces. Hundreds of pieces. That's why it takes so long—and costs so much."

"Still, I'd like to do a story on it. A break from crime and corruption."

Maynard hesitated. "I don't think it's ready to talk about yet. No sense stirring things up."

"Curiosity, expectations—what?"

"All that, maybe mischief, too. Why draw attention to it? It isn't news till it happens, right?"

Craddock seemed not to hear. The pool players had finished their game and were racking their cues. He was watching Durkin, J. W. Whitlock and Othello Biggers as they left the table, chairs scraping noisily, and moved toward the pool tables, passing directly in front of Craddock and Maynard. Durkin was frowning, chewing his lip. He noticed Maynard and stopped, glaring at him as if about to speak, but Biggers bumped him from behind and Durkin moved on.

"Gents," murmured Biggers, then he too stopped. His eyes swept them briefly. "Rack or two of balls? Friendly game? A little wager, maybe?"

J. W. was grinning, diligently excavating with a toothpick. "Sure, join us—'preciate the company. Way it is, I'm outnumbered. Mister Craddock, right?"

"Right," Craddock said. "Maybe I will. Shake hands with Captain Gaylen."

Biggers stared at Maynard, his face expressionless. "The aviator, right?" He stuck out his hand. His grip was like a spring clamp. They shook hands all around, except for Durkin, who glowered and busied himself chalking his cue, and then Biggers gestured at the table.

"Not me, thanks," Maynard said. "Payday is too far away."

Durkin shrugged and began to collect the balls, sweeping them together in the triangular hardwood frame. Biggers and J. W. Whitlock selected cues and began to chalk them.

Craddock turned to Maynard with a wry grin. "Let's see if there's anything more to learn about Vega's packhorse," he said, his voice low. He put down his beer and walked a few steps to the cue rack, where he too took a cue. They lagged to see who would get the breaking shot. When it was his turn, Craddock bent his tall, skinny frame over the table, cocking his head so his cigarette smoke curled free of his face. "I couldn't help overhearing what you boys were saying about that fella Vega and his packhorse. There's a good story there."

Durkin flushed and glared at J. W., but said nothing. Biggers looked from one to the other.

"That's all it is," J. W. said. "A story. We missed our chance, Red, couple gunnysacks full of diamonds. We could've filled our hope chests."

"Still," Craddock said, "a great yarn. Somebody put that horse in the barn, right? Say you put your heads together, go over the facts, jog your memories. Maybe take a run down there and go over the ground again, how about that?"

"Mexico is one place to stay clear of," Durkin said. "Them poeple don't forget. Especially they don't forget Vega."

"Who's to know us?" J. W. said suddenly. "I mean, hell, we aint the same people anymore." He slapped his big belly. "Spose we went together?" he said to Craddock. "Two newspaper guys, right? Take a big Kodak."

Durkin, about to shoot, stopped, frowning suspiciously at Whitlock. Biggers said, "I just heard you say there wasn't nothing to it."

"I'm saying me and the redhead missed our chance, is all. It was there, all right, so where did it go?" He waved a big hand, grinning. "How about it, Captain? You like to take a charter down, couple hunderd miles is all?"

"Anytime." Maynard grinned.

"You go to Mexico," Durkin growled, "by god, you aint going alone."

Craddock caught Maynard's eye and winked. "The way I see it," he said, "it was too much of a load for a man to walk off with, but suppose, let's say he filled a sock and then hid the rest someplace. How's that sound?"

J. W. grinned. Consciously or not—Maynard wondered—he let his hand touch his necktie. Two diamonds flashed, one on his finger, one in the stickpin. "What do you think, Red? Had to be something like that, wouldn't you say?"

"That's what? Seven years?" Biggers said. "He would've gone back before now, cleaned it out."

"Hell he would!" Durkin blurted. "You don't know Mexico. It's still goin on down there—they only just croaked Pancho Villa *this year*! July, it was."

"Maybe," Craddock offered, "with that sockful, say the guy was pretty well fixed for a while, didn't have to go back. But suppose a time comes, he needs some investment capital? Could happen anytime, couldn't it?"

Durkin and Biggers exchanged glances. J. W. Whitlock flexed his shoulders to free his cuffs and turned to the table. "Hey, my shot?"

Emilio Kee, short and heavy in a black suit, drifted along the other side of the bar, nodding at Maynard with a slight smile. Maynard leaned over and said softly, "A day or two more, all right?"

"Seguro," Emilio said. "You the captain."

Maynard turned back to the table. J. W. was shooting, looking pleased even when he missed an easy shot. Durkin was chewing his lip, his frowning stare directed at the back of Whitlock's neck. Then Craddock leaned down to shoot, and for a moment his eye caught Maynard's. One eyelid drooped, ever so slightly. Maynard turned and left the room.

LATER, J. W. Whitlock couldn't remember when it stopped being fun and started getting ugly. The drinks kept coming. J. W. was comfortably loaded but shooting good pool. He swept the table a couple of times, which didn't help Durkin's mood. J. W. remembered card games under the stars in Mexico, cards and Mex silver on a saddle blanket, plenty tequila—and the old redhead was a sore loser then, too.

So Red was still burned up about the damned packhorse. Which, in the first place, gave J. W. the idea. Let the redhead think what he wanted. Maybe, if J. W. had something the redhead wanted, it would sweeten him up some when J. W. got around to asking for a piece of their liquor business, which is why J. W. skinned out of Fort Worth and drove all the way here. He needed a deal, needed it the worst way. . . . Something the redhead wanted. It didn't hurt a thing to make it look like he had, the way the newspaper guy put it, *investment capital.* It was Vega's packhorse that bought Red Durkin's loyalty to the crazy Cuban, and losing the packhorse must've broke his heart. Broke *my* heart, too, but, shit, never look back with tears in your eyes. My motto.

I mean, J. W. would think later, going back over it, I didn't plant the idea—mostly it was the newspaper guy, Craddock. He's the one. After he said I got away with a sockful of diamonds, then Red Durkin knew, for Chrissakes, *knew* I had a sockful of diamonds! *His* diamonds, the way Red looked at it. And then Biggers caught it, too. Maybe that's when it got serious, when Biggers started believing it. Should've kept my trap shut, but, shit, I half believed it myself after a while—couple more drinks, I was ready to charter the ace and his airplane, go back down there and find where I hid it.

Durkin was losing, so after a while he quit, sat there nibbling on a glass of tequila, chewing on a lime, and every time Craddock pumped in another line of thought on Vega's packhorse, J. W. could see Durkin *twitch,* see the gears grinding around in the redhead's ugly skull. At the same time Biggers was taking it all in, not missing a thing, J. W. realized later. *My kind of guy,* he would always think, *but only when he's on my side.* As soon grab a tiger by the ass as have that son of a bitch against me.

Along about three in the morning, Kee's place was pretty well emptied, except for the pool shooters and a few spectators. A card game was still going on in one of the alcoves, and four Kees sat at a table in shirtsleeves whispering in Chinese, going over their accounts, Emilio clicking beads on an abacus.

J. W. had to hit the latrine, was joined there at the metal trough by Shorty Blaine, a bowlegged little cattleman from Sonoita, and another guy, one of the watchers, a stocky drifter named Leopold Genereux, from St. Martinsville Parish, Louisiana, killing time until the 6:20 westbound freight. So, three streams going at once, hissing off the zinc.

Craddock walked in at that moment and heard Blaine say, "A sockful of diamonds—that right? Couldn't help hearing."

Craddock watched, amused inwardly but keeping a straight face as J. W. grinned affably and shrugged. The cattleman went on, "What better way to carry your money? You can put it in your pocket and walk away anytime you're of a mind to, which you sure as hell caint do if it wears horns and blows bullsnot all over you."

J. W. laughed. Craddock observed then that the other guy, the dark and stocky drifter whose name of course was unknown to Craddock, with a lumpy, battered reptilian face that Craddock would later struggle to remember, was eyeing J. W., a sidelong look. But Craddock's attention was on the conversation.

Buttoning up, Blaine said, "Say, you know a cowboy with Vega name of John Wesley Simmons?"

"Yeah, I remember him. Friend of yours?"

"Worked for me once, you want to call it work—when he left, he stole a thoroughbred racehorse from me. I hope the son of a bitch croaked down there."

"He was still alive, last I saw of him."

"Too bad." Blaine clucked his tongue and shook his head as they walked out just ahead of Leopold Genereux. "Damn shame. He needed shooting something terrible—forty-four caliber would just about do the trick."

This was what Craddock was remembering, making a mental note for his file on Vega, stopping a moment to scrawl *J Wes Simmons* in pencil on an envelope—a lead was a lead, no matter how slight.

So it was getting blurry by then. J. W. heard himself bragging about how he was going to get a nice piece of property, a place where his kid could have a couple of pinto ponies. "That boy is my *heir*!" he said, and then the game was breaking up.

J. W. was glad to quit, a few hundred to the good, mostly from Biggers. J. W. needed the cash, not merely to pay for his hotel room, but to keep up the good front, along with his two diamonds and big Marmon touring car parked down the street, while he was negotiating with Durkin and Biggers. Old habit made him fold most of his winnings into a little square. He bent to tug at his cuff, and when he stood straight again the money was tucked away in his sock.

Durkin approached him, *anxiously*. "Where you holed up, J. W.? I got to talk to you."

Great, J. W. thought. "Cosmo House. Spose we have a plate

of aigs, maybe ten o'clock?" But then he couldn't resist it. "Oh hell, I forgot—me and the ace, we was going to have an early chat."

The look on the redhead's face was worth it—not only does he bite for the sockful, but there's more where that came from! I'm playing the redhead like a fucking trout, exulted the inner J. W. Whitlock, walking the dark street to his Marmon—his triple-mortgaged Marmon, if anybody wanted to know. He opened the heavy door, heard a voice.

"Hey, J. W., got a minute?" Soft voice, not the redhead's—there he was, standing back in the doorway of Avila's Shoe Store, stocky figure limned by a faint night-light in the back of the shoestore. *Biggers?* Without Red. Hey, that could be good! J. W. left the door ajar and walked over, hands in pockets, grinning, shambling a little. He never saw it coming. There was just an instant's blinding flash as the sap caved in his jaw. He grunted, buckled at the knees and dropped.

J. W. Whitlock was out cold for more than half an hour. His senses slowly returned. He could see, and move, with effort, but his memory function and reason were knocked into the middle of next week. There was a great red-hot cannonball in his jaw. The heat spread from his collarbone to the top of his skull. After a time he saw the open door of his Marmon. *Gotta get going.* He knew that much. *Get the hell out of here . . . Biggers . . . Yeah, Biggers hit me.*

Out on his feet, J. W. staggered to the Marmon and toppled onto the leather seat. An eternity later, it occurred to him to turn the key. He trod the starter with his heel and the Marmon rumbled to life. Ground the gears noisily, pulled out into the street. What's wrong? No lights. He turned on the big headlamps. He knew where the highway was—came in that way couple days ago. He was in second gear for twenty minutes. Had to get there. Where? How the hell do I know? Somewhere pull himself back in shape. Couldn't talk to the redhead and Biggers this way. Bastards tried to kill me!

* * *

J. W. Whitlock drove east through the old Apache country, pushing a fan of light from the Marmon, the car weaving, fish-tailing on the graveled highway, now fifty, skidding, slowing to twenty as J. W.'s foot fumbled on the accelerator. A herd of sheep crossing the highway stopped him. Dawn was flooding the sky and wind blew grit across the road in trailing wisps. It rattled on the side of the Marmon and stung J. W.'s face. He felt a familiar bulge in the leather map pocket on the door next to his left knee. Flat bottle of Mexican brandy. Aah-h-h, little pick-me-up. Burned going down, fireworks flashing in his skull from the pain, but then it felt better. A lot better. J. W. watched three Indians on stunted, ratty horses pushing the sheep. Took another slug, hearing the drone of an airplane overhead. It came into view through the windshield, a big bi-plane heading east.

9

DAYBREAK was a little after seven. The Jenny was airborne and headed east toward Dragoon Wells. It was fiercely cold in the cockpit. Lexie shook out the blanket and tucked it around herself. She pulled the cuffs of her jacket down over her gloved hands under the folds of blanket and buried her chin in her collar. Her cheeks felt numb. Her feet were icy in their jodhpur boots.

She watched the sharp ridges of the Rincons pass beneath the wings, startlingly close, the canyons dark and bottomless, the mountain's broad crown looming still higher above them on the left. The sun burst through a cleft in distant mountains almost dead ahead and limned the whirling propeller. The ground below fell away sharply toward the San Pedro. Its sandy bed lay across their path like a sinuous twist of pale silk cutting through a dark pelt of mesquite *bosques* toward the Gila, far to the north.

Something tapped her knee. Maynard was passing her a small metal clipboard with an attached notepad and pencil. On it was written *OK?* She bobbed her head, worked a hand loose and wrote *How high?* and passed it back. *About 2500, 70 mph!!* he answered. The earth was now red-tawny in the dawn light. Mile-long shadows streamed across the desert floor from saguaros that looked ridiculously stubby from this altitude.

She saw a herd of sheep crossing the white ribbon of highway, splitting around a stopped automobile.

Maynard tapped the cowling and pointed—ahead, between the wings, was a long, faint scar threading out of a distant canyon into a valley that was knobbed and studded with bizarre wind-polished rock formations, all that same tawny red color in the dawn light. He banked, and she looked down on a crumbling adobe building with a caved-in roof. Nearby were a collapsed shed and the scattered rails of an old corral. A dirt tank of water reflected the sky like a blue sapphire. *Land?* she wrote.

Maynard throttled back and glided down in a long sweep that brought them in above the straight stretch of road close to the old station. He added a little throttle, holding the nose high, hanging it up there with throttle, it seemed to Lexie, so that she could not see ahead at all. Huge rocks swept past on both sides, and then it was as if the bottom fell out. The Jenny dropped and Lexie gasped. But the ground was right there. She fell a foot, no more, hit down firmly, and then they were rumbling along the uneven road. Maynard wheeled the airplane to a stop and switched off the engine. Lexie was dizzy with the landing and sudden silence.

"When you said we were at twenty-five hundred," Lexie said, "what did you mean, exactly?"

"I meant above ground," Maynard said. "And the ground around here is probably three or four thousand above sea level."

She was getting herself untangled from the folds of blanket, climbing out. Maynard guided her foot into the step, and then she was down. She leaned against the fuselage, laughing as she pulled off her helmet.

"Thought you'd never make it, right?" Maynard said. "Not to make you nervous, but sometimes it's that way with me too."

"Oh, terrific," Lexie said. She opened her small leather

portfolio. It held her notebook, pencils, a small folding Kodak and a very old, leather-bound volume that had *My Diary* embossed across the front in faded gold.

"Here's what I've been doing," she said. "When I started writing these historical pieces, I didn't want simply to rehash old stuff from the files or from history books—Father Kino, you know, or the Gadsden Purchase. I wanted to find something personal to take the reader's imagination by the hand, if that makes sense"—she looked closely at him and he nodded—"something to *touch* from that other time. I called it 'Silent Witness.' There's a silent witness to the past in each one of the articles."

"Like the foot in the stirrup?"

"That's right. The bones of a man's foot, about size six, with a spur on the heel, still in an iron stirrup. Some Scouts found it on a hike and I worked it into the article about the Spanish explorers."

Maynard laughed. "When I read it, I thought Alexandra Clark would be a big strapping woman with her hair in a bird's nest on top of her head."

"Do I sound like that?"

"It just had an air of conviction . . . authority, I guess."

He had opened the turtleback locker, taken out a thermos and was pouring coffee into two enameled cups. Steam curled up in wisps. He put the thermos back. With it were a hatchet, blanket, a coil of rope, the picket pins. A heavy flat pistol in a scuffed holster with US stamped on the flap lay partly covered by a faded red cap with a cracked leather bill.

"Why do you have that?" Lexie said, holding her cup in both hands.

Maynard laughed and put the cap on, tugged it so it sat squarely, and gave her a salute, palm out, in the manner of the Legion. "This is my Legion *kepi.*"

"No, I meant why do you have *that.*" She pointed to the pistol.

"Just *because,* I guess. It's my service pistol."

"Shouldn't you have turned it in? The war's over."

Maynard grinned. "Maybe. A German officer took mine when I was captured. When I got back from prison camp a week or so after the armistice, the squadron exec was . . . m-m, disposing of stuff used by one of our fellows, boy named Archie Kimball, who had gone down a few days before the war ended. The exec said, 'Here, maybe you can use this,' and he tossed it to me, so I kept it."

Lexie thought for a moment. "How come it didn't go down with that boy?"

"After what happened to Frank Luke, he wouldn't carry it. When Luke went down he crash-landed—he was all right, see? All he had to do was put up his hands when the Kraut soldiers came. Instead he started blasting away with his forty-five, so they killed him. Archie was afraid that would happen to him."

"But he died anyway, didn't he?"

"He was on fire," Maynard said. "He hit the ground going straight down, so the gun didn't have anything to do with it."

"It gives me the creeps," Lexie said. "You should bury it."

Maynard smiled uncertainly. "No, I just keep it around out of habit, like a . . . a wrench." He pulled off the *kepi* and tossed it back into the locker.

A quail called nearby. She shrugged and made a small face. "All right. Here's what we're doing—" She held up the leather-bound diary. "After my first article, I had a letter from a lady in town. I went to see her. She was very, very old and very tiny, like a little bird. She wanted me to read her diary, and that's what got me started on following the old stage route. She was married at an army post in New Mexico in 1859—that's sixty-four years ago, can you believe it? She was fifteen years old. Her husband was being transferred to Tucson, so she spent her honeymoon on the stage trip. From what her diary says, it was simply ghastly. Terrible, except for one little part, and we'll get to that later. I want to follow the trip she described in this diary, picking it up here, where we are now, and see if anything still looks the same, or if it's changed, how it's changed."

"What was her name?"

"Marietta. Marietta Ricks, although at that time her name was Applegate. She outlived three husbands."

"Durable."

"Indeed, but a lot more than that. I've had this diary for a few weeks now, and she has come to be very dear to me. Marietta Applegate is . . . she's a heroine, I have to say it."

Maynard smiled. "She outlived three husbands—I believe you."

"I mean it. You don't understand."

"No, I do understand. I have heroes myself."

"You mean like Wilbur and Orville?"

"Sure, but I was really thinking of your Uncle Hector."

"You're joking!" Lexie was clearly annoyed.

"No, I'm not. The more I think of him, the more I think the old gentleman is a noble spirit."

Lexie's nostrils flared. Clearly, she didn't believe him. After a moment she said, "Let's get on with it, shall we?"

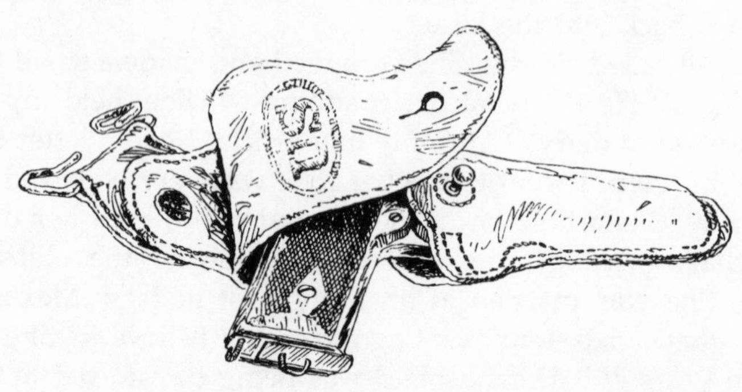

Jason awoke slowly that first morning, not letting his eyes open at first. He thought, my name is Jason Whitlock. That was the first and only thing he was sure of. Then he said to himself, where am I? Why am I here? And instantly his mind leaped to the question and tore it apart and it became: why was I born? And as the familiar hollow dread settled beneath his ribs, it became: I know I will die sometime—will I die soon? Asking the questions when he woke up was a kind of game. Pondering the answers could delay for long minutes his becoming aware of where he was waking up and what fresh misery the day was to bring.

Jason smelled dust first, then coffee through the dust. He let his lashes part slightly and saw the stained quilt that covered him, and then it all flooded back in a rush. He heard a slight scraping sound and twisted his head to look back. The door to the kitchen was open and the old man was standing at the sink with a cracked, steaming cup in his hand, and he was glaring out at the reddened sky.

Jason could not lie still any longer. He sat up and rubbed his gummy eyes with his hands, and then, knowing he had to, looked directly at the old man who, in the boy's eyes, looked remarkably like a great blue heron, his hunched and bony shoulders jutting from faded blue overalls, his head crested with spikes of white hair, the very movements of his skinny legs as he awkwardly planted his carpet-slippered feet suggesting the gawky bird.

And the old man, for his part, turned then and saw a runty, towheaded boy who appeared to be old before his time, a worried scowl etched into his face. Warily, they eyed each other.

"I'll make you a plate of grits," the old man said at last. "You like grits?"

"Yessir," Jason said uncertainly.

"Rise and shine, then. You can warsh up out yonder, in the pump house. Just turn off the water when you're done." The old man snatched a black iron skillet from the sink and hurled it onto the stove with a crash. He spooned a gob of bacon fat from a can and whipped it into the skillet with a snap of his wrist. Jason unrolled his corduroys and pulled them on. Remembering the sticker patch outside, he pulled on his socks and shoes too, and then went out the back door to find the pump house. He needed to find a toilet, too, but he was afraid to ask the old man where it was.

The back door, his malevolent enemy in the dark and windy night, opened easily onto the rickety steps. The wind had stopped blowing. A well-worn path led through a trash-littered, weed-grown yard. Sudden panic shot through Jason. Suppose he should be challenged this very moment and couldn't remember his countersign? His skin prickled with sudden horror and at that instant, unaccountably, the word *javelina* flashed into his mind.

"Dummy!" he whispered savagely to himself. He had to find that toilet in a hurry. Or maybe it would be an outhouse. Or even the *bushes*, the way he felt. He hobbled anxiously along the path and toward the wooden derrick of a windmill towering before him. Attached to one side of the derrick was a weathered pump house with a cable-strapped wooden tank on its top, like a plug hat, Jason thought. A small shed with a single window was built against one side of the pump house. The window was barred. The door was chained and locked and bore above it a board upon which was boldly lettered *DANGER—KEEP OUT.*

A cool breeze stirred. The windmill groaned on its derrick, and Jason saw that its tailvane was locked to one side to keep it from pumping. It groaned again, quivering, and he realized that if it had been unlocked during the windy night, it might have pumped itself to pieces. He stepped through the pump house door.

Inside, heavy cross-braced timbers formed the corners of the single open room. Jason smelled wet wood. The ceiling was the dark, damp-streaked bottom of the wooden tank. The floor was of concrete, sloping toward a drain in the center. Water showered down here and there from the leaky tank above and ran out through the drain. In the corner opposite the door, there was a stained metal trough cut from half an oil drum. A toilet seat straddled the trough, supported on two boards. Water from the tank above cascaded down onto the toilet seat. A large calendar for the year 1919 hung on the wall behind it. The heavy paper was water-stained and wrinkled from many soakings, and Jason saw that the calendar served as an umbrella for one sitting on the toilet, an amenity he now gratefully put to use. From his drizzly perch he observed a metal sink supported by pipe legs against the front wall. Overhead, a pipe ran along the ceiling over the center of the room. A lard can punched with nail holes hung from the end of it on a wire bridle. *Shower bath,* Jason noted appreciatively.

But how to flush the toilet? he wondered anxiously. He looked for a handle, water cascading down around him from the calendar. Then he saw a faucet on his left side, poised over a smaller, open-topped tank that was perched at a steep angle next to him. Water trickled from the faucet into this tank, which was less than half full. Then Jason saw that this small tank was mounted on a kind of axle, so that it rode on its mount like a teeter-totter. The weight of the water kept one end of the tank down, because the axle was off center. Jason was wondering why the axle was off-center when suddenly the tank, having filled to a certain level, rocked over with a crash and dumped its load of water into the big trough beneath the toilet. Jason squawked and nearly leapt from his perch as his bottom was inundated in the brief deluge. The tank beneath his seat was swept clean, everything having gurgled noisily down a drain at the low end. Emptied, the smaller tank rocked back to its former position and began slowly to fill again. Jason's heart thudded in his chest. He thought it was the most marvelous toilet he had ever seen. Finished, he remembered to turn off the water.

He washed his face free of grit and sleep at the sink. Sputtering, he reached for the dirty flour sack hanging on a nail at his left hand. This brought his eye close to a small knothole in the wall. Light on the other side caused him to put his eye to it for a closer look.

His view was restricted by the knothole to what appeared to be a bench or tabletop upon which sat a marvelous machine. Morning sun streaming through the window washed it in golden light. The machine was made of polished brass and had geared wheels mounted on polished shafts of bright steel, and a series of pivoting arms, all set in a brass openwork frame. Peering through the tiny hole with one eye, he could not be sure of the machine's size. It had to be less than a foot high, yet the light and something about the machine itself gave an illusion of loftiness, of vast scale, so that Jason instinctively thought of it as a huge and monstrous thing. Nothing about it indicated its purpose.

He squirmed for a better look, but the hole was too tiny. Reluctantly, he pulled away. He finished drying his face and ran his broken pocket comb straight back through his wet hair, neglecting the back and sides. He could feel the combed strands springing up, loosening tiny rivulets of water to course down his neck, tracing muddy tracks into his collar. Suddenly, Jason was hungry. He darted out the door and ran along the path, back to the kitchen door. Halfway there he smelled bacon frying. Saliva gushed beneath his tongue.

"Slick as a peeled snake!" the old man cackled when he saw Jason. He cleared two places at the table by sweeping it with his elbow. Newspapers, a pair of pliers and a pie tin fell to the floor in a shower of crumbs and dust. Cockroaches scurried for cover. The old man slapped two plates down on the oilcloth, and the next moment he was dumping grits onto the plate from the smoking skillet. He buttered the grits with a table knife and then streamed a swirl of syrup onto each plate with a calligraphic flourish. He splashed coffee into his cup and filled a mug for Jason.

"Root, hog, or die!" he said. "Any man who bellyaches gets thirty days on bread and water!"

Jason nibbled suspiciously at a bite of grits. Butter, syrup and hot bacon fat melted together with creamy nodules of hominy in subtle and fragrant delectation. He filled his mouth, savoring.

Jason mopped up the remains of his breakfast with a cold biscuit. He was not used to drinking coffee, but the syrup that clung to his lips smoothed the harsh bite of it, and drinking it down gave him a feeling of manliness.

"Soldier grub is the best eats for hungry men." The old man was filling a broken-stemmed pipe mended with black friction tape. He raked a wooden match along the seat of his overalls and noisily sucked the pipe alight, then dropped the match into his plate where it sizzled out. "Now, then, spose you tell me just why you have come to roost here."

"It's only till Lexie can get a court order—on account of . . . my dad . . . he—"

"He what? A hard case, is he? Hard to live with, that it?"

Jason nodded. His nose suddenly stung and his eyes flooded. He blinked helplessly. How to tell the old man about J. W. Whitlock?—he saw him suddenly, sprawled in his chair at the kitchen table in the Fort Worth house in his underwear, a hand of solitaire laid out, a nearly empty bottle of whiskey and a quart bottle of beer at his elbow, his thick fingers fiddling with a dirty shot glass as he glared at Jason. The hand shot out and snatched at Jason's shirtfront, yanked him close to the red-stubbled face with the tiny purple veins and the square yellow teeth, whiskey reek boiling out hot and damp . . . Jason shook his head.

"I don't spect you can tell me. Don't know that I ever set eyes on your daddy—he come along after Sam died, if I've got it right. But I knowed your mama. Easy to shock, she was." The old man chuckled, sucking at his gurgling pipe. "She had no use for me, and I didn't do nothing to change her mind. It was more fun to tease her, play the ornery old fool, and that I done, just to be contrary, nothing else. But a man is judged by what he *appears* to do or be, remember that, young sir." He stabbed his pipe at Jason's chest and Jason flinched.

"Anymore," the old man went on, "I've fell out of touch with the family. I'm just too blamed busy to get around much. And I just don't hardly dare to leave the place, is what it's like."

"Why not?" Jason said. He was looking through a door into another room—a dining room or parlor, he couldn't tell for sure. Heavy brown oak furniture was almost obliterated under a chaotic litter of old newspapers, magazines, tools, bowls and plates full of matches, tobacco ash and taped pipes, along with odd garments, shoes, boots, socks, shotgun shells, hats, a cribbage board, decks of dog-eared cards, books, photographs, a stuffed hawk, a six-foot-long rattlesnake skin, a cavalry saber—all seen from where Jason sat, so there was no telling what other treasures the rooms held. It was as if nothing ever put down had been picked up.

"Why not?" the old man echoed crustily, his voice cracking. "I'm just damn near wore out from the work, since you ask, plus, if I did leave, they would break into the place, and I just caint, by god, take a chance on it." He thudded his pipe onto the tabletop, scattering coals. Smoke curled up. Jason reached out and brushed at the smoldering spots with his hand. The old man did not notice. He glared into space.

"You mean," Jason said carefully, "because of the agents?"

The old man's eyes swung back to him and widened, as if he were startled to see Jason there. "You don't know what it's like. They're everywhere and there aint but one of me."

Jason swallowed. He thought of the marvelous machine he had seen a few minutes earlier in the pump-house shed. "What are they after?" he whispered.

The old man frowned. "Dammit, I caint set here and jaw the morning away. I spect you can find something to do. I caint tolerate a kid loafing around. Maybe you'll want to go to school."

Jason's insides heaved. "My dad will just find me there and take me away." His worried scowl deepened. "Besides, I can help you here. I'll keep watch while you work."

The old man rose jerkily, like a wooden rule unfolding. He snatched the coffeepot off the stove, trailing a fine stream of coffee through the air as he swung the pot to fill his cup. Jason flinched. The old man returned the pot to the stove with a jarring crash and stalked out through the porch where Jason had slept and on out the back door, leaving splotches of spilled coffee along the floor behind him. Outside the door, he stopped and looked back.

"It don't matter a damn to me whether you go to school or not. I only just got through the fourth reader myself. A couple of the bigger boys laid for the teacher and give him a thrashing, so he quit and that was the end of my education. After that it was hard knocks done the trick." He turned and stalked past the rear of the house on the stony path to the pump-house shed. Jason, leaning as close as he could to the kitchen window, could see him unlock padlocks on the shed door, one, two, three of them, the last linking heavy chain. The chain clattered loose, hinges squalled, and the old man disappeared into the shed.

10

J. W. WHITLOCK kept the pain in his shattered jaw at bay with frequent jolts from the bottle of brandy. The heavy Marmon slewed from side to side of the graveled road as J. W. cursed and raved and fought the wheel. A truck driver blew his horn at the crazy fool who careened through a bend and nearly ran into him, who then gave him the finger and bellowed something at him as he swept by. J. W. never saw the sign that told him when he crossed the state line into New Mexico. His eyes were trying to stay closed. The Marmon ran out of gas just in time. The car veered off the road and skidded up next to a cattle-loading chute about two miles from Lordsburg, New Mexico.

Alone after the old man went to work in his shed, Jason felt trapped in the strange old house, fearful of the dark rooms and appalling litter. He hurried to the back door and slipped outside. A few yards away toward the riverbed, there was a sandy knoll. Jason climbed it, threading carefully between clumps of buckhorn and ocotillo and prickly pear. The top of the knoll was a little higher than the house and he could see for miles.

Below him, the road he had traveled in the night wound across the sandy riverbed, a long gulch walled by eroded bluffs. Across the gulch he saw another house, not unlike the old man's, with its own windmill close by. A good place for agents, he thought, but then he saw a woman in the yard and a little white dog. As he watched, the dog barked and the woman's voice rose in querulous complaint. They can't be agents, he decided.

A steam whistle wailed in the distance, and Jason saw a freight train creeping slowly eastward along the brush-stippled plain, miles away. And on beyond the train, ranges of mountains thrust up from the vast, smooth sloping plain like islands in a sea, the highest peaks brushed with red and gold where the morning sun licked at them. Even as he watched, the light burned slowly down, melting the cold purple left by night. Coronado rode there, Jason thought, and he felt himself among the Spaniards, a burnished helmet heavy on his brow, bit chains jingling and saddle leather squealing to the pace of the march. Jason shivered.

He walked a few steps around the top of the knoll to where he could just see the pump house and shed. Something fell to the floor of the shed with a metallic crash, and Jason heard the old man's voice mumbling testily. He could make out nothing through the dirty window, but he fancied he felt the old man's eyes on him through the glass and he was stung by a pang of guilt. He wondered if looking around outside the house was the same as loafing. Jason hurried down the slope and back into the house.

He smelled scorched coffee. Brown froth was bubbling up out of the coffeepot and running down onto the stovetop, where it sizzled and spat steam. He moved the pot to the cold side of the stove and then stood back and looked uneasily at the sink and wooden drainboard, mountainous with dirty dishes, pots, pans and utensils, all splotched with dried food and liberally peppered with mouse droppings. Something his mother had said came to him. He could almost hear her voice. "No guest need be too grand to help wash up a few dishes."

Jason saw a chipped dishpan under the piled dishes. He

found a chunk of brown soap and a tatter of stiff rag. He cleared room to work and then poured hot water from the blackened kettle on the stove into the pan. The high drainboard cut into his breastbone. He kicked a wooden crate free of its burden of trash and skidded it over in front of the sink to stand on. Lettering stamped on the crate said *RED CROSS EXTRA DYNAMITE—60 PERCENT.* Jason was pleased. He felt bold and daring, stepping up onto a dynamite box. It made him think of the book he had just read, of Legionnaires mounting the firing step on the parapet of the fort in the desert. Jason looked to right and left, frowning grimly. He saw the bodies of his dead comrades propped in the embrasures, rifles at the ready under their dead fingers.

"The swine are re-forming for another charge," he murmured. He ducked a near miss as an Arab tribesman fired at him. Laughing in grim disdain, he moved along the parapet from one embrasure to the next, firing each Lebel rifle in turn until cartridges littered the parapet and the air stank of burned powder. Stacks of dishes mounted on the drainboard. He scalded them with hot water. The kettle in his hands was the breech mechanism of a small fieldpiece. He skidded it back onto the stove.

"Empty!" Jason snarled. "With a hundred rounds of ammunition, we could hold the devils off!"

In the shed, old Hector Callard carefully dressed a small piece of brass with a jeweler's file. His mind commenced to wander, as it often did when his hands were busy, the work repetitious.

He felt the warm Mississippi sun of ancient memory on his back. There were six of them, a detail from Company B of the 7th Illinois Volunteer Cavalry, and they were skirting an open field that was fringed with spindly pines. They splashed across a shallow creek. Hector felt the big chestnut he was riding lurch in the water, and it stumbled when they trotted up the far bank.

He said, "Shep, I b'lieve this jughead has throwed a shoe." His friend Walter Sheppard laughed and said something Hector did not catch. At that moment, a piece of fabric flew off the back of Shep's blue blouse and spun away and something spattered Hector. Another part of a second later, as Shep was falling backward over his horse's rump, a single shot rang out. A puff of smoke drifted through the pines across the field, a quarter of a mile away. The corporal yelped, "*Move,* goddammit!" and Hector grabbed for Shep's arm, but the horse bolted out from under him and Hector's fingers tore loose.

Looking back, he saw Shep bounce and roll, his arms and legs limp as rags. They pulled up in the shelter of some pines a minute later to let the horses blow and to collect their wits. Hector looked down and saw tiny flecks of blood and flesh drying on himself, and then felt it on his face too, pulling at the skin the way blood dried and pulled at the skin at dehorning time. His throat constricted in a sudden spasm of grief and shock, and tears streamed down his cheeks, and the same shock and grief bridged the whole vast chasm of time, the sixty years from that moment to this, and old Hector Callard sitting at his bench felt his throat torn with rage again, and blinked away tears.

It was a single shot, not even a skirmish. Nothing gained or lost except, in a split second, the life of Hector's friend Shep, nineteen years old, from Bosworth, Missouri. Of all the battles and fights and all the times that Hector had seen death, sudden and violent, this was the time that came back, and back and back again. He shook his head and rubbed his eyes.

Movement at the kitchen window caught his eye. He sucked in his breath. His spine prickled. Then he remembered. That damned kid. Hector rubbed dirt from a windowpane over the bench and peered out between the bars. The kid's face was there, above the sink. At that instant, the face dropped from sight. It reappeared in another place, then disappeared abruptly again. Puzzled, the old man watched. Next he saw the canvas blind on the screened porch pushed aside. The kid peeped out warily, looking from right to left, then ducked back. Another moment and he was back at the sink. The old man saw his lips move. *The kid was talking to someone,* and all that skulking and spying was to make sure Hector Callard did not overhear them.

Hector threw his file down. I thought I warned the kid. Now someone has wormed his way in there, askin questions. At least the kid don't know nothing. Dammit, where did I put my shotgun? Adrenaline pumped. Hector's pipe hung quivering from his jaw. Whoever it is, I've got to talk to the son of a bitch, find out what his game is.

He rose jerkily to his feet, looking down at the Juggernaut. Ought to pull it to pieces, the way he always did when he left the shop, but there wasn't time. He reached down and pulled the flywheel off its shaft along with the linkage that drove it, and put them up high on a cluttered shelf between the studs. Even if they was to photograph it with a Kodak, it won't tell them what they want to know, he thought.

Hector slipped out the door. He did not intend to be out of sight of it, so he didn't lock it. He circled around behind the pump house through the brush to the door, avoiding the familiar path. The kid, bent over the sink and looking down, had not seen him approaching, but his lips were moving and now the old man distinctly heard his voice.

"Someone will have to try to get through for help, or we're finished—"

The old man hurled the door wide and leaped through. Jason stumbled backward off the dynamite crate, his arms flailing soapy water. The old man stalked toward him, his stubbly chin thrust out and quivering, his skinny neck corded and his pale eyes glaring.

"All right, who were you talkin to? Where is the son of a bitch?" He advanced another step.

"N-nowhere," Jason stammered, his heart beating wildly. "There wasn't no one—anyone. It was a . . . kind of a game, is all." His hand twitched and water slopped onto the crate.

The old man looked down. His eyes widened. "Great Lord of Hosts, where in hell did you get that?" He pointed at the dynamite crate.

Jason swallowed. "It was right there under a mess of papers and stuff. I just took it to stand on."

The old man's fury subsided. He scratched his spiky hair. "Damn! I wondered where the stuff had went to. It set out at my claim shack for a long time, and I was afraid someone would bust in and take it, so I brought it back here, and then—well, damn if I could remember where I put it." He knelt down and fingered the wooden top. "I better have a look at it."

The old man's voice now sounded moderate and reasonable. Curiosity overcame Jason's fright. "What is there to look at?"

"I think the stuff has went bad." The old man pointed to dark brown stains on the wooden corners of the crate. "It's old. I don't even remember how old. See them marks? That means the stuff is leaky. The nitro has dreened out of the sticks, and when it's done that, you want to walk mighty damn careful, understand?"

The old man took a piece of kindling from the wood tub by the stove. He put its sharp end against the joint where lid and box came together and tapped it with a heavier stick. The lid loosened and he pried it up. "You don't want to use iron tools on dynamite, see? Just wood." Inside, the crate was full of sticks, their paper wrapping stained a slick, shiny, brownish black.

The old man recoiled. "*Shew*! Look at the color!"

Jason flinched. He wanted to run.

The old man pulled out a stick and squeezed it. The paper split and black mush spilled out. "It's bad, all right. I mean real bad. She could go anytime."

Jason's heart lurched within his breast. "What are you going to do?"

"Aint but one thing we *can* do and that's burn it."

"I think I want to get out of here," Jason whispered. His tongue felt dry as a shingle.

The old man laughed sharply. "You do, do you? Then who's a-going to help me? Answer me that. So just you bring some paper and matches and foller me." He gently cradled several blackened sticks against the bib of his overalls and went out the back door. Jason took a deep, shaky breath, then snatched up some old newspaper and followed.

The old man led Jason on a blurred path through the brush and cactus. A lizard scuttled beneath a rock. A spidery branch of ocotillo plucked at Jason's sleeve. Some forty yards from the house they came to a cleared area with a circle of rocks and a pile of ash and scorched cans, bottles and odd pieces of charred trash.

Hector opened a pocketknife and slit one of the cartridges, spreading it with his fingers to expose the blackish mush inside. He put it down on wadded paper, then struck a match and held the flame to the paper. Smoke wisped up. Paper curled and blackened and the mush began to smolder.

"Oh, gawd," the old man said with a sudden shudder, *"she looks like she's a-goin to blow!"*

Jason's belly sucked flat with horror. His hackles bristled. A grunt burst through his clenched teeth as he wrenched himself around and ran, scrambling and stumbling on the rocky path. Tears of fright blurred his vision. The ocotillo slashed his cheek and ear. He heard himself whimper as he ran, the sound torn from him with each frantic stride. The ground broke into eroded trenches near the bluffs. Jason hurled himself into a gully, facedown, his hands over his ears, his eyes clamped shut.

The earth did not heave beneath him. There was no blast. He slowly opened his eyes. Inches away, a red ant strained backward, pulling an enormous burden. Dust puffed beneath Jason's nostrils, and a bright bead of blood from his torn cheek balled on the sand. He uncovered his ears and heard a strange cawing sound.

Jason peered over the rim of the gully. The old man was doing a kind of shuffling jig-step. He was making the cawing sound, too, and Jason understood then that the old man was laughing at him. Shame welled up in him, shame and horror and self-disgust and loathing of the old man. His throat knotted, his nose burned, and tears sprang to his eyes.

"Dirty old son of a bitch!" he choked aloud, lurching to his feet—the first time he had ever dared say the words. Oh, God, he thought, you never answer my prayers, but couldn't you just make that dynamite blow up now, while that old man is standing over it?

Jason drew a shaky breath and forced himself to climb out of the gully and start back toward the fire. He wiped his eyes and nose, careless of the blood that smeared his face, and thrust his jaw out. Don't let him see me cry, he thought.

Now the old man had a hand on each knee and, so bent, was awkwardly stalking around the fire in a circle, his laugh reduced to an occasional convulsive bray. Foul, sharp smoke stung Jason's nostrils. The old man slit another stick and opened it flat and placed it at the edge of the fire. He brayed once more. Jason stopped a few feet away, his face set.

"Well, now," Hector Callard gasped, "what you have done is learn how to do away with old dynamite, and if anyone ever says it aint a scary proposition, you can tell em you know better—which is no more nor less than any good powder man knows." He had stopped laughing. He cocked his head and smiled at Jason, an expression of unaccountable tenderness. "Now, spose you trot back and bring me the rest of the stuff, a few sticks at a time, so's we don't have the whole lot here at once, then you can feed some to the fire, too."

Jason was surprised and grateful that the old man made no attempt to rub his nose in his humiliation. He carried the sticks as he was told, his hatred slowly subsiding.

"Are we through?" he said when the last stick was burning.

"No, sir, we aint," the old man said. "The wood in the box

is soaked with that old nitro, too, so you run get the box and something to break her up with."

Jason retrieved the box from the kitchen. He started to take the hatchet, but then he remembered—use no iron tools on dynamite. What, then? Some kind of mallet. Back outside, he noticed the shed door standing ajar. He left the house and entered the shed.

A workbench ran along the front wall beneath the window from the door to the pump-house wall. The back wall held rough shelves loaded with metal parts and scrap—cigar boxes, tin cans and dynamite boxes full of it. On the plank floor, other boxes overflowed with more of the same scrap. The bench top was littered with small tools, more cigar boxes and scraps of brass. Close to the door sat a small machine which Jason identified at once as a lathe mounted on an iron sewing-machine table, its bed half buried in curled whiskers of brass, its drive wheel connected to the treadle mechanism. All this noted in a quick scan as Jason stepped inside the shed, for his eye immediately found the strange machine he had seen earlier through the knothole.

Seen in the open, the machine no longer seemed to tower into space, but its ingenious interplay of geared wheels and pivot arms was fascinating. Jason looked for a motor or some means of driving it, but there was none. He thought he remembered a large wheel mounted on one side, which might have told him its purpose. Was it, he wondered, a water-driven machine?

He stepped closer for a better look, so absorbed that he did not hear the old man's thudding footsteps on the path or the slap-slap of the baggy overalls—and then the old man was upon him, a clawed hand digging into his shoulder, jolting him into the workbench.

"Now, by god, sir, I'll be damned to the fiery pits, but just what in hell is your business in this here shop?" Hector Callard was gasping from his run. Wind rasped in his throat. His spiky hair stood out as if charged with electricity. His fingers dug into Jason's shoulders. Certain he was about to be throttled, Jason caught the old man's wrists to keep the hands away from his throat. There was no resistance. The wrists he held were thin as turkey legs. Jason realized the old man was leaning on him to keep from falling. He eased him to a seat on a tall wooden stool, where the old man sat gasping.

"I was trying to find a tool to break up the box with, is all," Jason said shakily. "You never told me not to come in here."

Still wheezing, the old man lifted his head and glared balefully at him. He lurched to his feet and felt behind some boxes on a high shelf. Satisfied, he plucked a rag off a nail and hung it over the brass machine.

"Well, then, if I didn't, I'm a-tellin you now, young sir. Nobody, and b'god, I mean not a livin soul, is to set foot in this shop." He waved a hand. "Oh, I spect you meant no harm, but dammit, don't you see, the bastards is everywhere and there aint nothing they wouldn't do to get their slimy hands on the Juggernaut. Lie, cheat, steal or kill, it's all the same to them."

Jason shivered. "The agents, right? But who are they?"

"The awl companies, that's who. They've already broke up the steam-car people. You know that, don't you?"

Jason had never heard of an awl company, although he knew about steam cars—Stanleys, Whites and Dobles. He shook his head. "I don't know anything about awl companies."

"Well, sir, by god, it's time you did! Stannerd, Shale and the rest, and old John D. hisself—they're all in it together and he's the head alligator. Stop at nothing, I'm a-tellin you. Sons of bitches . . ." His voice trailed off. Motes of dust hung in the light of the window.

"What is it they *do*?" Jason said softly.

"By god, they run the show, is what they do. Look what they done to that cabber eater—stole it, is what, to keep it from the people! Christ, we'll never see it now!"

There was anguish in his voice. To Jason, whatever it was

that had happened to the cabber eater sounded darkly sinister. Trying to understand, he said, "Cabber eater?"

The old man's eyes, staring, were pale blue, like melting ice, the pupils hardly showing. "Yes, the one that give over a hundred mile to the gallon." He slapped his palm onto the bench. "And by god, they stole it!"

Understanding washed over Jason, and embarrassment for his apparent ignorance. *Of course* he knew about the legendary carburetor, and how the oil companies had stolen it from its inventor and destroyed it to keep it out of use. Any kid who knew anything at all about cars knew about the carburetor. Anxious to redeem himself, Jason blurted, "I know what a juggernaut is."

The old man's head jerked around fiercely. "You do, do you? Then spose you tell me about it."

Jason was a bookworm. He had a good memory for words and a curiosity about them. "In India, it means 'lord of the world.'"

The old man shook his head, puzzled. "No, that aint it."

"They have a god there, Krishna, in statues and things, see, and they would put this god up on a huge cart—"

"No! Hell, no, it aint anything like that!"

"—and they rolled this great big cart through the streets," Jason went on, "and people would get crushed under it, so—"

Hector wagged his head. "It's nothin to do with any of that, I'm a-tellin you."

"But wait. So now what it means is a thing or object, like a machine, that can roll over and batter to pieces anything in its path. It's the powerfullest thing in the world."

"That's it! Now you've got it!" The old man laughed sharply and squirmed on the stool. "That's the Juggernaut!"

Errare humanum est
[Lat.] To err is human.

Cui bono?
[Lat.] Who benefits by it?

Contra bonos mores
[Lat.] Against good morals.

Anguis in herba
[Lat.] A snake in the grass.

11

RED DURKIN was awakened that morning by a call from Augie, the watchman at the airport. Durkin pulled on his trousers when the bellhop's knock woke him. Suspenders dangling, he grumpily took the call on the hall phone.

"The captain, he took off at daybreak, some guy with him—too dark to see who. You wanted to know, right?"

Durkin got dressed, went downstairs in the Territorial for a plate of ham and eggs and hashed browns in the coffee shop. In his mind, he chewed the matter of J. W. and Vega's packhorse the way he chewed bites of gristly ham. Easy enough to find out if it was J. W. with the pilot. Durkin finished eating and walked two blocks to the Cosmo House in the bright morning sun. He asked at the desk for J. W.'s room number, went up the stairs to the third floor, rapped on J. W.'s door. No answer. Down the hall, a hotel maid was working with her cart of sheets and towels, softly singing "La Golondrina." Durkin waited until she was in one of the rooms and then he opened the door on the third try with one of his numerous passkeys.

J. W.'s bed was made up. The maid has already been here, Durkin thought. Durkin quickly went through J. W.'s things, a couple of suitcases, the pockets of a suit hanging in the closet, a toilet kit on the dresser. He inspected the linings of the suitcases carefully. Nothing. He lifted the mattress, felt the pillows, ran his hand behind the steam radiator. Oh-oh. He looked in the toilet tank too.

J. W. and the ace have went to Mexico, he thought. It couldn't be nothing else. But J. W. wasn't no idiot. He wouldn't be taking his roll or whatever was left of that sockful of diamonds back to Mexico. Hotel safe? No, he decided, why give them people ideas? So, he's stashed it with his kid.

Durkin helped himself to a hefty slug from the bottle of scotch on the dresser and left the room. As he came into the lobby from the stairwell, he saw the newspaper guy, Craddock, at the desk talking to the clerk. Him and J. W. was pretty thick last night, Durkin was thinking. He knows plenty about Vega and the whole thing. He knows J. W. is making his move and he wants to be in on it. Durkin kept walking, right on out the door, while Craddock's back was turned. It was too early to wake up Biggers. Durkin wanted to do some serious thinking. He went back to his own room in the Territorial, where he stripped to his union suit and laid out a hand of solitaire. Left his hat on.

Woodie Craddock saw that he had two cigarettes burning at once, one on the edge of the ashtray, and one hanging from his lips. He grimaced and stubbed out the shorter of the two. He was getting nowhere with his editorial, the subject of which was "Does this town need storm drains?" His idea was, why not let the streets themselves carry away the water, since it only rains a few times a year anyway?

But his mind kept lunging off target: Lexie, Rodrigo Vega's packhorse, Captain Gaylen, Lexie . . . and J. W. Whitlock. Craddock was disappointed in not finding J. W. in his room at the Cosmo House.

Abruptly, Craddock spun in his chair and whipped out his manila folder labeled *Vega.* It contained notes and clippings going back to 1916. He had started a file on Vega that year when he was still with the Baltimore *Sun.* He couldn't remember exactly why—something to do with the numbers of people Vega was said to have killed. And he had kept on adding to the file once he got to Arizona where Vega's name was well remembered.

A scribbled note read: "Costello—SP dick—ex-Pinkerton." He picked up his phone and called the Southern Pacific offices, asked to be put through to Costello. A few minutes later, he was in Costello's office on Toole Street, next to the railroad tracks. Little guy in his fifties with a drooping mustache, voice like chipped flint, eyes about the same. Wore a dark suit with a blue flannel shirt and black knit tie, high-heeled boots on his small feet. Craddock noted a single-action Colt in a worn shoulder rig hanging from a coat tree.

"I've been working on putting together an article about Rodrigo Vega," Craddock said, "and if there turns out to be anything to it, a follow-up piece on his packhorse. And maybe you could tell me something about a fellow named Red Durkin."

Costello laughed. Started talking.

As he talked, Costello pointed out a few of the numerous framed photographs on the wall across from his chair. One showed Costello and several other people sitting in the wreckage of a big touring car in what appeared to be a village plaza—there was a fountain, anyway—in Mexico. The car's fenders were gone, its headlights cocked at crazy angles. It was down on the shattered spokes of its wheels and the engine was full of holes, sprouting a tangle of wires and tubing. Costello had one arm in a sling, and the people were all looking severely battered although they were smiling happily for the camera. A little to one side stood Red Durkin, wearing a big Mexican hat, a nasty, crooked grin on his face. A U.S. Army sergeant was holding his arm.

"I spect you'd like to know what happened to Vega," Costello said, "and I take considerable pleasure in being able to show you." He tapped another photograph. Craddock saw a picture of the corpse of Rodrigo Vega sprawled on a rocky patch of ground that was littered with broken prickly pear. Several U.S. cavalry soldiers stood around grinning—and again, there was Red Durkin.

Some time later, Craddock said, "To do the packhorse story right, I ought to go over the ground where it happened. You know anyone who could give me a lead on that?—or better yet, go with me?"

"You know that bridge over the Santa Cruz, the machine shop there? Talk to Jack Perrell, owns the place. Tell him I sent you—and don't forget to mention Red Durkin." Costello laughed again and pointed to another figure in the photograph of the wrecked touring car. "That's Perrell right there. The lady next to him there is his wife, Amanda. Her name was Sibley then. The way it happened, Vega had us all locked up in a mine building down there, but Perrell got that old car going and we broke out."

Craddock peered at another photograph. Tapping it, he said, "That's General Pershing, right?"

Costello laughed again. "Right, and Red Durkin standing next to him. You see, Durkin was Vega's chief lieutenant, but he later claimed he shot Vega himself, to protect U.S. citizens, meaning us. Pershing rewarded him by enlisting him in the U.S. Army—no doubt to his eternal regret."

Craddock drove out to Perrell's shop in his Buick. Perrell was a compact, square-jawed man of about forty, and he was busy welding some steel tubing into a weblike framework, following a drawing laid out on a bench. Perrell took off his mask, handed the torch to the young Mexican who was helping him and said "Run the bead right along there." To Craddock, he said, "That's an engine mount for an airplane, in case you're wondering."

Craddock told him about his visit with Costello. When Craddock spoke Durkin's name, Perrell laughed too. "I don't know why I'm laughing," he said. "The so-and-so did his best to kill me." Craddock opened his notebook and began asking questions.

"Sure, I was right there where he lost the packhorse," Perrell said, "but I didn't know anything about it because we were locked in a boxcar, four of us. Got a glimpse through a bullet hole, you know, dust, gunfire, horses down and kicking. It was a mess. But I could find the place again—there were low hills and some scraggly trees along the railroad tracks where the *federales* strung up prisoners they captured. Later, maybe a week or so, Vega and what was left of his Gringo Legion, including Durkin, took over the mine where we were working, place called Baroyeca—I mean they ran that town up a tree. There was an old wreck of a car locked up with us—we managed to get the thing running and break out of there . . ." Perrell's voice trailed off. He half turned toward a back corner of the shop, and Craddock now saw the chassis of a huge touring car sitting there.

"Costello told me a little about all that," Craddock said.

The frame of the car was enameled red, with gold striping. The engine, the massive snout of the radiator and glistening nickeled grille were mounted on the chassis. Seats newly upholstered in red leather sat off to one side along with acetylene headlamps and other parts and pieces, all perfectly restored.

"That's it." Perrell grinned. "The Thomas Flyer. I went back down there after the war, in twenty-one, found it in Cusichic over in Chihuahua, just where we left it. It was a wreck, but that's dry country, you know, no rust. I had the wreck hauled to the railroad and shipped back here. I want to have it finished in time for my wife's birthday—she was with us through that whole thing, and the Flyer was something special to her. But"—he waved Craddock to the back door of the shop and pointed outside to another machine—"if you want to go find the place where Vega's packhorse went astray, we'll go in that."

Craddock saw a big Stanley Steamer tour coach—he knew it because he had ridden to the top of Pike's Peak in a machine just like it in 1915. "I bought it here when a tour outfit went broke," Perrell said. "My wife and I take it on camping trips in the desert. It carries enough fuel and water to go a thousand miles."

Looking over his notebook later, Craddock saw a gaping hole in his day's work—neither Costello nor Perrell knew anything about J. W. Whitlock. If there was a wild card in the deck, it had to be J. W.

Othello Biggers awoke just before noon in his room in an old adobe in the same walled block as the old San Agustín cathedral, or what had been a cathedral a half-century earlier—it was now a run-down hotel and restaurant. The adobe room occupied by Othello Biggers had served then as the mother superior's quarters in a convent, which was now ostensibly a boardinghouse run by a Mrs. Tatum. But the cubicles built for the nuns in 1870 were ideally suited to Mrs. Tatum's real endeavor, which was running a whorehouse. Her girls were known to the town's sports as Mrs. Tatum's Sweet 'Taters. Decorum was assured by the presence of Othello Biggers, in return for his quarters at the end of the building, along with privileges Mrs. Tatum called his "season's ticket."

Othello Biggers' concentration in the game of pool at Jimmy Kee's had faltered badly once his attention was drawn to the possibility that J. W. Whitlock might indeed have gotten his hands on Rodrigo Vega's treasure, and Biggers had dropped a few hundred, much of that to Whitlock himself. Later, disgusted with himself, still wide awake, he had exercised his ticket holder's privilege with a plump red-haired girl who now snored softly next to him.

He threw back the sheet and looked down at her. She lay on her side with her hands nestled between her drawn-up knees. Bluish veins were visible under her pale skin. Her lips were puffy and there were dark bruises on her rump. Biggers reached out and slapped her on the bottom. She came awake with a cry.

"Beat it, Darlene," Biggers said. She pouted, frowning, then a slow smile tugged at her lips and, catlike, she stretched.

"Beat it, I said."

"You dint say nothing like that this morning," she said.

He smiled thinly, slipped out of bed and padded over to the deep-set barred and shuttered window, where he poked a finger through the shutter slats and peered out across Convent Street. Biggers stood five-ten and weighed 220. "There aint enough fat on him to grease a skillet," one of the girls had told Darlene. The girls fancied he bore a resemblance to the beast on the tobacco-sack label, and among themselves they referred to him as Bull Durham Biggers.

Biggers, thinking about Rodrigo Vega's packhorse, teetered on his toes and watched a skinny yellow dog making the rounds of garbage cans set in the mouth of an alley.

Darlene looked at the leather folder standing open on the chest of drawers against the far wall, beyond the foot of the bed. The folder's velvet lining was covered with medals—military decorations—dangling from colored ribbons pinned to the fabric. Nearby were a comb and brush, a pair of scissors and a roll of adhesive tape. Darlene had an idea. She moved silently from the bed and busied herself quickly with the decorations.

"Hey, sojer, whatayasay?" she said softly, seconds later.

Biggers turned. Darlene grinned merrily, her hand raised to the brim of Biggers' campaign hat in a military salute, her naked shoulders thrown back in an exaggerated parade-ground pose. A Silver Star hung from her left breast by a bit of tape, its ribbon draped over the boldly thrusting nipple. A Purple Heart hung from her right breast and, below, the Croix de Guerre, Medaille Militaire and Expert Rifleman glinted on a cushion of crisply curling dark auburn hair. She swayed her hips and the Croix de Guerre chinked against the Expert Rifleman.

Biggers' nostrils flared. His eyes stared and a vein wriggled in his temple. Darlene's smile faltered, then vanished as he lunged for her. She snatched at the dangling medals, hurled them onto the chest of drawers and was out the door with a whinnied squeal, slamming it behind her. Biggers picked up a fallen Croix de Guerre. The pin carried a tight curl of hair. Biggers' lips twitched in what might have been a smile. He replaced the medals in the leather folder, polishing each with a handkerchief.

Thirty minutes later, in the dining room of the San Agustin, Darlene was telling the other girls what had happened, over breakfast. Her friend Charlotte was doubled over her hashed browns, laughing. She straightened, tears bright on her lashes. "You're jist lucky," she gasped, "he dint swat you with that thing of his. You'd of been *squarshed*!" She gave way to another fit of gasping merriment. Darlene hissed and prodded her.

The girls fell silent. Othello Biggers stood in the doorway. He was freshly shaved. His dark suit and derby had been sponged and brushed and his black shoes gleamed. His wing collar was fresh. With a gloved hand he lifted his hat, smiling his thin smile. "Ladies," he growled. Darlene shivered, but Biggers merely seated himself at another table and shortly was ordering *huevos rancheros* from Narciso, the waiter.

Biggers ate slowly, staring, oblivious of the girls whose guarded giggling echoed softly in the lofty room. Above, frescoed saints with distinctly Indian features floated serenely in painted clouds. Biggers was thinking about J. W. Whitlock. A uniformed policeman looked in the door, grinned and wagged his nightstick at the girls and then moved on. Biggers finished his coffee, threw a dollar onto the table and went after the policeman, catching up with him on the corner.

"Ferd," Biggers said. "You remember J. W. Whitlock?"

"Sure. He's back in town, I hear."

"Right. Know anything about his family?"

"Sam Callard's family, that was. Sam was a railroader, passed away a few years back. J. W. married his daughter. Me and her was in school together. She was a hot little job . . . but now she's dead, too."

"Anybody else J. W. might have been close to?"

The policeman laughed. "Not Sam's other daughter. She moved away from home, account of J. W. Name's Clark now."

"I mean someone he could've wanted to see again or maybe park some of his stuff with."

"Mm-m, tell the truth, only one who had much use for J. W. was his wife, and now she's gone. Left J. W.'s kid. Way it happened, the lady got pneumonia and died in Fort Worth while J. W. was gone somewhere. Sam's daughter Lexie—the one who moved out—went to Fort Worth and brought the kid home . . . his mother too, in a casket."

"Okay, much obliged." The policeman nodded and left. Biggers walked slowly toward Congress Street. He was thinking, J. W. is not going to leave valuables in any old hotel room or boardinghouse. No one in that family cared for him except his wife and she's gone. That leaves his kid. Last night J. W. said he wanted to see his kid, too. Said the kid was his heir. Heir to what? Vega's packhorse, that's what.

Biggers went into a drugstore and turned to listings under *Clark* in the telephone directory. *Clark, Alexandra* was first of three names. That would be Lexie, he thought, and made a note of the address. Thirty minutes later, Biggers parked his Essex in front of the house on East Ninth Street. He got out and went to the door. He was wearing coveralls and a cap and was carrying a metal toolbox. He rapped at the door. No answer. He let himself in with a simple passkey.

It took Biggers three minutes to determine that there had been a small boy staying in the house, but that he had apparently departed, leaving only some laundry and an old pair of shoes, size three. Biggers left the house and drove away in his Essex. If the kid had left or been taken away from the house where his sister lived, then naturally she had been in on it. Maybe we're lucky today—let's say it could be family, start with old Sam Callard's side.

Biggers went to his room and left the coveralls. Dressed again in his dark suit, he went to the railroad yards, parked the Essex and went into the shop. He found the foreman and asked him if anyone there might have known Sam Callard.

"I knowed him myself," the foreman said. "Twenty years anyway, if that's long enough. What's up?"

"I'm working for a lawyer in Phoenix," Biggers said. "Trying to trace the Callard family to hand out a small bequest. A hundred dollars each, is all. I found his daughter and delivered hers, but I heard later that there was another relative, or might be, let's say."

"Couldn't the daughter tell you?" the foreman said.

"I didn't actually speak to her. She's out of town today, and I left hers in a letter at the paper where she works. Thing is, I want to head back this afternoon. It would cost me money to stay on overnight."

"Well, I damned near said there wasn't nobody else, now Sam's gone," the foreman said, "but I would've been wrong. There's one other Callard, used to stop in here when Sam was alive. Always tinkering with something, the old gent was, and Sam would help him, but hell, that's years ago. I spect he's croaked by now."

"D'you know his name, where he lived?"

"Name was Heck Callard. He lived on a homestead somewhere, way the hell out in the desert, but I wouldn't know where."

Biggers went to the courthouse. A clerk helped him to look up the homestead. The claim was filed in 1896—*Callard, Hector and Hattie M.* He located the property on a large-scale wall map.

Biggers went to the old Territorial Hotel. Loose tiles tinkled underfoot in the lobby and a moth-eaten elk stared glassily down at him from the wall. He went to Red Durkin's room on the second floor. Durkin was sitting in his underwear with his hat on, smoking a black Mexican cigarro and playing solitaire.

"I been thinkin about your old pal J. W. and that goddam packhorse," Biggers began.

"You aint the only one," Durkin said sourly. "He's nowhere to be found today. Neither is the fucking ace. That tell you something?"

"How'd you find that out?"

"I called Augie at the airport from Kee's last night, told him I wanted to know every time that pilot left the ground. Well, he left before daybreak this morning with a passenger—Augie couldn't tell who the passenger was in the dark—and the airplane aint back yet. You seen how J. W. talked to him last night about flying a charter?"

Othello Biggers explained his idea to Red Durkin, that J. W. had to have left his *valuables,* one way or another, with his kid, and Biggers was willing to bet a sawbuck that the kid had been dumped with a relative, namely an old geezer who lived on a homestead not far from Papago Junction. It was worth, said Biggers, a run up to the Junction and maybe a look at the homestead.

12

LEXIE SAID, "The old stations were about twenty-five miles apart, sometimes closer, depending upon water," Lexie said. She consulted Marietta's diary.

"They were already five days on the road when they reached the Apache Pass station. Marietta says she was beginning to get over being seasick from the pitching of the coach. Her entire body was bruised and sore from the constant battering. The accommodations for sleeping were such that women were put together in one room and men in another. Marietta's roommate was a hard-bitten laundress from Fort Bowie who remained drunk most of the trip. Listen to this: 'The nights are made hideous by her cries and snorts and thrashing about. I have been married almost a week and have yet to spend a night with my dear Lucian.'"

Lexie skipped a few lines. "'This is the place where Silas St. John lost his arm. He and two American companions were building the station and corral with three Mexican helpers. On the night of September 8, the helpers fell upon them and murdered his two friends. Silas was left for dead with one arm severed by an ax and the ax left buried in his hip. He fought off coyotes and Buzzards for 72 hrs as those Creatures would have made a meal of him. Lt. Mowry came along and found him, a doctor was sent for all the way from Ft. Buchanan so the poor man did not have proper care for most of a week yet within six weeks he was able to travel.'"

Lexie photographed the building with her folding camera and made some notes. The sun was now well up and it was much warmer. The first thing Lexie noticed when they took off was that the air was beginning to get bumpy. The old stage road was considerably north of the highway, which served towns that had not existed in 1858. They circled low over stations at Thimble Creek and Corralitos, but the adobe buildings had melted down to little more than their outlines and there was no good place to land. The road faded and was hard to follow through the mesquite forests near the San Pedro, and Maynard had to double back twice. They landed in a field near a little town in a valley below the Galiuro Mountains. Coming in, Lexie saw a barn with *Willcox* painted on its roof.

On the ground, Maynard said, "We don't know where we'll be by lunchtime. We can pick up some groceries and I'll get a couple of cans of gas. It never hurts to top off the tank."

They walked a half-mile to a general store, where Lexie bought some boiled eggs, oranges, canned fruit and a loaf of bread just baked by the proprietor's wife, along with half a cold roast chicken. Maynard got two five-gallon cans of gasoline from the pump, said he'd leave the empty cans out at the field if that was agreeable. Hundred percent, the man told him, long as you don't try to git me up in that thing.

Maynard stood on a wheel and poured fuel through a piece of chamois in a funnel, into the tank. Just before they took off, Lexie said, "I'm praying we can find the old Atascadero station on the San Pedro and land there. Marietta left something behind there and I'd like to take it back to her."

Maynard was incredulous. "After all these years?"

Lexie smiled. "If we can land there, you'll see."

"We'll land there," Maynard said.

Lexie began to laugh. She was barefoot, on her knees in damp sand next to the Jenny's bogged wheel. She pointed at the barnlike adobe stage station squatting grimly on high ground a hundred yards away. "This was called Atascadero Station—*atascadero* means something like 'mudhole.' We should have known."

"It begins to look complicated," Maynard said. He had a long twisted pole set across a mesquite log in the sand, its far end under the Jenny's axle, close to a wheel. He bore down on the end of the pole, and the Jenny lurched up a few inches, its tire making sucking sounds as it pulled free of the boggy sand. Lexie stuffed brush and small branches under the wheel.

"I've landed on beaches," Maynard said. "Long Island . . . New Jersey. The trick is to watch the color of the sand. There are three bands of color—light, where it's dry, is too soft. Dark, where it's shiny, is too wet. In the middle the sand is damp and firm."

"And here?" Lexie said, smiling.

"It looked okay from above, but obviously the riverbed under the sand twists back and forth. We should have landed over there." Maynard nodded toward higher ground, a gravel bench twenty yards away. Their tracks were clear and straight along the riverbed, ending where the Jenny had bogged down. Maynard had swung her tail around and the two of them had begun to pull her out tailfirst, a few inches at a time, having chopped brush with the hatchet and carried it there in bundles.

"We've come four feet in about an hour," Lexie said. "At that rate we'll get it where we want it by the middle of next month."

"A team of horses would help," Maynard admitted. "When we were landing, I saw plowed ground and a little house a few miles downstream."

She sat on a flat rock and brushed sand from her feet and put on her socks and boots. They walked north along the sandy stream bed, sharing a piece of roast chicken and an orange as they walked. It was well past midday. The sky was brilliant cobalt, cloudless, and the sun was hot. They crossed tracks of mule deer, rabbits, coyotes, javelina, various mice and small birds, and a trail made ornate by scalloped undulations.

"Sidewinder," Lexie said. In an hour they reached a small adobe house set among cottonwood trees on a stretch of bottomland. Chickens scratched and pecked under brush. A patch of corn stood inside a deer fence of twisted mesquite branches and spiny ocotillo arms. Three pigs in a small pen squealed and ran in circles when they approached—whether from fear or hunger was not clear. There was a pole corral, empty except for horse droppings. A damp clay *olla* hung from a branch near the adobe. Clay dishes and an iron pot were neatly stacked on a wooden bench. A ring of stones held cold ashes. Maynard rapped at the plank door, but there was no answer. He pushed the door open. Inside was a rope-bound bed with a cornshuck tick and a folded serape on it. A crucifix hung over the bed and a chromolithograph of the Virgin and Child was tacked to the inside of the door. Shelves made of wooden boxes held various pieces of clothing.

Maynard closed the door. They walked around outside. "We have a man, woman and apparently a little girl living here," Maynard said.

"They have a dog, a horse, some chickens, and she's a very tidy housekeeper," Lexie said. "But they aren't at home. The pigs will need feeding, though, so that means they're due home very soon." She took out her pocket notebook and began to write.

"What are you saying?"

"We are at the big adobe house. *Ayuda, por favor* . . . Please help. *Avion atascado*. That means stuck—same word, see?"

"What if they can't read?"

Lexie drew a simple, childish sketch of a biplane with only the upper half of its wheels showing above the line representing ground. Next to it, she put stick figures of a man and woman, both smiling, with their arms up as if waving, and next to that, a building with a big doorway. Maynard put the note under the door with a silver dollar on it and then they walked back to the old station.

* * *

"'The Atascadero station is a huge structure,'" Lexie read from the diary, "'built with an open passageway in the middle so as to allow a coach and teams of horses to drive inside under cover if the Apaches are attacking.'"

She and Maynard were standing in the open passageway, now littered with cans, bottles and papers. It was some fifteen feet wide and the sheet-iron roof lofted more than twenty feet above their heads. Bright rods of light drilled down through holes in the iron roof. Birds flew in and out under the broad eaves.

"It's a fort," Maynard said. "The passengers could just pop out of the coach and into these rooms."

"But now listen to this. 'Supper was the usual beans and cornbread, with a dish of tough shredded meat in chillie gravy that set my tongue afire. Mrs. Heaney and the man Haugen drank mescal licker from a stone jug and their behavior grew steadily more raucous. He kept guffawing and touching her in the most familiar manner. Her response was to cackle the more. Lucian and I quit the table early and took a short walk along the river. When it was time to repair to our rooms, he took me to my door. The room was pitch-dark. I discovered that the bed was heaving like a ship in a storm. It was occupied by Mrs. Heaney and Haugen who were both groaning and mumbling'" Lexie stopped. "I'm not sure I should go on with this."

Maynard could not restrain a grin. "It's graphic, all right, but don't stop now. That would have been one of these rooms right here." He touched a door hanging off one hinge, as she read on:

"'—like two pigs. Lucian, hearing me gasp, entered behind me. Without a word, he took my arm and led me outside. We gathered our two blankets and my carpetbag filled with necessaries, that Lucian always calls impossibles, and went along a path outside for some distance to where a spring issued from a low cavern in the rocks. Hang the savages, Lucian declared. Surely they will keep to their wickieups this one night. I asked if we should not build a fire. It would warm the hearts of the Apaches, said Lucian. We must not tempt them too far. We will keep one another warm with a different fire, and he embraced me ever so tenderly.'"

"Go on," Maynard said.

Lexie shook her head. He saw tears glittering, clotting her lashes, and he put his arm around her. After a moment, she brushed at her face with her hands and took a deep breath. "As long as we're here, I want to find that spring if we can." She stepped away from him and they went back outside.

Rocky, cactus-studded hills rolling down from higher country broke up along the riverbed. A narrow arroyo spilled a tongue of sand into the river course just above the old station. They followed a trail of animal tracks into the arroyo. The walls steepened and the sky narrowed overhead. The sun was beyond the crest of hills now, and after the bright sunlight along the river it seemed dark in the arroyo. Maynard touched her hand. Thirty feet away, a wildcat lay on a ledge, its yellow eyes fixed on them. As they looked back, it eased to its feet and backed carefully away until it was out of sight behind the rocks.

"*This* is the mudhole!" Lexie exclaimed suddenly. "The *atascadero*." Their feet were in reddish sandy mud. They walked on around another turn and the mud became a pool. Water trickled down a face of rock from a low cave. "This is why they put the station where they did," she said. "When the river was low, they could always get water here. Soldiers dug out the spring and made that little cave above the pool."

A few feet to one side of the cave, the rocky wall jutted over a sandy bench that was overhung by palo verde and buttressed on the upstream side by the bony skeleton of a toppled saguaro.

"We're standing in Marietta's honeymoon chamber," Maynard said.

Lexie was silent for a time, then she suddenly said, "I've got to find Sibbie."

Maynard laughed. "Sibbie?"

"Marietta was only fifteen, remember. Sibbie was her doll, her faithful companion since she was a baby."

"What happened? Did she lose Sibbie?"

"No. This is what she wrote . . ." Lexie settled herself on the fallen saguaro trunk and opened the diary. "'I learned in Lucian's arms what it meant to be a woman. When we arose at daybreak I beheld Sibbie looking brightly at me. So filled was I with joy that I hugged and kissed her and said Sibbie you must stay here now for it is not seemly for a married woman to have a doll. I found a little perch for her and promised to come back one day. Later I wept oceans, called myself a wretch and would have gone back for her except we were on that accursed coach, swept along like leaves in a gale. My beloved Sibbie!'"

Lexie got up and walked along the rock wall, looking into crevices. She started to put her hand in one, but snatched it back. "That was silly. My dad taught me always to look out for scorpions and snakes." She picked up a stick and raked the crevice with it. "I don't see Sibbie, though."

"Think of all the years, all the rains—floods must've swept this place clean," Maynard said. "Don't count on finding her."

She flashed him a stricken look.

They went back to the Jenny to see if anyone had come to help them. The sky over the looming mass of mountains to the west was flaring red by then. Lexie said, "I was so certain they would be here!"

"Do you want to camp in this trash pile," Maynard said, indicating the littered stage station, "with the ghosts of Mrs. Heaney and her friend Haugen—or follow Marietta?"

Lexie grimaced. "Marietta, by all means."

They carried their food, blankets and a canvas cockpit cover back to Marietta's camp. Maynard also carried the hatchet and his service pistol. It was dark and growing cold by the time they finished eating. Maynard opened a can of peaches with his knife and spilled some into Lexie's cup.

"You're very quiet," he said.

She frowned. "This is absurd. Do you expect me to be happy about it?"

"Why not? *I'm* happy about it. To be, what was the word? . . . *atascado* . . . with a beautiful girl? In Marietta's camp? I couldn't be happier."

Nettled, she merely shook her head. "Shouldn't we build a fire?"

"If you want. Lucian preferred *another* fire." She gave him an angry glance but refused to answer. He put some twigs together a few feet out from the overhang, struck a match to them and then began adding small sticks. When the fire was burning well, he sat back against the rock wall. Lexie sat down across the fire from him and pulled a blanket over her shoulders.

"It'll be warmer on this side, where the rock will catch some of the heat," Maynard said. She ignored him. "It's going to be close to freezing before morning," he said. She opened her notebook and began to write by firelight.

Biggers and Durkin arrived at Papago Junction just at dusk in Biggers' black '22 Essex sedan. The Junction had also been a stage station in the old days, called Papago Wells then, but now the Junction existed because of the Papago Queen mine. There was a settlement of miners' houses scattered back from the highway, a couple of stores with gas pumps, a Chink restaurant and pool hall owned by a cousin of Jimmy Kee, and the old Papago Queen Hotel.

They checked into the Papago Queen and were shown to a second-floor room. The bellhop, who cultivated a certain brassy gall, waited expectantly with his hand extended far enough to make his meaning clear. Othello Biggers turned and stared bleakly at him. The bellhop shivered involuntarily and hastily left the room.

The two men ate supper at Kee's, where for a dollar extra each, they got the familiar Kee specialty, gin over crushed ice in place of water, and rice wine in their teapot with dinner. Biggers, who had spent two tours of duty in China, ordered with a passable pronunciation of the names of the Cantonese dishes. Later, they went into the poolroom in back and shot a couple of racks. In seemingly idle chatter with the regulars, they confirmed that an old geezer named Callard lived out on the Gulch road near Farney, the day-shift foreman.

"He aint but about a hundred and ten," one of the men said, "always messin with crackpot inventions—you know, perpetual-motion machines, that kind of stuff."

They returned to their room. Biggers said he thought it was worth a recon in the morning—see what was out there. Durkin said it wasn't work for two men. Biggers agreed and said if Durkin could catch a ride back to Tucson on one of the ore trucks, he could spend some time checking on what the ace was doing. And see if J. W. had showed up yet.

Durkin stripped to his underwear, leaving his hat on, and sat down with a deck of cards, a glass and a pint bottle. Othello Biggers opened his leather valise and took out his folder of decorations, which he stood on the dresser. He too stripped to his union suit. He hung up his dark suit and sponged and brushed it, and then he polished his shoes until the naked light bulb reflected as a bright point of light on the toes. He started bath water running.

Biggers got down on the floor and did a hundred push-ups. He turned over and did one hundred sit-ups, and then he did twenty-five one-armed push-ups on each side. His pale skin was slightly flushed when he finished. Durkin went on playing, taking an occasional drink.

"You gonna climb in the ring with Dempsey?" Durkin said.

"Anytime," Biggers said with flat conviction. "Only I wouldn't be wearin gloves." When he had bathed, he slapped lotion on his face and rubbed hair oil into his thinning dark hair, which he combed carefully to cover a shrapnel scar on his skull. Biggers climbed into bed with a dictionary he took from his bag. He opened it to the *Foreign Words and Phrases* section. Watching him, Red Durkin frowned.

"What the hell are you readin?"

"Per angusta ad augusta."

"Okay, what does it mean?"

"Through difficulties to things worthy of honor."

"I don't get it. What's the point?"

"Honor's the point. *Mens sana in corpore sano.*"

Durkin made an explosive snort and threw down a card. "I give up."

"A sound mind in a sound body," Biggers said. *"In omni paratus*—ready for all things, see?"

"Shee-it!" Durkin said.

Hours later, it seemed to Maynard, Lexie shook his arm. The fire had burned to darkly glowing embers. Lexie's teeth were chattering. He scrambled up and added wood to the coals. While he was nursing it into flame, she spread the cockpit cover where he had been and then spread both blankets and her coat over it. She glared at him. "If you say one word about Lucian and Marietta, I'll murder you." She slipped under the blankets on the side closest to the fire. Maynard stretched out next to her. She was still shaking, her back to him.

"We can either suffer," he said, "or get warm. I care for you and I'm inflamed by your presence, but I don't want to offend you. In fact, I will perish first—"

"Sh-shut up, Lucian," she said through chattering teeth, "and hug my back."

Later, much later, when their seeping warmth had spread beneath the blankets, he drifted out of sleep again. The Pleiades were gone. Was that bright V Taurus? The far wall of the canyon was bathed in light from half a moon. Maynard turned his head. Lexie's eyes were open and she was regarding him silently. After a time he moved his head slightly and kissed the tip of her nose. She did not move, but continued to look at him silently. He moved closer and kissed her on the mouth. There was no response—at first. Then her lips softened, moved with his own and parted as he drew her close to him. Even so, her kiss was tentative; there was a distance to it, her hand on his arm merely touching. He pulled back and looked at her again.

"Back to sleep, Lucian," she whispered huskily. "The accursed coach leaves at dawn."

He bent to kiss her again, but she said, "No more, please." He kissed her anyway, kissed her eyes, her chin, the hollow of her throat, her mouth, lingering, their lips wet now, but when he touched the buttons of her shirt she caught his hand. The fingers of her other hand tightened on the back of his neck. Suddenly she shrugged away and sat up. "No, Maynard."

"What happened to Lucian?" Surprised, he tried to banter.

"It was different with them. I'm just not going to throw away my freedom for a quick roll in the hay with a—"

"It's nothing like that to me!"

"I started to say, with a bootlegger." She was on her knees now, the shirt buttoned. He gave her a startled, angry look. She leaned forward and kissed him lightly. "A nice bootlegger, I admit it. But I'm thinking of what happened to my sister when she fell for J. W., and it's just not going to happen to me that way—that's a promise I made to myself." She was shivering again. She gathered up her coat and started to put it on. He caught her arm.

"Not necessary. Nothing's going to happen if you don't want it to happen."

She hesitated.

"It's okay," he said. "I've made myself some promises, too—this situation is covered." He stretched out again, turning his back to her. She settled herself next to him and, after a moment, she roughed his hair with her hand and then snuggled close to his back.

13

JASON and the old man were having grits again, with bacon and two fried eggs apiece, on Jason's second morning at the homestead. Jason had dreamed about the Juggernaut in the night, dreamed he was riding it and it was like the giant Ferris wheel he had ridden at the fair in Fort Worth, except that he looked down in the dream and was horrified to see that it was spinning free of the earth, beginning to wobble crazily so that he could barely hang on and he looked down again and saw his mother crying and calling up to him.

"When I looked at the Juggernaut," he said carefully, watching the old man for any sign of an explosion, "I didn't see a motor, or a steam boiler or piston. How are you going to make it go?"

The old man stopped eating, frowned suspicion. "Never you mind. She'll go."

Jason's face wore a puzzled scowl. He started to speak, thought better of it and returned to his breakfast. The old man was moved by Jason's expression to elaborate: "The thing of it is, she'll run so fast, she's likely to tear everything to pieces, so keepin her slowed down is what worries me. I'll need some kind of brake that won't just turn red-hot and burn up."

"Can't you just cut back on your throttle?"

"Like with a steam locomotive, you mean . . . nothin wrong

with steam, but you're burnin all that coal, see, and when you're out of coal, you just plain quit rollin. Not the Juggernaut. You don't have no throttle."

Jason was incredulous. "Like a Nieuport scout, then. The engine turns around the crankshaft, and the way you slow it down is to blip the ignition."

The old man grinned happily. "No ignition."

"Ah-h," Jason said. "It's a diesel. You burn oil!"

"*Shew!* Wouldn't the awl companies love that! They wouldn't need to steal her. No, sir, she don't burn awl, nor gasarene neither."

"What then?" Jason persisted. "Alcohol? She's got to burn something!"

"Says who?" the old man said loftily. "There's other kinds of energy. Wind, sun, magnets—"

"Is it one of them?"

"I aint sayin it is or aint. I'm sayin what it *could* be, maybe, by chance or happenstance, and that's all I'm sayin." The old man shoved his plate aside and heaved himself to his feet. "Now, is it too much to hope that a man can go to work without all hell breaking loose around his ears? Life is like a sock full of sand with a hole in the toe, understand? The sand is a-runnin out. My sock is damn near empty, young sir, and I've got a heap of work on the Juggernaut yet to finish. She's a scary proposition."

The old man stalked out the back door and went to the shed. Left to himself, Jason looked around. His labors of the previous day had scarcely made a dent in the mountain of chaos that surrounded him. Standing on another dynamite crate, an empty one this time, he washed the dishes from breakfast and the previous evening. He carried encrusted skillets and pots to the back yard and scoured them with sand.

The sun was high by the time he finished, and hot on his back. He was tired and beginning to get hungry. The biscuits were gone. There was no icebox. He lifted the lid of the Dutch oven. It still held beans, but the beans were cold and streaked with fat; and Jason saw again with horror the fat and wrinkled nipple projecting from the sowbelly. He dropped the lid with a crash.

At that moment Jason heard a cry like a strangled bleat. He ran to the back door and beheld a large woman of sixty or so hobbling toward the door. She wore an apron over a faded cotton housedress and carried a splint basket covered with a flour sack. Her hair was pinned in a loose coil on top of her head. She was the woman he had seen across the canyon. "*Whoo-oo!*" she screeched breathlessly. "Mist' Callard, whur-rat're you keepin yourseff?"

Jason opened the door. She cried out and lurched backward. "Gracious! How you startled me, young man!" She charged up the steps and brushed past him into the house, darting glances at the disarray. She marched to the kitchen table and put the basket down. "I thought I seen Mist' Callard had company, so I brought ye a little bite. I spect you're his grandchile?"

"He's my great-great—" Jason started, and then he gave up on that and finished lamely, "I'm Jason."

"Indeed, and I'm pleased to make your acquaintance." She dropped a girlish curtsy, lurching slightly. "I'm Olive Farney and I live just yonder." She waved vaguely cross-canyon. "My land, this place is a hawg-pen!"

"I'm working on it," Jason said.

"A hawg-pen!" she repeated. "Don't he never put nothin away? The answer to that is N—O, that spells *no,* he don't."

Chain rattled at the shed door. Jason looked out and saw the old man hurrying toward the house. The screen door squealed. Inside, he glared at them like an outraged heron. No, *buzzard.*

"I see you wasted no time getting here, Olive."

"Good intentions speak for theirseffs." She whipped the flour sack off the basket, exposing fried chicken, a pan of cornbread and a glass-capped jar of milk. Steam curled off the cornbread and the jar was beaded with moisture. Jason licked his lips.

Olive Farney quickly set the food out on the table. She steered Jason forcibly into a chair and skidded it forward until Jason's breastbone was jammed against the table. A moment later, with her hand relentlessly steering his own, Jason found his mouth stuffed with cornbread, butter running off his chin.

"You'll naturally start school tomorrow, won't you?" she screeched.

Jason, startled, shook his head, but she went on without a pause. "The one at Papago Junction, for the county chillern? You don't want to miss no more classwork, do you? Where'd you go last? What grade are you in? Fifth is my guess. You have the look of a scholar. Fifth grade, you said?"

"Sixth," blurted Jason through his cornbread. It did not seem to matter to her that she was giving him no time to answer. Her own surmises appeared to satisfy her lust for information. Hector Callard glared briefly at her and tore at a chicken leg. With practiced deftness, she opened a snuff tin without removing it from her apron pocket, conveyed a pinch to her mouth under cover of a bandanna and tucked the pinch under her lip while appearing delicately merely to wipe her mouth and lips. Fascinated by her sleight of hand, Jason missed the drift of her words until he was suddenly jolted alert.

". . . and since my sister's husband works for the board of education, it's my duty to have him call here, you see, so his office is kept abreast of matters. I tell you, that pore man sees whole families where the chillern aint in school, where they aint even fed! Families livin in hawg-pens, is what it is." She fixed her gaze on the old man who, savoring her cornbread, was not listening, but shaping in his mind a part for the Juggernaut.

Dread clamped down on Jason's heart with iron fingers. He

could not understand how the conversation had ever reached that point. The old man had pushed back from the table and was holding a match to his gurgling pipe, punching the tobacco down with a forefinger.

Olive Farney, seeing the water tracks on Jason's grimy neck and cobwebs caught in his hair, the charcoal smudges on his face and clothing, itched to tear the shirt off his back and plunge it into a scalding tub of suds and then to go after the boy himself with a soapy washrag.

"Next time," she said grimly, "we'll have a good scrub before we set down to the table." She looked through the door into the porch and saw the rumpled quilt, the piles of trash. A mouse scuttled under the cot as she watched. She shuddered. "Any county man worth his salt would snatch you out of this sinkhole so quick it would make your head swim. *Unspeakable* is what it is, and that don't begin to tell the story!"

Jason's eyes widened. His mouth was full of chicken, which prevented his having to speak. Instinct told him to say nothing and hope her outburst would subside. He wondered—chicken sticking dryly in his throat at the thought—what would happen to him if the county man did snatch him out of here. *Jail,* most likely, he thought, or an orphanage, until J. W. found him. His jaws, paralyzed by dread, ceased to work. A sick feeling spread beneath his ribs. He thought he was going to throw up. He wiped his mouth on his sleeve and sat back.

Olive Farney, clearing the table, disgruntled by a feeling of outraged impotence, stared hard at the old man. "Pumping that filthy smoke through your lungs is a pore example to set for a chile!" she exclaimed, and then she was out the door and striding away with her basket over her arm.

"Damnation!" the old man said. "Fire and fall back, that's her style." He sucked on the offending pipe.

"She *chews,*" Jason said. "I watched her put snoose under her lip."

The old man slapped his knee. "How come I never seen

that? She makes old Farney go out in the yard to smoke his cigars, too."

"She says the county officer will be calling on us to make me go to school, or maybe even to take me away."

"She said that? I don't half listen to her." The old man frowned. "Mess around with the Juggernaut, that's what's on her mind. By god, I won't have it! Don't you let no one in the door—not a livin soul."

"Even a county man?"

The old man squinted craftily. "Hell, you don't know who he might be. They'll tell you anything. You just don't know how I've had to fight the bastards."

"I mean," Jason persisted unhappily, "spose he had a badge?"

"Piece of tin. A badge don't mean nothin. I'd tell him to send his superior officer with a court order. It takes a court order to get anything done legal, and by the time they could get one, I'd be out of here and holed up in my tent at the claim."

Jason squirmed, thinking of himself left alone to face the wrath of the law. The words "county man" triggered in his mind a picture of a huge hulking man in a uniform with a Sam Browne belt and a big pistol and, of course, a badge. He felt he had to turn the old man's thinking around before it got them both into trouble. "If the county man does come and all he really wants is to put me in school, I could just *go*—that would lead him away from the Juggernaut, even if my dad finds me there." He shrugged to indicate an indifference he did not by any means feel.

The old man thrust out his bristly chin and wagged his head. "Badge or no badge, the son of a bitch is not to set foot in my house. He'll have his orders, don't you see? I know what they'll be and who gives em, what's more. The damned awl companies, that's who. They think they can run roughshod over anyone they please, but by god they are messin with a citizen and a war veteran, and I don't mean no paper-collar soldier! We was *fighters*!" He smote the table and a plate sailed against the wall.

"You mean the county man gets his orders from an oil company?"

The old man jabbed a bony finger into Jason's chest. "Most people can be bought, you understand that? They'll do anything for money. And why not? When a man is pore all his life, a little cash money is like a piece of heaven. The awl people know that, so they *own* just about everbody, from the president to the courthouse janitor, and don't think they don't!"

"The President of the United States?" The thought was staggering to Jason.

"*Shew!* Them birds don't even run for office without they get the nod from the big companies. Democrat, Republican or Bull Moose, it don't matter."

Jason was struggling to understand the mechanics of such transactions. "How do people get bought?"

"A few greenbacks under the table, that does the trick. Or sometimes favors, like lettin a man be a judge or mayor, if that's what he wants."

Jason pictured a dark room and a big table with a green baize cover, and men sitting around it smoking cigars. A bald man sat at the far end of the table where the light was dim, so that only the top of his head and his cigar and a curl of smoke showed clearly, and he had a shopping bag full of greenbacks and he was tearing the wrappers off the bills and passing them on, sheafs of them, all under the table.

The bony finger jabbed again. "But, you see, there is some of us that caint be bought." The old man fixed his gaze piercingly on Jason and lowered his voice to a dramatic whisper. "No amount of money, understand? We know what the bastards are doin, but we won't fall into line and sing their tune. Hell, money don't mean a thing to me! I've had my share of it too, you bet. I could have all I want of it now, too, if I was to go on back out there to m'claim and burn a little more powder." He tapped his nose and winked.

"Gold?" Jason ventured.

"Plenty of it. Tungsten too, a mountain of it—all we need to do is put in a rail spur so's we can ship it out easy."

Jason had heard of tungsten, but had never thought of its having monetary value. "Why not go ahead then and dig it up?—use the money to finish the Juggernaut."

The old man sighed. "It would be tainted money. Oh, I could do it all right, but who would profit from it?" He stared hard at Jason.

"If you sold it, you would," Jason offered hesitantly.

"Oh, sure, I'd make a piece of change," the old man said airily, "but only a particle of its value. The *munitions makers*! They're the boys who would clean up. And they'd put it into more cannons to kill more boys. Hell, that's what they're in business for—to run fine boys through the meat grinder! Sons of bitches, they're right in it with the awl people. Why should I profit them?"

Jason shivered, picturing in his mind young soldiers in khaki doughboys' uniforms being tumbled head over heels into the gleaming hopper of an enormous grinder, with blood and limbs and pieces of meat being ejected from a grinning orifice at the side.

"Anyway," the old man sighed, "I already told you—there aint time for that. The sand is runnin out on me. The ball is pret near over, is what I'm sayin. I'll be eighty-nine next July the eighth. When she all runs out, there aint no more."

Jason thought of the overwhelming, incomprehensible finality of death, and wondered how the old man could speak of it so calmly.

"So the question I had to ask myself," Hector Callard went on, "is, do I put them blood-suckin sons of bitches in the way of more profits?"—his voice broke off sharply on a high, questioning note, and he held himself rigid as a statue while the last of the sand ran out of the glass, whereupon he rocked forward and slapped the table so hard that Jason recoiled—"*or . . . or*, I say, do I do somethin for *the people*?"

"What people?"

"Well, dammit, just the people."

"You mean the ones who get paid under the table?"

"No, no. Everyone aint gettin paid off. I'm talkin about the poor stupid bastards that caint help theirselves, that just keep on lettin the big companies and the politicians suck em dry because they don't know no better."

"If they just sit there and let that happen, I don't see they've got any favor coming. But what could you do for them?"

A smile stole across the old man's face, lending it sudden and unexpected sweetness. "The Juggernaut," he whispered. "I aim to give em the Juggernaut."

"But what would they *do* with it?"

The old man blinked and the smile vanished. "Why, dammit, don't you see? It would get their necks out from under the yoke forever!" Seeing Jason's worried frown, he leaned forward until his eyes were only inches from the boy's. "What, you may say, is to prevent me from keepin it for myself and makin a mint off of it? I'd be rich as old King Midas and live out my last days in silks. I'm too old to need it, is why. My ticket across the river is already punched. I just aint climbed aboard the boat yet, is all. It could happen any minute, any second, but I'm holdin her back, see, holdin her back until I finish the Juggernaut."

Jason took a shallow breath. The idea that the old man might be only seconds away from pitching forward in death was very uncomfortable to live with from minute to minute. And he was still without one crucial piece of information. Having only glimpsed the Juggernaut for a matter of seconds, all told, he had taken from it a sense of vast scale and purity of design, but nothing at all of the machine's function, its purpose.

"How will it get the yokes off their necks?" he asked. In his mind, he saw an endless column of Chinese coolies carrying buckets suspended from the ends of neck yokes, the buckets springing as the coolies trotted, and he wondered if they were talking about the same kind of yokes.

"*Power*, that's how. Unlimited power and no cost to run it. That's the Juggernaut! The way it is now, you see, we've got the awl companies and the damned utilities, and they've got a strangle holt on the people, chargin em triple prices and worse, and the people put up with it because they don't know no better! And power, anyway, is one thing you caint do without. So they're helpless. With the Juggernaut, they won't need all that. The way I aim to set it up, all the power will be generated by the Juggernauts, the big ones to run the electric plants and the little ones to run the cars and trolleys. The people will pay for the machines, which they do now anyway, but there won't be no need for the awl and gasarene and coal, so the money the people been a-payin for that will just stay in their pockets, to be spent as they please. Don't you see the glory of it? The big companies will be left suckin a dry tit! And that's why they will stop at nothin to get their hands on the Juggernaut!"

"But what is it that runs the Juggernaut?"

The old man pursed his lips. "*How* is a matter of great secrecy, but I can tell you the *what* of it. *Momentum* is the key. To put a harness on *momentum* is like turnin lead into gold, which is what them old-time chemists tried to do."

"Alchemists," Jason said.

"All right, so you know about em." The old man heaved himself jerkily to his feet. "You know they never done it. If they had, gold wouldn't have no value. They couldn't see that. But *power*, now, is different. We can use all of it we can get, and the cheaper the better, if the people are to benefit. See here, now, the world is still a-tryin to crawl out of what you might call a hand-tool age. There's a scarcity of goods—I mean, dammit, people are sleepin on the ground and starvin to death! The Juggernaut will turn scarcity into plenty, and the people won't have to pay through the nose for it the way they pay the big companies now, because what I'm doin is, *I'm givin the Juggernaut to the people*!"

Jason was startled to see a tear seep down the old man's cheek. Hector tried to say something more, shook his head helplessly with a slight wave of his hand, and then turned and went out the door. Seconds later, Jason heard the clash and rattle of chain at the shed door.

14

MAYNARD and Lexie awoke at daybreak. He scrambled out and got a little fire going. On his knees by the fire, he laughed suddenly and said, "Next time I'll be sure to bring some coffee and a pot."

"Next time?" she said tartly. She went to the pool and dipped her scarf in the icy water and washed her face with it.

They each had a boiled egg for breakfast, and then they shared a can of pears and an orange. Lexie was cool and distant with Maynard, answering him curtly when he spoke. Above them, the notch in the dark canyon walls was glowing fiery red as the sun crept into the sky. Maynard looked up and watched as the fire licked out along a feathery mare's tail. At length he said, "Something is sadly out of balance here."

She flared. "What is that supposed to mean?"

He smiled wryly. "This is, or let's say *could* be, the most beautiful morning of my life. I've just slept with a beautiful woman. So long as I live, I'll never forget it—yet you're miserable." She frowned exasperation, but he went on doggedly. "Look, we're in a beautiful place. No one is going to shoot us today. We're in no danger. I admit we're . . . slightly inconvenienced. But not threatened. And because I want the memory of it to stay with me, dammit, I'm going to take pleasure in every minute of it." His smile was slight, rueful. "This minute

I see red light from the sunrise on the side of your face. It's beautiful. Understand me?"

She regarded him levelly. Her frown faded. She leaned forward and kissed him quickly. "Shall we go to work now?"

An hour later, she was following Maynard, picking up greasewood brush as he cut it. The sun was well up, but it was still cool. A few yards away, the Jenny sat at a different angle—having packed brush under the wheels, they had lifted the tail and swung it back and forth, working it backwards half a foot at a time. Maynard paused, looking at the zigzag tracks in the sand.

"We can either cut more brush and keep working at it, or we can start walking. There's a ranch house near Alamos Creek, and that's fifteen, maybe twenty miles."

"And five more to the highway after that," Lexie said. "Another day to bring horses. Suppose we work until noon—if we're not making real progress by then, we start walking." She gathered her armload of brush and held it like a dancing partner and then began to dance, humming, waltzing toward the Jenny.

"More brush, Lucian!" She laughed merrily. "Cut more brush for the accursed coach!"

Her voice choked off. Maynard looked up and saw them, too—a young Mexican man carrying a singletree over his shoulder and leading an old horse. The horse was in harness, and on its back sat a young woman and a little girl.

Maynard knotted a rope to the stout ash tailskid that was bolted firmly inside the fuselage and snubbed against shock with a five-turn wrapping of bungee cord. He ran the rope from the tailskid to the singletree and tied it off. He showed the woman and the little girl where to push with him, against the sturdy leading edge of the wing. Lexie took a picture with her camera and then ran to help as the young man, Lázaro, urged his horse into the collar. They all heaved together and the Jenny rocked free of the wet sand and rolled backward, up onto the gravel bench. Lexie took another photo of them all, triumphant. Maynard gave Lázaro his hatchet. Airborne, Maynard flew low along the riverbed and wagged the Jenny's wings above the family while Lexie waved.

As they were cresting the long slope of the Rincons, Maynard passed something to Lexie under the cockpit cowling. Thinking it was the clipboard and notepad, she took it. Instead, it was a floppy-legged wooden doll with a painted face and shoe-button eyes. The tan-and-white-checked calico bonnet and dress were powdery with age. Lexie's eyes filled with tears beneath her goggles. She saw Maynard's eyes watching her in the mirror. She pressed Sibbie to her cheek and mouthed the question, *Where*? He passed her the notepad. *Up inside cave*, he had written, *on a rock*.

Instead of heading for town and the airport, Maynard veered north and west, letting down slowly over the Catalina foothills. Lexie signaled, questioning. Maynard wrote *Must see Jason*. Looking for an indication of wind direction, he saw laundry hanging limply on a line behind the house that sat across the canyon from the old man's place. A woman was standing in the yard shading her eyes and looking up at him. He banked to make a wide swing that would put his landing run toward the house, instead of toward the old adobe shack where his cognac was stored. A boxy black car caught his eye. Its sharp-cornered coach, uncompromising as a coffin, triggered *Essex* in his mind. It was a quarter of a mile north of the house with the laundry—he saw its tracks leading away from the road. Near the car, sitting on a knoll, was a man in a dark suit. The man raised binoculars and looked at him. Real-estate guy, Maynard thought idly.

Maynard landed the Jenny and taxied to the end of the once-plowed ground, not far from the old man's house. Jason ran toward the airplane, followed by the old man, as Maynard cut the engine. Lexie jumped down and hugged the boy, whose answering hug appeared indifferent to Maynard. The boy was looking at him with a tense and somehow drawn and expectant expression.

Maynard shook Jason's hand and murmured, "Mesquite."

Jason exhaled gratefully. "Javelina," he whispered. "Can we talk?"

"Sure." Lexie, a few feet away, gave the old man a peck on the cheek, accepted austerely as he eyed Maynard and the aircraft with a degree of suspicion.

Jason said in a voice husky with dread, "There's an old woman over there"—he pointed—"who wants to put me in school, or maybe even take me away. She says this is a sinkhole and she's going to call the county man. If he takes me away, I can't do my mission."

Lexie swung toward them, frowning. "What county man?"

"It's Olive Farney's doin," the old man said. "Turrible old busybody and a damned fool, to boot."

"I don't want Jason in school or anyplace else but right here," Lexie said firmly, "until I've had a chance to get this straightened out in court. No matter who calls." She took the old man's arm and turned with him, lowering her voice. "But, Uncle Hector, I think I see what's on her mind. If anyone should show up, it would be a good idea, don't you think, for Jason to be cleaned up—a bath and a change of clothes?" The old man seemed startled by her proposal.

As she went on, Maynard murmured to the boy, "You might watch out for a man in a dark suit."

"An agent?" Jason asked. Maynard shrugged slightly and Jason said, "Maybe he's the county man."

"Oh, I doubt that," Maynard said.

"He could've been bought," Jason said, "you know, under the table."

Maynard's eyebrows shot up. "By whom?"

"The awl companies and munitions people—they own everybody from the president to the courthouse janitor, right?" Jason gave him a look so level, unflinching and filled with truth that Maynard was jolted. He tried to maintain a conspiratorial calm.

"I doubt if the county man is really an agent," he said, a trifle lamely. "After all, what's in it for the munitions people, way out here?"

Jason squinted, his face torn now with turmoil. "My uncle, Uncle Heck, is working on something they're after. I can't tell you what it is—he's pledged me to secrecy. I . . . I don't even know yet, for sure." He bit his knuckle intently. "Do you . . . I mean, do *our people* have to know what it is?"

Poor little devil, Maynard thought, this is getting deep. "I can't tell you for sure, of course, but if it gets to be a matter of *national* concern . . . to the *people,* you know . . . you'll have to decide, I guess."

"It's *for* the people," Jason said desperately. "He's going to give it to them. Right now, we're trying to get his Ford running, case we have to get out of here in a hurry."

Lexie and the old man were returning. "We'll have to talk again later," Maynard said, "but look—I almost forgot!" He took his old Legion *kepi* out of the Jenny's locker and placed it on Jason's head, where it settled over his ears. "Your *kepi,*" he said.

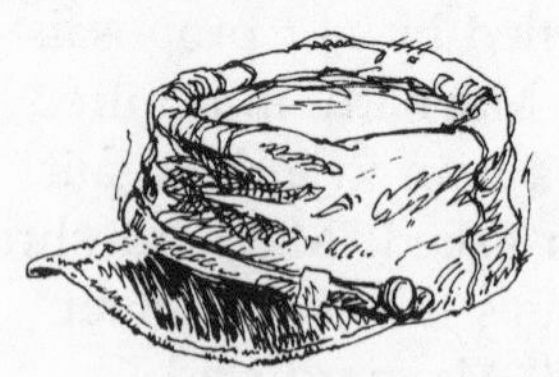

Jason's fingers sought the stained and battered red cap. His scowl of dread gave way to a strained, incredulous smile.

Maynard turned to the old man. "What's the problem with your car? Want to show me?"

Somewhat stiffly, the old man led him to the old Model T.

"She's got gasarene and she's got a spark," he said, "but she won't fire."

"Plugs clean?" Maynard said. The old man shrugged uncertainly. Maynard unscrewed the fuel cap and thrust a stick into the tank. When he pulled it out, about an inch of the stick was wet. He sniffed it. "There's part of the trouble right there. The gas is old and it's gone bad. If you'll drain that tank, I'll get some out of the Jenny." The old man gave him a can and Maynard drained half a gallon out of the airplane's tank and poured it into the Ford's tank. He set spark and throttle levers, spark up, gas down, and cranked. The engine made sucking noises, then it fired up and ran raggedly, backfiring and emitting clouds of dark smoke from the exhaust.

After a minute Maynard switched off the engine. "Your plugs are dirty and the carburetor is all varnished up from that old gas. I'll bring some acetone to clean it, next time I come. Jason can clean the plugs and we'll get this baby running like a top." Maynard unscrewed one of the spark plugs with a wrench and showed Jason how to scratch the carbon off the tip with a knife blade. He turned to the old man. "You're lucky to have a good man to help you. This will leave you free to work on your project. I wish I had someone to help me—I'm nearly ready to get my engine out of the crate and install it."

When she was getting into the cockpit of the airplane a few minutes later, Lexie said to Maynard, "I wish you hadn't done that. Uncle Hector is too old to be running around in that car."

"It gives them something to work on together," Maynard said. "Anyway, they're not going anyplace on a couple of quarts of gasoline."

Othello Biggers watched the airplane take off and bank away to the southeast, toward Tucson. He had seen the pilot and J. W.'s good-looking little sister-in-law give something to the kid, he couldn't tell what. So, the pilot was back from taking J. W. to Mexico. And now the girl was involved too. Biggers was a methodical thinker. Everything he had seen made perfect sense. And now there was a new and more urgent complexion on the whole affair. He was too far away to learn anything specific, the way he was going now. He peered again through the binoculars. The old man and the kid were working on the Ford. That added to his uneasiness. Biggers ate his sandwich and drank from his canteen and watched for another hour, and then he decided he needed a closer look.

The old man watched Jason scrape the spark plugs. "Feller's right," he said. "It don't take two of us to do this, and I've got work piled up to where I caint see over the top of it."

"Maybe I could help you on the Juggernaut too," Jason said.

"Crocus cloth and elbow grease is where I could use some help. We'll see." The old man went back into his shed. "And mind you keep an eye skinned for that damned county man, hear? If the son of a bitch shows up, I'll skin him alive."

Jason was terrified of a clash between the county man and the old man, and he was glad to see the old man go back to the shed—the more so when, minutes later, his keen ears caught the sound of a distant automobile engine. He stepped back from the Ford and looked across the riverbed. A flash of light caught his eye and he saw a black car turn onto the road. It dipped down into the canyon and stopped. A man in a dark suit got out and raised the hood of the Essex. After a moment he began walking toward the old man's house. Jason's insides heaved.

Car trouble was as good an excuse as any, Biggers thought. He saw the kid look up from the Ford's engine. The kid was scruffy and dirty. His forehead was deeply furrowed and his eyes squinted painfully. He appeared to be trying to twist his lips into something resembling a smile. A rapid pulse was visible at his throat. He swallowed hard when Biggers stopped before him.

"I'm afraid my car has boiled over," Biggers said.

"I . . . I'm Jason Whitlock. I been expecting you," the kid said in a dry voice.

Biggers planted his feet wide apart and clasped his gloved hands behind his back. He frowned balefully. "You have, have you?" What does the kid know? he wondered.

The kid nodded jerkily. "Mrs. Farney said you would come. She said the county would send a man."

"Um-m," Biggers said. "Praps she said what the man would do."

"She said he—you would come to put me in school."

"Well, now." Biggers' lips peeled back affably. "Nothing wrong with that, is there? He was startled and a little amused to be taken for a truant cop, a breed he ranked just below dogcatchers in the worlds affairs, and it made him think suddenly of his own epic battle with Holsclaw, truant officer back in Slade County—himself fourteen and still in the sixth grade, but his stocky body already packed with muscle from cutting and hauling beef and hogsides in the slaughterhouse, standing over Holsclaw, who, after Othello called him a "turd-face son of a bitch," had come at him with a cane, which Othello Biggers took away from him and hurled up onto the roof of the slaughterhouse before tearing into him with his fists, and Holsclaw down in the dirt then in front of the whole skinning gang, holding his bloody nose and crying out, *"I warsh my hands of ye, by god! You're the sheriff's work now!"* About 1901, that would have been, and Othello Biggers had caught a southbound freight out of town a couple of hours later.

The boy had not replied. "I say *is* there?" Biggers repeated.

The boy swallowed with difficulty. His smile had faded and his face was gray with the strain of contending with forces massive beyond his strength or ability to deal with them, a look Biggers well knew among soldiers. "No," the boy said, "it's just that I won't be *living* here. I'm just visiting, sort of, for a day or two, until my father comes for me, so it wouldn't hardly be worth starting school for just really no time at all. . . ." He spread his hands earnestly, reasonably, and tried to smile again as if to show the futility of such a move.

"The county don't pay me to decide if you should go to school," Biggers said. He had learned as a corporal never to get caught in a direct lie. "The rules is all wrote out. It aint of my doing."

A faint sigh, like dry leaves rustling, escaped the boy. "Spose it's only two days," he ventured, half a question.

"Ah," Biggers said, "so your dad will be back in two days?"

"Maybe. He didn't exactly promise." The boy had been almost whispering, Biggers noticed, and now he cast an uneasy glance over his shoulder toward the pump house, as if, Biggers thought, he did not want their voices to be overheard.

"And where did he tell you he was going?" Biggers purposely raised his voice.

The boy winced. "He didn't say. Fort Worth is where we lived before. It might be better if you talked to my aunt."

"Long as I'm here," said Biggers, "I'll have to see the house, and I may's well talk to Mr. Callard." He stepped around the boy and walked purposefully along the side of the house and up the front steps and entered the house, the boy trotting helplessly after him.

"But he's busy working," the boy was saying, "and he told me he wasn't to be disturbed on no account . . . *any* account."

"He did, eh? And what's he workin on? I understand he's a pensioner."

"Well, he is. He's a *veteran*. But he works all the time in his shop . . . on . . . stuff, I guess, for his claim—he's got a mine—or maybe for his car, I don't know."

"Is that all? I understand he's supposed to be an inventor." Biggers looked curiously at the littered room. He touched the six-foot rattlesnake skin, then pressed on through the hallway toward the kitchen.

"Is that what people say, an inventor?" the boy said lamely.

Biggers smiled icily. "Ask anybody. No doubt he is inventin something of great worth to mankind." He thought the boy flinched slightly. "Of *great* worth to mankind," he repeated in a manner intended to be ingratiating, not realizing the chill his words engendered in the boy's belly. "What are my chances of getting a look at his inventions?"

"He won't allow *anyone* in his shop, not even me. He's really cranky that way."

"What a shame. How I do admire a man who's talented in the ways of machinery." Biggers scanned the kitchen, filthy except for the sink and a few pots. His top-sergeant's instinct prompted him to reach out suddenly and draw a finger along the wooden plate rail above the table. His finger came away with a thick wad of cobwebs and dust adhering to it. He grimaced. "It appears his work don't leave him much time for housekeeping."

Jason sagged against the door frame. He had been expecting the county man to get around to this. "I *know* she said it was a hawg-pen. She said you wouldn't let me stay here if you saw it, but I been working on it. Honest." Jason's voice caught in his throat. He hastily snatched up a wet rag from the sink and scrubbed at the offending rail. "You just caught me before I had time to finish, see?"

Biggers dusted his hands. "Now you mention it, I believe she did call it a hawg-pen. She was tolerble worked up about it, wasn't she?"

Jason nodded dismally. "She said I would catch the plague, but that was before I even started to clean it up."

Biggers grunted noncommittally, frowning. "And no doubt she told you exactly what we should be doing about it?" He waited, but Jason said nothing. "Or should I just look it up in the ree-ports? It's all there, you know."

Trapped, Jason said, "She said it was *unspeakable,* and she said any county man worth his salt would snatch me out of this sinkhole so quick it would make your head swim."

"Well," Biggers said, holding his palms up, "you see the position I'm in, don't you?" Years of penetrating the subterfuges of hapless soldiers had trained Biggers for this moment.

Jason's shrug carried surrender. He looked away, blinking rapidly. "Where would you have to take me to? I mean, what if my dad or my aunt come for me and I'm gone? Will they be able to *find* me?"

"Before we get into that, I need to know exactly what he left with you in the way of money, for expenses and such."

"Nothing," Jason whispered. "There wasn't time."

"Nothing! Not a red cent?" Biggers took an envelope and pencil out of his pocket. He licked the lead and began to write. "D. . . . E. . . . S. . . ." How do you spell *destitute*?"

Jason spelled it for him and Biggers scribbled grimly.

"If you can spell it, I guess you know what it means. The board aint going to like that. Now then, one more thing—this could help with the board—did he leave any valuables at all with you? Such as maybe . . . *jewelry*. It could make a difference in what I tell the board."

Jason held his breath for a long moment, and then shook his head. "Nothing."

"How about with the old—old gentleman?"

"No. I would have known. My aunt, she brings groceries."

"That aint the same," Biggers said. He was certain the kid was telling the truth. "It takes the board a while to act in these matters. Of course, if things is *desperate*, I can always act on my own authority." He looked searchingly around the room, as if to seek out even more that was *unspeakable*. His gaze fixed, through the window, on the pump house and shed. No use getting the old man all worked up—best keep it between the kid and me. He smiled suddenly, intending to enlist the kid's trust now that he had him paralyzed with fear. "Until I've had time to make my report to the board, spose we keep this between you and me?"

The boy nodded carefully. I rode him pretty hard, Biggers thought.

"Why, maybe you and me could persuade Mr. Callard to let us see the invention he's workin on. Maybe we could even sell it for him for a lot of money." He distinctly heard a gasp from the boy and saw him flinch. "Probly a pot full of money!" he went on expansively. "You wouldn't be in this predicament then. I hear all the time how people invent things and make theirselves fortunes." Biggers grinned warmly, reassuringly, not realizing that his face was no more built for smiling than a cobra's.

"Oh, no!" Jason protested. "He isn't ready yet—"

"Not while he's still working on it. I spect he'll hold out for a while—they all do—but watch him come around when you and I wave a bundle of greenbacks under his nose."

Greenbacks! Jason thought with a shiver of revulsion. "No, he just plain aint interested," he said stoutly. "Besides, it's just a piece of junk. No one would want to buy it."

Biggers felt the boy's trust melting away, and pressed to regain it. "You never know. A big company could get interested in it if we was to take it to them, and they are the boys with the real money. You and I might just do that ourselves and *surprise* Mr. Callard. Maybe next time I come, you can get me a look at that invention, what do you say?" He again bared his teeth, but inexplicably to him, the boy's face paled even further, causing the water tracks on his neck to appear suddenly chalky white.

"No," Jason whispered, "I couldn't do that."

Biggers fished a gold watch from a vest pocket. "I've got a board meeting in just an hour. Spose we talk about it next time I see you. Say tomorrow, if the board gets to your case by then." He had turned and was already moving briskly out of the house and down the steps to the road, heading for the Essex. He did not take water for the radiator.

Jason was stricken. The worst had befallen him, for there could be no doubt that the county man was an agent of the big companies, bent on stealing the Juggernaut. The blame was bound to fall directly on himself, for the county man would not have come around except for him.

Jason dared not interrupt the old man. He waited miserably.

After a time, he heard the clash of chain. The old man was beaming happily when he entered.

"By the eternal! I had her pumpin water! She sucked it up like a weaner calf. Now if I can just get the reverse take-off workin—" He did his little shuffling jig-step.

Jason waited until he was seated at the table and put a cup of coffee in front of him, and then, resolutely, he said, "I tried to stop it, but we've been infiltrated. The county man was here and I think he"—Jason watched the old man's bushy eyebrows shoot up, felt his own nose burn and tears of shame and fury spring to his eyes so that the words were torn from him in a rage—*"I mean I know—the son of a bitch is an agent!"*

15

HECTOR CALLARD listened, sipping now and then from the chipped cup cradled in his weathered hand, as Jason told him about the visit of the county man. Jason had been expecting an explosion, but the old man remained strangely calm. When Jason finished talking, Hector nodded.

"It don't surprise me none. I been expecting the bastards for a long time. Years, in fact. I started workin on the Juggernaut, the *idee* of it, anyway, long before the war, and back then I done a damn sight more talkin than I should've. Then when the war was on, I realized what it would mean to the damned Huns if they was to get their hands on it. After that, by god, I was careful, but too many people had at least heard about it. They been a-watchin me ever since. The thing is"—he wagged a finger at Jason—"the bastards never could penetrate m' dee-fenses!"

He stared hard at Jason. "You say he never give you his name? Well, then, that leaves two possibilities. Maybe he's the real county man and they've bought him off, so he's usin you as an excuse to get at the Juggernaut. Or, he has infilterated the county office so as to get at us. And hell, maybe he shot the real county man down in cold blood and left him stretched out in a pool of gore."

Jason shivered. "How you going to tell which it is?"

* * *

Ulysses Farney, home from the Papago Queen mine, paused in his rocking as he watched the old Ford lurch across the canyon, bucking and smoking, and pull up before the house. Two figures climbed down and walked toward the house.

"Libby," Farney called softly, "we've got company." He went inside to bring more chairs out onto the gallery. "My stars!" Olive Farney exclaimed when she saw them.

Hector Callard gravely removed a black hat when bidden to take a seat. Freed of the hat, his damp hair sprang out in wild spikes. His freshly shaved chin bore a piece of tissue stuck to a small razor cut. He wore a clean white shirt, collarless and unironed, beneath an ancient, round-skirted suit coat. Cut for the strapping six-foot-three he once was, it now hung loosely on his shrunken shoulders.

The boy's hair was slicked back, too. Gone were the water tracks and smudges, sluiced away under a cold-water shower in the pump house. He wore clean cords and a checked cotton shirt with fold marks creased into it.

"Now, Olive," the old man said softly, "we've knowed one another for twenty years, give or take. There was times when I was disposed to devil you. Pure cussedness, call it. Mother, three sisters and two wives, I never could set still for a female tellin me what to do. And I know you done the same to me." He waved a hand as she started to speak. "No matter. No offense intended, either way. Now, though, we come to the matter of this county man you meant to call down on us—all in a good cause, no doubt—but Olive, did you—"

"No," she said, "I didn't make the call."

"That's right," Farney said. "Libby thought better of it."

"I believe you. Now, Olive, if you *had*, who would you have expected them to send out here?"

She hesitated. "Harold Emmons, my sister's husband. You'd know him."

"Skinny dude, right? Wears that straw boater with the ribbon on it."

She nodded. "I seen a black car over near your place this morning. Was it—"

He again held up his hand. "So far as you know, Olive, is there any other man doin that job for the county now?"

"None. Pore Harold, he is worked like a slave. S . . . L . . . A . . . V . . . E!" she spelled.

The old man and the boy exchanged glances.

"What's this all about, Heck?" Farney said.

The old man shrugged. "Me and the boy is just settin our house in order, is all. Olive, we've got the place tidied up like a funeral parlor, and we aim to keep it that way. No need of the county steppin in."

"Oughtn't the chile to be in school, though?" she offered.

Hector Callard smiled civilly and rose to leave. "All in good time, Olive. Now we've got to get back. Our supper is on the stove." He turned to Farney. "And I'm wondering if you might do me the kindness of a short-term loan of a gallon of gasarene? I've brought a can."

Othello Biggers, having interviewed Jason and driven away, decided that he had to continue his surveillance of the old man's place. He pulled the Essex off the road a mile away and walked back along the riverbed until he found a good path up the bluffs and a well-situated knoll from which to watch. He had his binoculars, his canteen and dictionary, which he leafed through contentedly, now and then glancing up to see what the old man and the kid were doing, hearing a considerable slamming of doors, clattering, banging and such noises as the two busied themselves. The sun had fallen far down in the west and he was savoring the marvelous place names in the *Pronouncing Gazetteer* section when he heard the noisy clatter of the old Ford's engine and then watched the old man and the kid drive away.

"Damn!" he murmured. He couldn't follow because his own car was too far away. But it was a perfect opening to let him check the place out. He left his knoll and hiked through the cactus and brush to the house, where he entered by the back door. Having already seen the house once, and been appalled by the mess—which was comparable in his memory only to the shell-blasted villages he had seen in France or to back alleys, odoriferous in memory, of cities like Manila and Shanghai—Biggers was startled to see the transformation. The screened porch was tidied and swept and clear of trash. The kitchen was cleared of its stacks of newspaper and boots and such, and the dishes were put away. The parlor was by no means emptied of trash, but the piles were at least more orderly. Biggers realized with pleasure that it was his own visit that had prompted this rush to cleanliness and order.

A few minutes' search turned up nothing in the house, though he curiously examined some of the weapons he found there: the old man's cap-and-ball .44-caliber Colt with holster, belt and cap box, a cavalry saber and an ancient black-powder shotgun. He paused before a tintype of a sturdy young trooper standing at his horse's head. The trooper's expression was flinty and resolute, his stubbled cheek bulging with a chew. Biggers felt a kinship with the trooper, and then suddenly it came to him that the trooper was the old man whose house he was searching. He put the picture down and went outside.

Chains and padlocks drew his attention to the pump house shed. A peek through the dusty window showed him a littered workbench, no more. He walked around the shed, which he found stoutly built, and then he went into the pump house. He saw the metal trough with the raised, thronelike toilet seat perched above it and half a metal drum cocked on its axis at one side under a faucet. Biggers had been trained in a field artillery regiment during one hitch in China—he saw that the drum was mounted on trunnions, like a cannon, so as to be elevated or depressed. He turned on the faucet and watched the water fill and then dump and pour in a rush down the trough. Biggers' face, usually impassive as sheet iron, split in a delighted grin.

He found the knothole through which Jason had first seen

the Juggernaut. He loosened the board with a kick and then pushed it, nails squealing, until he could wriggle through into the old man's shop. Biggers examined the clutter of tools and parts with interest. It appeared to him that the old man might be working on clocks, from the nature of some of the pieces. It also occurred to him that the old man might very well be doing a clever job of hiding J. W.'s hoard of jewels in something like a clock. Very clever of him, thought Biggers. But whatever it was that the old man was working on, Biggers thought, *he had to have taken it with him,* because there was no clock or mechanism of any sort in evidence, except for an oddly ornate, openwork brass frame that might conceivably have been a mount for the works of a large clock. So the old boy was toting it around with him, and that was the clincher—it was clearly something of great value.

Biggers saw, with a surge of hope, small cubbyholes set between studs here and there, up above bench and shelves. He felt around in them, one after another, finding odd parts and pieces of machinery—clock parts again, so far as he could tell—wrapped in pieces of flannel. Assembled, they might have made the works of a clock of some kind, apparently one powered by weights. But there was nothing in the way of jewelry or stones except a tiny glass jar holding a few clockmaker's jewels.

Biggers replaced the flannel-wrapped parts in their cubbyholes, making certain that each was returned to its proper place. He was certain now that he was on the right track . . . all the secrecy hinted at by the kid. All the locks and chains. All the hidden parts of this strange clock. And the comings and goings of the airplane.

The sudden noisy clatter of the Ford startled Biggers. He watched as the old truck wheeled into the yard and stopped and the kid and the old man got out and went into the house. Biggers crawled back into the pump house, pulled the loosened plank into place behind him and then slipped out the door and ducked away into the brush. He had seen enough for the time being—had to get back to town, find the Durker and see if he had located J. W.

Walking toward the house from the Ford, Jason uneasily began to sense the alarm and growing agitation in the old man, whose steps were erratic and whose breath came in short gasps. They reached the steps, and the old man caught his arm and clung tightly to it, leaning heavily on him as they climbed.

Jason led him into the kitchen, where he sagged into a chair. "Do you want your pipe?" Jason said.

The old man shook his head. He pointed to a cupboard with a shaky finger. Jason opened it and saw a squat bottle among the pots and pans. The old man nodded. Jason poured from the bottle into a teacup. The old man drank. A tremor ran through him. He drank again. The smell stung Jason's nostrils and he shuddered. He was no stranger to a liquor bottle, and he was uneasy in its presence because whenever J. W. and whiskey got together, Jason could count on being thrown into an unpredictable, chaotic and often frightening train of events. But now, the old man poured himself another small dosage, thumped the cork squealing into the bottle and pushed it aside. He tapped his ribs in the region of the heart.

"For man or beast," he said, "an uncommon good tonic." His eyes roved around the room. "You see the fix we are in, young sir. The bastards have closed in on us."

"He wasn't the real county man at all." Jason's relief at realizing he would escape or at least delay being dragged off to school or to an orphanage gave him a twinge of guilt.

"No, he was an agent, all right. No question about it. There aint but one thing in our favor in this mess, and that is, they don't know we've saw through em. Slow and easy, that was their game while they worked the net around us, but by god, once they know we've tumbled, you can bet they'll strike like a rattlesnake!" His hand darted out and he struck two clawed fingers into Jason's forearm. Jason recoiled.

"Couldn't we go to the police?"

"Police!" The old man snorted and spat dryly at the floor. "*Shew!* They would've been on the payroll from the beginning. Before we're through, we'll no doubt lock horns with that bunch too!"

Jason regretted he had mentioned the police. "Can't we trust *anybody*?"

"To what end?" the old man growled. "I trust Farney, down the road there, but to do what? He caint help us. No, we are betwixt the hawk and the buzzard, with no one but ourselves to count on." He lurched unsteadily to his feet and staggered a few steps, turned and staggered back. "You see, I aimed to finish the Juggernaut and get her workin—and dammit, I'm almost there!—and then, at my *leisure,* to set about givin her to the people! And don't think I didn't know there'd be battles there, too! But hell, that's all down the drain now!"

Jason was shocked at the anguish in the old man's voice. "Why is it down the drain? We've still got the Juggernaut."

"Spose I kick off? Time is on their side, see? They've . . . hell, they've already waited *years*! We're in a race against time. If we don't get the Juggernaut into the right hands before I croak, then the *people* lose, don't you see?"

"Whose hands?" Jason pleaded. "Whose?"

The old man stared past him into space. "Wait here like a couple of snared rabbits? No! By god, we won't do it!"

"If you're thinking of leaving," Jason said, "we can take the Juggernaut with us, but how could you finish it without your shop and tools?"

"Couple boxes will carry all the tools I need now," the old man said. "It aint the tools I'm worried about, it's *me*. I'm nearabout wore out."

"Can't I help? I fixed the spark plugs today."

"Yes, you did, and a first-rate job, too, but there's more to it than the shopwork. It's got to be protected, whatever that takes, and dammit, it could come down to gunfire, with them bastards after it! And then it's got to be handed over to the people in a legal and orderly way, so the damned companies can't just grind her out under their heels. It damn near kills me to have to say it, but we need help, there's no way around it. Someone who aint mystified by the work, who aint afraid of a fight and who knows the meaning of *honor*, because the sons of bitches will be after him with sacks full of greenbacks, if they don't shoot him first."

"Captain Gaylen," Jason said. "He could do it. He was in the Foreign Legion and the air service, and he's building a whole airplane by himself." For a moment he thought the old man wasn't listening.

"Maybe you've got it," the old man said after a long pause. "He *told* me they was after him, too, first time I seen him. This will take some deliberation, young sir. My experience is that it's a rare soul indeed who is stout enough to shoulder the load when honor, not riches, is the burden. Only, we caint do it tonight. We need rest. So if you will light the lantern and come with me, we'll check our outposts and pickets before we turn in."

Jason did as he was told. Together, they walked outside and took the path to the pump-house shed. The old man unlocked the padlocks and chain and opened the door, holding the lantern up. Breath hissed through his teeth. Jason looked in.

"They've been here," the old man whispered. "Look at the tracks. I salted the floor with flour before I left. We've been *raided*!"

16

MAYNARD helped Lexie down from the cockpit of the Jenny after landing back at the airport. He asked her if she would like to take a minute to see his Dragonfly. She said, somewhat coolly it seemed to him, that she was in a terrible rush to get to work on her story. He asked her to have supper with him that evening. She told him that she would be working on the story all day and probably right up to deadline at eleven o'clock that night—and by then, she said, she would be ready for the boneyard. But, as she was getting into her car, she turned and said, "It was sweet of you to find Sibbie for me."

"It took me a while to realize that it was important to you." He hesitated. "Mind reading, I guess I'm not too sharp, but this thing . . . the bootlegging . . . it bothers you, doesn't it?"

"Certainly not," she said crisply, "if it doesn't bother you."

"It doesn't. There's just nothing to it—"

"Don't bother to explain."

"I started to say that I'm not going to try to explain it or alibi around it."

"That's fine with me." Lexie's voice was tart.

He grinned suddenly and shook his head. "No, it isn't and I know it isn't, but I'm not going to say any more about it for now. Saying *anything* would make it more important than it is."

"You mean you're ignoring it, right?"

"Right. It doesn't bother me. *You* bother me, though. Look, please take one minute and look at my Dragonfly."

Reluctance clear in her expression, Lexie followed him to the hangar. He rolled back the door and they stepped inside.

The hangar was covered with corrugated iron. In the summer it was an oven, but this time of year, with the sun on it, it was merely warm without being unpleasant. The army tent that was his bedroom sat in one corner on a wooden platform. In the summer, when the heat became unbearable, he hitched a truck to the platform and dragged it outside and at night slept with the tent flaps rolled up. Near the tent against the wall of the hangar was an iron sink on pipe legs, and next to the sink was a small iron stove with a coffeepot on it. A packing crate held a skillet and cooking pot and some canned goods. The rest of the hangar belonged to the Dragonfly.

The fuselage skeleton with its high vertical fin sat on two sawhorses. Work tables held stacks of ribs and spars and a partly assembled wing. Spruce lumber and sheets of thin mahogany plywood were racked against the back wall, and a workbench and various tools stood against the side wall.

Lexie walked between the work tables and paused by the fuselage. "It's much smaller than the Jenny, isn't it? Will it have two wings?"

"Yes, but not placed one over the other, the way they are on the Jenny, and it won't have all those wires and struts. All the framing and bracing is internal, and the real strength comes from the skin—*monocoque,* the French call that."

She walked on and stopped before his tent. The flap was tied back, and inside she saw a wooden-legged army cot, a footlocker, a small chest of drawers, and a bookshelf full of books next to a small table that was littered with drawings.

"What are you thinking?" Maynard said.

"Whoever lives here is . . ."

"What, a wild-eyed visionary? Obscure genius?"

She laughed. "He's busy, anyway. No time for frills. I never dreamed an airplane had so much in the way of *innards*. Now, I do have to get home and change and go to work. Seeing the Dragonfly makes me feel indolent and lazy."

Maynard watched her drive away. He was used to being alone, but her going left a feeling of hollowness that he found disturbing. He couldn't fill it by eating or drinking or ease it by scratching, yawning or stretching. He wrenched his attention to the Jenny.

Maynard was concerned that the wheel bearings might have picked up some sand from the San Pedro. He blocked up the Jenny's axle and took the wheels off, washed the bearings with solvent and repacked them with grease. He added a quart of oil to the OX-5 engine. Since she was parked next to the gasoline pump, he topped off the fuel tank. He looked for brush slashes under the wings and found a little tear in the fabric under the bottom wing on the right side and patched it with a piece of fabric and dope. His mind was still churning with thoughts of Lexie (her eyes gleaming in the moon-bright canyon), but he forced himself to roll back his hangar door and go to work.

Sibbie leaned against a vase of flowers on Lexie's desk, staring brightly. Lexie took her up onto the roof of the *Courier* building and photographed her in bright sunlight, and when Craddock came in at noon, she asked him if she could run a cut with her story of Marietta's journey, a cut being a metal plate, a photoengraving of pictorial material.

Craddock was grumpy. He felt strung out and sick and he was well aware that Lexie had not so much as checked in at the office the day before, after her flight . . . not that he had expected her to go right to work, but she might at least have looked in the door. When she hadn't, a suspicion began to build up that she might have been enjoying the captain's company. The suspicion had a physical presence under his vest somewhat on the order of that coiled adder he described to her only a few days earlier.

"How *big* a cut?" Craddock snarled through a cloud of cigarette smoke.

"Say, four columns by eight inches—I want a picture of Marietta and one of Sibbie to be vignetted into an 1862 map of the stage route."

"That means a *combination* line and halftone. Do you realize what it will cost?"

"I know it costs a little more than either by itself, but it will *make* the story."

"Who the hell is Sibbie?"

Lexie told him about finding the doll after its sixty-five-year sojourn in the cave. She showed him an ambered portrait of the youthful bride. After a minute, he threw up his hands irritably and said, "Okay, you want to bankrupt us, run it."

Pleased, Lexie took her roll of film to a photographer's studio a few doors up the street, where Hernandez, the photographer, promised prints by three o'clock. She went back to her desk and worked at her story until then, when she went back and picked up the prints. In the office, she laid out a print of the map and positioned Sibbie's cut-out figure in the upper-right-hand corner, with Marietta in the lower left, gazing serenely eastward from an elliptical frame which Lexie outlined in India ink. Pleased with the effect, she called the engraver's shop on Toole Street and they sent a boy to pick up the artwork.

She was typing furiously, stopping now and then to scribble corrections, when Craddock picked up the pictures and thumbed through them. There was one of Lexie leaning jauntily against the propeller of the Jenny with a crumbling adobe building in the background. His interest quickened when he saw the one showing a horse hitched to the Jenny's tailskid and the people pushing against the wing.

"You didn't tell me about getting stuck out there," Craddock said. Lexie shrugged, cocked her head slightly, and went on typing. Craddock frowned. "How is J. W.'s kid getting along with your uncle?"

She stopped typing. "He was all right when we landed there this morning, except that he really needed a bath—and it seems that a woman down the road—an old busybody, according to Uncle Hector—has threatened to send a county officer to put him back in school, or even take him out of there. She called the place a sinkhole. I may have to go see her myself . . . try to calm her down."

But Craddock was thinking that if Lexie and the pilot had landed there this morning, it meant—didn't it?—that they had not gotten back from their flying trip yesterday when they should have. So, where had they spent the night? His eye fell upon the photograph of the bogged Jenny hitched to a horse, and Craddock felt helpless fury nudge against the adder under his vest.

Maynard backed his Ford into the hangar, close to the aluminum racing-car engine he planned to mount in the Dragonfly. He lifted the engine with a chain hoist, set up a plank ramp and then let the engine down and skidded it into the van. He climbed into the car and drove to Jack Perrell's shop over by the Santa Cruz River. Perrell had Maynard's engine mount all welded. He carried it out to show Maynard how light and strong it was.

"We'll adjust the mount to the engine for a perfect fit," Perrell said, "and then drill the holes for the bolts. After that I can make the exhaust manifold and mount the carburetor."

"And we can make final measurements for the fuel tank," Maynard said.

"I had the race-car shop in L.A. send me an electric fuel pump," Perrell said. "You can't use gravity feed in this setup because you can't put your tank any higher. It's another twenty-five bucks, but it's worth it. Besides, you'll have constant pressure, even in inverted flight—ever think of that?"

Maynard grinned. They talked about the design of the exhaust system.

Durkin checked with the desk clerk at the Cosmo House to see if J. W. Whitlock had returned. The clerk said he had not. Durkin decided it was time to go see the ace, find out where he had left J. W. It was clear enough, anyway, that the ace had dropped J. W. in Mexico. What Durkin had to do was find out when he was going back to pick up J. W. And the stuff.

Durkin fought his wrinkle-fendered Model T out of town on the road to the airport, narrowly averting disaster at every corner. Durkin hated cars. At a time when a whole generation of young men—*his* generation—was learning to drive automobiles, Durkin was doing a stretch in the old Yuma pen. Shortly after he got out of prison, he got into trouble again and had to go to Mexico in a hurry, which was how he got into horse-soldiering with Rodrigo Vega—*that crazy goddam Vega!* he thought—and later with Pershing in Mexico, and that led to more soldiering, and time in the guardhouse, in France, and then guardhouse in the States, and he damned near drew a double sawbuck in Leavenworth, *a fucking twenty, for Chrissake*! except that Thel Biggers, top sergeant, no, master sergeant by then, told a different story at the court-martial than the one the supply sergeant was telling, which got Durkin off with only sixty days instead of the double sawbuck. So, between the army, Vega's Gringo Legion and the pen, he never learned to drive, at least not a regular car. Of course he could drive a Ford, *anyone* could do that, but he didn't exactly drive it, either—he *fought* it, like a square-wheeled buckboard pulled by a couple of ornery studs. Hated cars!

He hated them most of all when he passed, as he did now, Perrell's Automotive and Machine Works, a stuccoed adobe building next to the bridge across the Santa Cruz, which brought back a rush of memory of a miserable time in Mexico in '16 when he and Vega and what was left of the Gringo

Legion ran themselves half to death in the Sierra Madre trying to overtake an ancient Thomas Flyer automobile driven by this same Jack Perrell.

He passed Perrell's shop. Almost drove off the road into the river, for there was the ace, talking to Perrell. They had an engine on a dolly and were both using their hands as they talked. Damn, Durkin didn't want to talk to them both at once. He knew Perrell was carrying a grudge for him, and it would be hard to crowd the ace with Perrell standing there. He swung around at the next corner and headed back to town. Had to pass the shop again. He scrunched down in the seat, but Perrell looked up just then and saw him. Perrell grinned crookedly at Durkin, waved, shaking his head as if at some shared joke. Durkin, knowing the joke—for he himself was the butt of it—swore under his breath, ignored Perrell and fought the car back toward town.

He drove along Convent Street, saw the black Essex parked at the curb by the old convent. Durkin swung into the curb—almost blew a tire ramming it—and went in to see Biggers.

They exchanged information. "Way I see it," Biggers said, "this thing is like a grenade with a loose pin. Do we let the pin fall out when we aint looking, or do we pull the pin when it suits us to pull the pin?"

"We pull the fucking pin ourselves," Durkin said, liking the idea.

"Check. Then you keep the ace under tight surveillance and I'll go back out to the old man's place. That way nothing gets past us. Meet me back here at Kee's tomorrow. By then—"

"We pull the fucking pin," Durkin finished for him.

Lexie's audience with Judge Polhemus of the Superior Court took only a few minutes. It left her uneasy, frightened, and only a little hopeful of getting guardianship of Jason without a lengthy and painful process.

"I can't do what you're asking," the judge told her, "without a good deal of proof of your allegations. The rights of parents in our society concerning their children are virtually unassailable. And Mr. Whitlock will have to be allowed to defend himself in court, in any event, if he so chooses."

"Supposing it's a matter of abandonment?" Lexie said. "He has threatened to uproot Jason, but now he's disappeared."

"The law doesn't say he has to be a stable, dependable parent, or even a kind and loving parent. Supposing we hold a preliminary hearing next week. I'll issue a court order for the boy to be left in your care, however, until the hearing."

"I can hardly risk that. If he can get his hands on Jason, he won't bother with a hearing—he'll simply take him off to Texas or the coast. Your honor may recall that he has already jumped the jurisdiction of your court, in a matter involving other people's money."

"And no doubt he's now laughing at us while I support his rights. Kangaroo courts and quick hangings have much to be said for them, but I'm afraid they are things of the past. Is this progress?"

Lexie went back to the *Courier* office and copyread a page proof of her story. Its title was "The Terrible Journey of Marietta Applegate." When Craddock came in, she showed it to him. His response was little more than a grunt. He was still fuming inwardly, thinking, in spite of himself, that something was taking place between the pilot and Lexie. He busied himself writing his editorial. Its title was "Ask City Council—Will the New Chief Come from the Same Old Crowd?" Bring in a man from outside who would owe no favors, who would clean up the department—that was his tack.

Lexie left to cover some kind of meeting. Craddock frowned at her back as she left. Suddenly he picked up the telephone and called Costello. "This Whitlock fellow still hasn't turned up," Craddock said. "There's something going on here and I can't put my finger on it, but Whitlock is the wild card. If you were me, how would you find the guy?"

"Problem like that," Costello said, "I just fire off a telegraph message, multiple addressees, from here to Nome or New

York, whatever it takes. Spose I put out the word? It aint strictly railroad business, but it can't hurt, either."

Leopold Genereux, the drifter from St. Martinsville, Louisiana, crawled out of a boxcar in the Los Angeles yards. He was careful to avoid being seen—he didn't want to have a yard dick shake him down, because when they found a sap on a man, they were apt to use it on him. Wasn't just the sap, either. He made his way out to the city street. He walked to the depot and went into the public restroom where he shaved and cleaned up. When he went back out on the street, he was wearing a diamond stickpin in his tie and another diamond on his finger. He walked along Main Street until he found a pawnshop. Five minutes later, he was on the street again, furious—the pawnshop guy wouldn't give him a nickel for the stuff. Said it was worthless. Threatened to call a cop.

17

J. W. WHITLOCK awoke very slowly, hearing noisy snoring. After a while he discovered another guy in another bed across the room from his own, so he decided he wasn't in his room at the Cosmo House. The guy had his leg elevated in a sling, and there was a plaster cast on the leg. J. W.'s jaw and neck felt red-hot. He found out that his teeth were wired together. He was wearing a kind of flannel nightie—he wondered where his clothes were. Pawing at his bed covers, he discovered that his diamond ring was missing.

Later, a nurse came—he guessed she was a nurse. She was wearing a cotton housedress with yellow flowers on it, and a nurse's cap on her head. She was skinny, with graying hair, and when she saw him looking at her, she said, "Well! About time you was waking up!" She put a glass of orange juice into his hand, and without asking him guided the glass straw into a gap between his teeth.

"Where'sh m' diamond?" J. W. mumbled, holding up his naked pinkie finger. "Tiepin too?" Only it didn't sound much like that, saying it through his wired teeth.

She faced him. Weighed about 85 pounds. "Listen, pal, before you say anything more, check your socks."

J. W. felt around his ankles, found he only had one sock on. Felt a lump there, pulled out a square of folded bills.

"Go ahead and count it," she said. "When I got you ready for bed, I found it, so I left the sock on. Now, don't tell me nothing more about it." She started to turn away.

"Hey, wait," J. W. said, peeling a ten off the wad. "How about you fix us up with a little eye-opener?"

"Stuff it, big boy," she growled, picking up a clipboard. "Give me your name—for the record."

"Not yet, not till I find out . . . where'n hell I am. . . ." Later, a one-legged Indian came in to sweep the room, and when J. W. asked him to fix them up with a little eye-opener, the Indian said, "Sure, cowboy."

After Hector Callard found the footprints on his workshop floor, he made a hasty search. He found all the pieces of the Juggernaut where he had put them. Either the agents had now known just what to look for, which seemed to him unlikely, or they knew better than to take the Juggernaut before it was finished, assembled and running. He packed all the pieces and the brass frame into a dynamite box and slept with it under his bed, his shotgun leaning against the headboard. In the morning, he and the boy ate breakfast early. Then Jason wrapped some gunnysacking around the box and carried it to the Ford, Hector walking beside him with his shotgun at port arms. Hector poured the gallon of gas from Farney into the Ford's tank and fired up the engine.

Maynard worked with Jack Perrell until quitting time, and then Perrell took him home for supper. Home was up in the foothills of the Catalinas, a rambling adobe ranch house with a tile roof and carved doors from Mexico. Perrell made a drink for Maynard and himself. His wife Amanda came in then, a lovely woman with a streak of gray in her dark hair. She took off a smock streaked with oil paint, and while they drank, she showed Maynard her paintings. Supper was *puerco adobado*, a dish of grilled pork strips in a red sauce or gravy, along with salad and black beans.

Maynard told about his flight with Lexie and finding the doll Sibbie, and then without really meaning to, he found himself telling about Jason and his ordeal. Amanda's face wore a worried look as he finished.

"I know Lexie. She did an article on my paintings. Promise me you'll tell me when that child is back with her. I'll be having nightmares, thinking about him."

"I promise," Maynard said. He left about nine and drove back to the hangar. When he got there, he began to prepare the firewall of the Dragonfly to receive the engine mount. It was after two before he went to bed.

Maynard awoke early as usual and made coffee and ate a grapefruit standing by the stove, and then because he felt the momentum churning, driving him, he went back to work, lost in his design. When he heard the familiar sound of a Model-T Ford engine outside, he thought nothing of it until it backfired just before it was switched off. Maynard opened the hangar door a crack and saw the kid and the old man. What the hell, he thought, annoyed.

And Red Durkin, coming around the rear of the hangar, stopped, flattened himself against the wall. He pushed aside a branch of greasewood and took a peek around the corner, saw the old man's shotgun, the kid holding a box on his lap, like it was full of eggs.

They climbed down from the rickety cab of the truck. Maynard, too, saw the old man's shotgun leaning against the seat inside. The kid was wearing Maynard's old red *kepi* on his head and carrying a box wrapped in sacking. The old man looked to right and left, along the length of the hangar and the empty runway, and then walked slowly with the kid toward the hangar, one hand on the kid's shoulder. For support, Maynard realized with a pang. His annoyance fled and he stepped out to greet them.

Jason was matching his steps to the old man's. His face

wore its customary scowl. The old man's expression was distant, austere, troubled.

"Captain," he said softly, "this intrusion caint be welcome."

"It couldn't come at a better time," Maynard said. "You're just in time to help me kill a pot of coffee." Jason swallowed anxiously, looking intently at him, and then Maynard remembered. *"Mesquite,"* he murmured.

"Javelina," Jason whispered. As they stepped through the door into the hangar, the scowl left his face. Both—the boy and the old man—walked slowly, looking at the long tables and multitudes of wooden parts until they came to the fuselage. They circled it at a respectful distance, the old man stepping in close to peer at details of the framework and once to put his hand on the varnished wood and stroke it gently. Maynard set out a camp chair for him and then got the coffeepot and some cups.

Outside, Red Durkin settled himself, leaning next to the open window, and lighted a black Mexican *cigarro.* He caught a little of what the pilot was saying—and he was beginning to think he was wasting his time.

"It's still in pieces, but you'll notice it doesn't look much like the airplanes you're used to seeing. Most airplanes today look pretty much like the one Bleriot flew the English Channel in, back in 1910. Our fellows trained in those Bleriots. They weren't too bad—tricky little devils. We banged up a lot of them. Anyway, my idea is that Bleriot picked up a lot of problems, the way he went, and after him the others went the same direction, more or less, both sides, all through the war, copying Bleriot first and then each other."

"What kind of problems?" Jason asked.

"Stability mostly." Maynard felt the excitement creeping into his voice. "They're all too easy to stall, and when they do stall, they want to spin. It's a deadly combination. What I've tried to do is forget Bleriot and Sopwith and Fokker, change the whole *look* of the thing, to get rid of that built-in stall."

"It might help," said the old man, "if I knowed what a stall is."

Maynard laughed. "Of course. Say the airplane is going too slow, it reaches a point where the wings won't hold it up"—he demonstrated with his hand—"and it just quits flying and drops. That's a stall."

"She's like a shot crow," the old man offered.

"Exactly." Maynard reached under a bench and took out a scale model of the Dragonfly and set it before them. It was sleek white, glistening, with no exposed wires or struts, and the two wings were set in a startlingly strange configuration, the smaller of the two jutting from the nose itself. Jason's breath blew out in a long sigh. "See, I've gone back in some ways to the Wright brothers, only without all the wires and struts."

"Do ye have an engine for her?" the old man asked.

Maynard nodded. "It's a four-cylinder air-cooled job with an aluminum block, designed for a race car. The guy went broke and I got it at auction."

"Burns gasarene, does she?"

"Alcohol originally, but we're switching to gasoline."

"Now we are coming to the nut of the matter," the old man said. "Spose you didn't have to burn *nothing*?"

Maynard grinned and shrugged. "Tell me more."

The old man looked around uneasily. "Can we talk here?"

"Perfectly safe," Maynard said. "I believe I told you that I have to be very careful of my own work, too."

Reassured, the old man uncovered the dynamite box, took out the delicate brass frame and placed it on the table, and then he began unwrapping other parts and assembling them despite a pronounced tremor in his hands.

"It's called the Juggernaut," Jason said.

"This is the first time eyes other than my own have saw this machine all put together," Hector Callard said. "The principle of it has to do with *momentum*. Once your flywheel here reaches a certain speed, then momentum takes over, understand?"

"Momentum becomes your fuel?"

"In a manner of speaking."

"Have you had it up to speed yet?"

"Oh, hell, no!" the old man said. "I wouldn't *dare*! Without a brake on her, she would just burn up and fly to pieces. The brake is what I'm workin on now." He had assembled and positioned a number of weighted lever arms, and now locked a flywheel into place. He turned a crank on the flywheel, and the lever arms began to spin smoothly around a central shaft. He cranked until their motion became a blur, the machine emitting a whirring sound.

Maynard read pride and ecstasy in the old man's fierce gaze as he cranked the Juggernaut. He saw with a jolt that Jason somehow mirrored the old man's expression. The boy stared, mesmerized. Hell, *bewitched*! Maynard thought. Reluctantly, the old man ceased cranking and withdrew his hand. The machine slowed, the whirring became a ticking, and then it stopped.

"You see, don't you, how I just don't *dare* let her get that speed up?" Hector said, his voice husky with profound regret. "On the bigger ones we'll be putting into our power plants, we'll run that flywheel up with a little electric motor, but once she's up there, by god, stand back, boys!—for there'll be no stoppin her this side of the moon! Do you see the glory of it?" The old man laughed and slapped his thigh, his eyes bright with elation. Jason's gleeful laugh echoed Hector's.

"M-mm," Maynard said carefully. But suddenly, Jason sobered. His scowl returned.

"We better tell him about the agent, Uncle Hector."

The old man slumped. "Hell's fire! I was damn near carried away." He proceeded to tell Maynard about the visit of the counterfeit county man, and the certain proof that he was an agent. "So, you see, the bastards want to snatch it away from the people! They've got to be stopped. I've got to finish the work . . . and I need help! It shames me to say it—if it wasn't a matter for the *people,* goddammit, I would cut my tongue out first—but I am drove to it. I need *your* help, Captain. You see, I . . . I am just damn near . . ." His voice trailed off with a helpless gesture of his bony hand.

"His sand is running out," Jason supplied. "His ticket across the river is already punched. He just hasn't caught the boat yet. He's afraid he's gonna croak before the Juggernaut is ready to give to the people."

"That's right," Hector said. "I could croak between here and the door, you want to know the truth. It needs *you.* I see the workmanship, the engineering"—his hand swept in an arc—"but more than that, I see dedication! This is a matter of *honor.*"

Maynard was aghast. How had it come to this? "Your Juggernaut . . ." he fumbled, then tried again. "It's a perpetual motion machine, right?" The old man nodded serenely. "You realize, sir, that perpetual motion is universally accepted in science as being impossible?"

"That's the glory of it, Captain. We've beat the game!"

"Have you considered the studies of Newton and Carnot and all the others after them? The principle of entropy? It all has to do with the second law of thermodynamics. A certain amount of energy is going to be lost because of friction, if nothing else. The system has to run down."

At the window, Durkin was lighting a second cigarro, wishing he were back at Kee's having a cold beer. The softly pitched voices he was listening to came to his ears as mostly little more than a mumble, but he caught the word *diamonds* and was suddenly alert.

"Jeweled bearings," Hector said. "I know we'll need *diamonds* in the big machines because of the heat buildup, but hell, a *bushel* of diamonds would be a cheap price—we're talkin about unlimited power! The goddamned *diamonds* will be worth a heap more thisaway than on some old woman's stringy neck, can you deny that?" His voice had risen to triumphant cadences.

At the window, straining to hear more, Red Durkin caught the continued references to diamonds, *bushels* of them. A pulse roared in Durkin's ears. He rocked back on his heels and raised his fists to the heavens. The pilot's voice was pitched almost too low for him to hear.

"No, sir, I can't deny it," Maynard said. "If diamonds will make this possible, then we owe it to ourselves—"

"To the *people,* goddammit!" the old man roared. "The diamonds are for them! It's power! The Juggernaut, the diamonds—it's all power!"

At the window, Durkin's senses reeled.

Maynard sighed. How in hell did I get into this? he asked himself. I can't let it go any further. Aloud, he said, "I have to tell you, though, that the only way the work on this machine will get done is if you do it—you and Jason, that is. You understand it. I just . . . personally . . . can't handle it," he finished lamely.

"It aint for ourselves, Captain," the old man whispered. "It's for Old Glory—for the *people!*"

"And the agents are after it," Jason said. "They're closing in."

Maynard saw tears glittering on the boy's lashes. He smiled uneasily. "Not *really,* Jason. That was some guy who was just stringing you along."

"Please, Captain, *believe* me," Jason whispered. *"The son of a bitch is an agent of the awl companies!"*

Maynard felt a crazy laugh working up inside himself—the kid sounded exactly like the old man! At the same time, he was shaken by the boy's anguish. "I know it must have looked that way, but the guy couldn't have known about the Juggernaut. He won't be coming back. You'll see. And if he does, you two are onto him."

"But how about my mission?" Jason said desperately. "Can't our people do anything?"

"We've got to study this thing a while longer," Maynard said. He knew he was floundering—he didn't know whether to keep up the charade with the kid—which humored the old man's delusions, too—or to try to get them to see the plain facts of the matter. "A few days more should clear it up—they haven't made a *hostile* move, really."

The old man was pulling parts off the Juggernaut, wrapping them and packing them back in the box. He seemed dazed. "I b'lieve we've said too much as it is. It appears to me the bastards have been here ahead of us," he mumbled in an aside to Jason, who turned his shocked and anguished face to Maynard.

"Have they bought *you*?" Jason said.

"You know better than that!" Maynard said.

"Don't expect no one to admit it," the old man said with finality. "We've got to be on our way, young sir." He lurched to his feet.

Jason stared bleakly at Maynard, who started to speak again, but caught himself—no use making it worse. He went into his tent and took a certain book off the shelf and then followed Jason and the old man outside.

"You must be about out of gas," Maynard said. "The gas pump is right there—let me fill your tank." He hurried out to the pump and began working the lever back and forth, gasoline gushing up into the glass cylinder, filling it to the ten-gallon mark. Pumping, he saw a man walking rapidly along the side of the hangar, to disappear behind the building. Crazy! he thought. The guy looks like Red Durkin. He stopped pumping, stuck the nozzle into the Ford's tank and let the fuel flow into it as Jason and the old man prepared to leave.

Maynard caught the boy's arm. Jason avoided his eyes, but took the book that Maynard pressed into his hands.

"I want you to read this," Maynard said, "especially the part about the studies of Newton and Carnot that were developed into the second law of thermodynamics. Think about it—

it'll help you understand the Juggernaut better." Jason turned away, clutching the book, his eyes brimming with tears.

When they were seated, Maynard cranked the Ford. It shuddered into life. Maynard stepped close to the old man. "I'm glad you came to see me. I'm not making light of this. I'll be out to check on you, and if . . . anything is going on, I . . . we'll take care of it together."

The old man looked right through him, nodding a little, saying nothing. Maynard stepped back. The old man trod on the *go* pedal and jerked the throttle lever down. The Ford backfired and lunged away. Maynard saw Jason's face turn to stare back at him. His face was twisted with anguish under the red *kepi*.

He waved and watched the Ford until it was out of sight, and then walked back along the side of the hangar. Wind-driven sand lay in smooth drifts against the base of the wall. Beneath the window near his tent he saw boot prints. The prints were scuffed and shuffled, and there were two black butts of Mexican cigarettes stamped into the sand, so he had been there a while. The prints trailed back the way they had come.

That damned Durkin, Maynard thought. He's after the cognac.

On the way home, Hector stopped next to the big canal north of town. He climbed out of the Ford and cut a bundle of willows from bushes on the canal bank, stowed them in the truck and headed for home. But when they reached Farney's house, Hector swung the Ford in next to Farney's workshop and turned off the engine. "You go tell Olive—Mrs. Farney—that I'm returning her husband's gas can. If she wants to feed you, let her do it. I need about three minutes out here."

Jason walked toward the house. Hector heard Olive's little dog barking, and then the screen door slammed. He went into Farney's shop. It was more like a storehouse. Farney's years at the Papago Queen had allowed him to outfit himself handsomely with every manner of tool and supplies, all arranged in orderly fashion. Hector quickly took down a hundred-foot coil of three-quarter-inch manila rope and two five-gallon cans of gasoline and stowed them in the truck.

He scouted further. There it was, under some gunnysacks. Two cases of dynamite. Farney, like most mining men, used dynamite the way other men used shovels, or axes, for ditching, say, or blowing stumps. That was how he dug the holes for Olive's oleanders. Dynamite. Hector pried up the lid of the topmost box and quickly filled his own box from it, leaving only a few sticks in the bottom. He put the lid back down and covered the boxes again. He found a box of caps and some fuse. Helped himself. He stowed the wooden case in the back of his truck and went back into the shop—for Farney in his foraging had not neglected the Papago Queen's commissary. Shelves on the back wall were stacked with canned goods of every description. Hector helped himself generously, filling two good-sized crates—no telling how long he and the boy would be living out of the truck. Took plenty of Eagle Brand condensed milk—a boy should have milk.

Hector heard the screen door slam again, heard the screech of Olive's voice. He went back to his truck and climbed in as Jason, his cheeks bulging with cornbread, came down off the gallery, carrying half an apple pie on a tin plate. Hector gave Olive a serene wave as he wheeled the Ford out onto the road.

Back at his own place, Hector turned to outfitting the truck. Jason's eyes widened when he saw all the equipment the old man was putting aboard, but he said nothing. It was perfectly clear, now that the agents were closing in on them, that they would have to leave. Jason collected tools and other articles as the old man directed, shovel, hatchet, baling wire. "You never know," the old man said at least ten times. Jason watched curiously as Hector took down the long ash springpole from his forge, the limber pole that operated the huge bellows. The butt end of the pole was reinforced with a steel leaf from an automobile spring. Hector stowed the pole, along with a light block and tackle. Seeing the boy's eyes upon him, he said again, "You never know . . ."

And then Hector brought out the lengths of willow he had cut back on the canal bank. He got an oilstone and whetted his pocketknife, saying to Jason, "You ever make a willow whistle? Back in Oregon, I showed my boys how." For a while they both cut whistles. Jason was tired of cutting whistles, but the old man said, "Let's keep at it—if you're going to do something, you may as well do it until you get it right." He showed Jason how to change the pitch of the whistle, and he said, "We'll have ourselves a regular pipe organ." Jason wasn't sure he wanted a pipe organ, but the old man was insistent, so Jason humored him. Got blisters on his fingers.

18

RED DURKIN screeched to a stop at Jimmy Kee's, went in the alley door to the poolroom, looked around for Othello Biggers who wasn't there, and ordered a beer and a shot of Mexican brandy. He was on his second beer and third shot, beginning to feel a comfortable buzz, when Biggers walked in.

The two men took a table and Biggers ordered steak and eggs with hashed browns and a glass of whiskey. Biggers told Durkin about his search of the old man's place the evening before. "There is something fishy goin on there, something pretty damned secret, unnerstand? The old guy locks the shed up like a bank vault whenever he leaves it. I skinned in through a board in the pump house. He's got stuff stashed all over, clockworks or something, but if he's got any of J. W.'s goods, he keeps it on him. This morning him and the kid was gone, so I went back and checked again, and now the clockworks is gone too! So the old geezer and J. W.'s kid"—he ticked them off on his fingers—"and the ace, they're all up to *something*, the way I read it, and the girl is mixed up in it, too. She took J. W.'s kid in the first place, and J. W. left his stuff with the kid. He *had* to, or we would've found it."

Biggers went to work on his steak. Durkin signaled for another beer and shot.

"I went to see the ace," Durkin said. "I'm thinking maybe he's been working for J. W. even longer'n we thought. *Possible,* right? Anyway, the old man and the kid drive up, so I hang around the window and listen. The ace—you know he's building a fucking *airplane* in there?—anyway, him and the old man are talking and the old man is showing him this gizmo, which could be some kind of clock all right, or maybe a motor, and the old man is saying to the ace"—Durkin leaned close to Biggers ear, whispering hoarsely—"that he needs *diamonds* on account of the heat is building up . . ."

"What heat?" Biggers mumbled through his hashed browns.

"How do I know? But he needs a fucking *bushel* of diamonds, he says. He says it's better to use em this way than to hang em around some woman's neck. It's all going to the people—what people, I don't know—but it's all going to the people anyway, and it's power, unlimited power, I hear him say."

"Sounds to me like they are putting the arm on some of J. W.'s goods." Biggers said. "They're pushing a deal of their own and J. W. picks up the tab, whether he knows it or not, and it's my guess he don't know it. What does the ace say to this?"

"He says he's got to think it over. The old man and the kid took their box of stuff and left. The thing is, the old man has bought some kind of ticket, across a river, I heard the kid say. His ticket is punched, but he can't go until they settle this thing about the fucking diamonds!"

"Whatever is happening," Biggers said, "is starting to move fast. If we don't get a handle on it, J. W.'s stuff is going to be scattered to hell and gone, and you and me will be sucking slop with the pigs. I say we go and tell the ace that he is working with partners, whether he knows it or not."

"What if he thinks he don't need partners?"

"He feels somebody's thumbs in his eyes, he'll be damn glad to go partners," Biggers said.

* * *

Lexie was back at her desk after covering an afternoon meeting of the city council when her telephone rang. It was Amanda Perrell. She said, "Lexie, what's happening with Jason? Captain Gaylen was at our place last night and what he said makes it sound like the poor kid is in a terrifying situation."

Lexie laughed. "Nothing as bad as all that. The captain just doesn't understand Uncle Hector. Anyway, it can't—" Her voice broke off as Maynard Gaylen walked in. "Oh-oh, he's here now—the captain, that is. I'll call you later."

Craddock's temper bubbled up again and when he said, "What brings you here, Captain?" it was like an accusation.

Maynard looked almost ill to Lexie. "Are you all right?" she asked him.

"Your Uncle Hector and Jason came to see me this morning. They brought his machine with them. They wanted my help and I . . . I'm afraid I turned them down."

"What kind of machine?" Craddock said.

Maynard and Lexie exchanged glances. A half-embarrassed

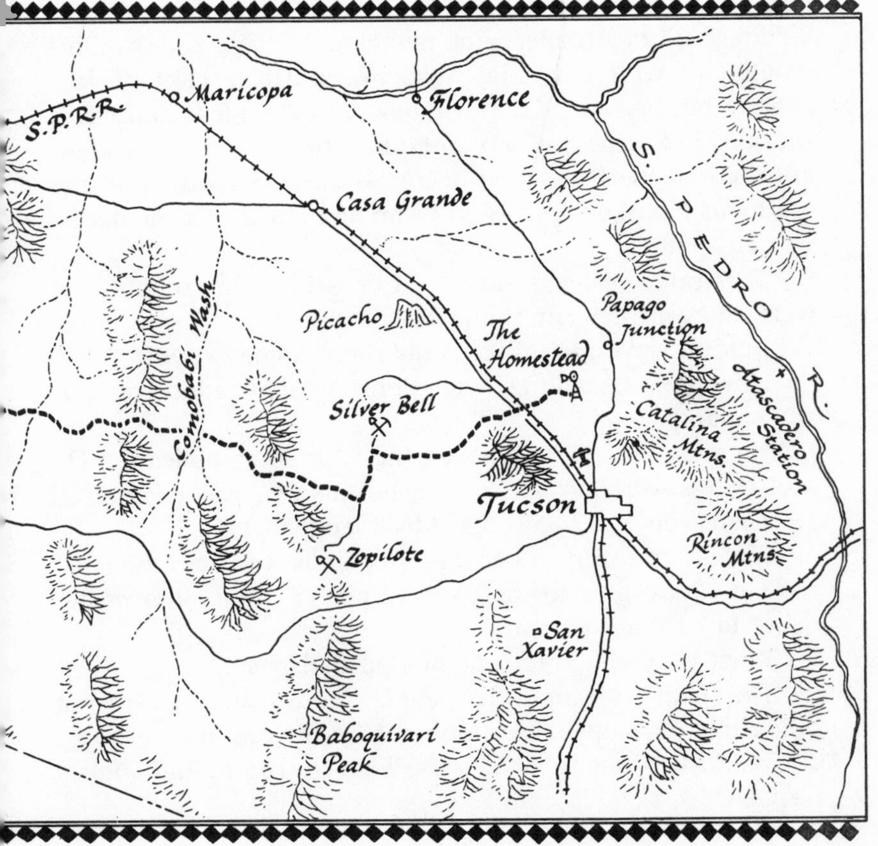

smile tugged at Maynard's lips. "Perpetual motion," he said.

Craddock laughed sharply. "Surely you could overturn the laws of science for them."

Lexie shot him an exasperated frown. "He never allows the machine to leave his shop."

"That's just it," Maynard said. "He thinks that the agents of the oil companies who are after his machine"—he looked uneasily again at Craddock and then went on—"are closing in on him. He says he found indications that his shop has been searched."

"That can't be so!" Lexie said. "Poor soul. How does Jason take this?"

"Like a little trooper. You're going to have to wash his mouth out with soap—he's picking up Uncle Hector's language—but he . . . *believes*. He talked to the agent himself. It sounded like some guy, a truant officer or something, was sent out there at the instigation of a nosy neighbor lady, and the questions he asked convinced Jason and Uncle Hector that he was an agent."

"That can't be too serious," Lexie said. "He thought you were an agent, too, first time he saw you."

"I didn't leave footprints in his shop. Somebody did."

"How could he tell they weren't his own?" Craddock asked, still smiling.

"He sprinkles a little flour on the floor when he leaves. He says things were moved around, but nothing was taken."

"There you are, then." Craddock laughed.

"No, it's critical now because they know the machine is almost ready to give to the people, and of course they're not going to let that happen."

"What people?" Craddock snorted derisively.

"*The* people, meaning the people of our country. He's not doing this for money. He's doing it for his country."

Craddock grinned. "Shall we call out the drums and bugles, Captain?"

Maynard stiffened.

"Woodie . . . *please*?" Lexie said.

"Can't we just drop this *Captain* thing for the time being?" Maynard said.

"I thought you took pride in your military title."

"Sure I did, before it got to be an epithet."

"Gentlemen?" Lexie said. "I think Maynard is only telling us how it looks to Uncle Hector. Maybe," she said to Maynard, "this is what you meant when you said he was a hero."

"Right. It doesn't really matter whether *we* think these agents are actually after the Juggernaut, does it? Uncle Hector and Jason *know* they are. These people will lie, cheat, steal or kill to get at the Juggernaut. The way it is right now, only an old man and a little kid stand between these sons of bitches and the loss to our country of the Juggernaut. When they asked me for help, I turned them down. Dammit, I *failed* them! That's what I'm trying to get at."

Craddock's ironic grin faded with Maynard's words.

"Forgive me, please," he said. "Both of you."

Jason felt strangely calm. Maybe it was the work of cutting all those willow whistles, but the familiar hollow dread in his middle was somehow shrunken and remote as he helped his Uncle Hector to finish loading the rickety Ford truck. Uncle Hector moved slowly, stopping often to rest, and he was calm, too, thoughtful and judicious, quiet spoken as he directed Jason.

"We're going to your claim, right?" Jason said.

The old man nodded. "Yes. I call her the Honest Citizen."

They packed a butcher knife, big spoon and the Dutch oven. Box of tools. Another smaller box of tools for working on the Juggernaut. A folded tarp. By the time they finished, it had grown dark.

"That's about it," Hector said. "It's a wise trooper who knows enough to spare his mount. We'll carry the Juggernaut up front. Now," he went on, "let us study this proposition. We'll go ahead and make supper as usual and bed down. They can't know we're onto their game. First glimmer of daylight, we'll be on our way. No breakfast. Save that for later, when we rest our horses."

Supper was sliced potatoes fried with onions and bacon. When the potatoes were cooked through, Hector poured half a cup of milk into the skillet, added some flour to thicken it, and a lot of pepper. "I call this Seventh Cavalry Spuds," he declared. "Trooper's grub, and none better." When it was hot, he served it out with some of Olive Farney's leftover cornbread. Dessert was Olive's apple pie. Jason thought it was the best meal he had ever eaten. After supper, he cleaned up the dishes and stowed two plates and the rest of their food in a basket, while Uncle Hector had a last cup of coffee with his pipe. He poured about a tablespoon of brandy into the coffee. The old man seemed preoccupied. From time to time he would look around the room as if examining it, shaking his head and clucking his tongue, once laughing, not quite silently, to himself.

"Had plans for this place, me and Hattie," he mused. "One year I bought two mules and plowed and planted. She was hotter than the hinges of hell that year. I took five sacks of beans off them forty acres yonder. Hattie said to me, this ground will grow nothin but gunpowder for the Devil's breakfast, and we'll join him at the table in Hell before we get a meal off of it ourselves. After that I went to work at the Queen. Me and Farney was on the same crew. He was a young sprout then, and me, hell, I was past seventy. Told em I was fifty-five. I done the smithin and was powder man, too. He made shift boss, and after that it wasn't the same no more. I had traded the two mules for a milk cow and a heifer, for Hattie. She sold milk and butter and eggs to the miners. I quit the Queen at the time of the strike when they brought the soldiers in. Hell, I got my head split open and done thirty days in jail, that's how I quit! I bought a burro and went to prospectin again, the way I done back in the eighties, and that's how come you and me are a-goin to hole up at the claim."

It seemed to Jason that Uncle Hector could dispose of the passing of ten years, or twenty, or even fifty, with a snap of his fingers, so that the scope of Jason's entire life was no more than the merest bubble in the stream of time.

"What will we do with the Juggernaut when we get to the claim?" Jason said.

"Do? First we see if we've throwed em off our trail. If we have, good—we'll hole up there and I'll finish the work on the Juggernaut, with you to help me."

"And what if we haven't throwed em off?" Jason said.

"They'll rue the day," the old man said simply, his blue eyes fixed serenely on Jason. "You've knowed me long enough to realize that I aint the type that holds a grudge." His face suddenly cracked into a devilish grin. "T'other hand, neither do I forget an injustice." He knocked out his pipe and stood up. "I've got things to do out in the shop. You best turn in, get some shut-eye." At the door, he said, "We'll ride at first light. No bugles. Muffle your bit chains and sabers." He lifted a hand and was gone.

"Yes, sir," Jason said. He was not sure if Uncle Hector was *serious* when he talked about bugles, bit chains and sabers, but he liked the sound of it. He got a dictionary from a shelf where he had spotted it when he was cleaning the place, and looked up *rue*. It said, "to suffer remorse, to repent of, to wish undone." It was from the Anglo-Saxon *hreowan,* to grieve or make sorry. *"Hreowan,"* Jason pronounced solemnly. "They'll rue the day."

He put his small suitcase on his cot, to pack his clothes in, and noticed the book that Captain Gaylen had given him at the airport. He had thrown it there in disgust earlier that day, disgust and bone-deep disappointment, for, looking at the Captain's Dragonfly, Jason had shared with the old man the certainty that Captain Gaylen was the man to finish the Juggernaut and get it into the hands of the people, and his disappointment at the Captain's refusal had bordered on heartbreak. Now he opened the book, which was titled

Addison's First Book of Science. On the flyleaf, he saw written *Maynard L. Gaylen—Lincoln High School—1908.*

Curious now, Jason looked up Newton, Isaac; and Carnot, Nicholas Sadi, in the index and began to read. Many of the words were unfamiliar. He looked them up, and then in certain cases had to look up the words that defined the words he was looking up. As he read, he was overtaken by a sense of uneasiness, of apprehension. He tried to remember Captain Gaylen's exact words when he refused to help them with the Juggernaut—even thinking about that stirred again the sickening feeling of betrayal—and the term *perpetual motion* popped into his mind. He looked for it in the index and found it at the end of the chapter in a summary. "As alchemy is to the science of chemistry," he read, "perpetual motion is to the science of mechanics. Perpetual motion, antithetical to the idea of *entropy,* is a will-o'-the-wisp sought by visionaries and crank inventors. It is rendered absurd by the immutable laws formulated by Newton, Carnot, Kelvin and others." Jason remembered that the captain had used the word *entropy* also, so he looked it up as well.

Jason's head nodded and slipped off his hand, upon which it was resting, and the sudden jerk startled him. Words like *antithetical, entropy* and *immutable* were beginning to skitter around in his mind. He could no longer focus his attention, but he felt that he was on the brink of being able to understand something very profound. Whatever it was, it hovered just out of reach, as if curtained from his sight. He put the book in with his few clothes, and then he undressed and got into bed.

Jason was very tired and yearned for sleep, but his mind was churning. *Absurd,* said the book. Yet Uncle Hector stated that he had beaten the game. How many other ideas must have been considered impossible at one time? He had read how Phoenician sailors building fires on a sandy beach had accidentally created glass. Supposing you told people, back then, in a time before anyone even thought of glass, that they could turn sand into a clear, hard sheet of *something*?—couldn't call it glass if it had never existed—something, anyway, that you could see through, that would hold water, that could be made to magnify. Crazy, he thought, they wouldn't even know what *magnify* meant. No wonder people laughed at inventors. How about sending words over wires?—or, even funnier, through the atmosphere? Talk about *absurd*! he thought, that was absurd. Jason laughed into his pillow. *Really* absurd! He wished he had thought to point that out to Captain Gaylen.

Out in the shop, Hector had a bundle of light canes before him on the bench—Olive Farney's tomato canes, in fact. He had baling wire, pliers, shingles, a cigar box full of willow whistles. Farney's box of dynamite at his feet. He busied himself by the light of the oil lamp. His mind fled down the corridors of time. He was in Oregon, at his forge, making chain for the log booms on the river. Chain links as big across as a dinner plate.

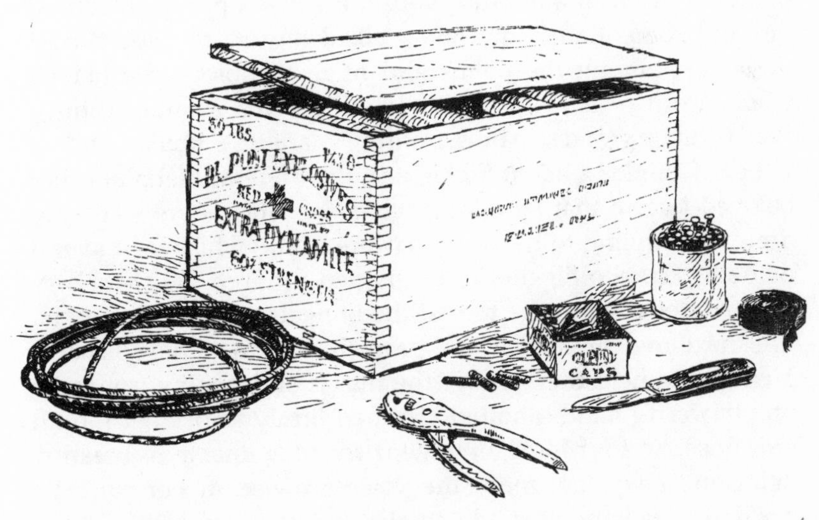

19

MARIETTA RICKS, once Applegate, lived with her spinster daughter Lucia in an old broad-eaved bungalow set in a grove of immense palms in a part of town near the dry bed of the Santa Cruz called The Hollow. It was well after sunset. Driving there from the *Courier* office, Lexie had to switch on the headlights in her little Durant Star. She didn't notice the black Essex running without lights behind her. When she parked in front of Marietta's house, the Essex pulled in behind her and someone got out and walked toward the house next door, lost among the palms and huge shrubs as she herself stepped out of her Star and walked into the avenue of huge *Washingtonia gigantea* palms fronting Marietta's house.

Lexie, thinking about Sibbie and the bride Marietta and her beloved Lucian that time long ago at the Atascadero stage station, was smiling to herself, unaware of the whisper of sound made by Othello Biggers as he slipped through the shrubbery and overtook her at the foot of the bungalow's broad veranda. The next instant, Lexie was propelled against the bole of a great palm, held there under the thatch of drooping fronds by one powerful hand, another clamped firmly across her mouth and nose, so that for the moment she was unable to breathe. "Not one peep, get me?" the voice growled in her ear. She nodded. The hand relaxed and she sucked in air. Still jammed against the tree, held there by a man's elbow and shoulder, she felt the shoe box with Sibbie in it taken from her, heard the lid being ripped off and dropped, and then heard the muttered grunt, a sound of pure disgust, as Sibbie was discovered and thrown down. Her purse was pulled from beneath her right arm, and Lexie—as if she were somehow perched a few feet away and looking down upon herself and this man whose breath hissed in her ear—marveled at her own detachment.

The purse was thrust roughly back beneath her arm. "Don't even *think* of turning around," the voice snarled. "Got it?"

Lexie nodded vigorously. Released, she continued to lean against the tree until she heard a car start up. She ran back a few steps on the path, but because of the trees all she saw was a dark, boxy car skidding into a squealing turn and tearing back up the street. Her knees suddenly began to shake. Still oddly detached, she thought, *I will not drop this on Marietta and terrify her too.* She picked up Sibbie and put her back in the box, decided *no*—it was too much like a coffin—put the box down and walked up the steps to the door with Sibbie sitting in the curve of her arm. She twisted the key to the brass bell set in the door.

The door swung back. Marietta faced her, a tiny white-haired woman in a dark print dress, buttons glinting on her high shoes. Lexie said, "I have someone here who tells me she very much wants to see Marietta."

"My dear girl—" Marietta started to say, and then she saw the doll. She fumbled for the spectacles that hung from a ribbon around her neck, peered through them. Her chin quivered and her breath caught.

"In fact," Lexie said, "she tells me she was beginning to think no would *ever* come for her!"

"Sibbie!" breathed Marietta, blinking rapidly as Lexie put the doll in her arms. She tried to speak, failed, tried again. "Come into the parlor, child. Do you suppose the law could forgive us if we were to have a drop of sherry?"

* * *

Maynard was cutting a long panel of plywood, using a fine-toothed handsaw, when Red Durkin and Othello Biggers walked in. He was so absorbed in the cutting that their coming was a complete surprise. *That damned cognac!* Maynard thought. It was still sitting in the adobe hut out at the old man's place where he had put it the first day he landed there. He had meant to go get the hoard of cognac, but hadn't yet found time—and Lexie's response to it, which had seemed most unrealistic and even a little childish to him, still had caused him to start *thinking:* if there are degrees of black and white or weight and balance, degrees of reckoning in almost any account, was there any such thing as a *little* corruption?

It made him laugh to think of calling the selling of a few bottles of French brandy in defiance of the Volstead Act a matter of corruption when in his heart he was still having trouble living with the nightmare memory of strafing German troops and horses on rickety pontoon bridges thrown hastily over the Meuse in their great spring offensive, when he could see the streams of tracers stitching down the writhing column of men and animals; pulling up then and coming around for another pass, seeing the horses down, kicking, sliding into the water, men sprawling, diving, trying to hide under the horses, himself behind shuddering Vickers guns smelling hot metal and bitter cordite, and then the solid *thunk* in his arm and shoulder and something that knocked his goggles down over his nose and mouth . . . some part of this flashed through his mind as he straightened from his work to face Red Durkin and Othello Biggers.

Durkin's freckled face wore an infuriating buck-toothed grin. He was wearing an ill-fitting striped suit, scuffed boots, sweat-stained stockman's hat, and he had a black Mexican cigarro in his mouth. He hooked his thumbs in the pockets of his unbuttoned vest and teetered on his heels. Biggers walked slowly down the length of a work table, noting ribs and spars, his lips pursed primly, nodding approval as he picked up a rib and looked closely at the cutouts and little mahogany gussets and varnished backstrap.

"Call this a rib, right?" Biggers said.

"That's right," Maynard said. The back of his neck felt cold and prickly with apprehension. Biggers, still holding the rib, turned to the Dragonfly's fuselage, which he examined dreamily.

"Scare me to death, get me up there," he said. He rapped the rib lightly on the fuselage. "And shit, they burn too easy, too. Guy could fry, couldn't he?"

"It's happened. Look, what's up?"

Biggers ignored his question. "My idea is, it took plenty nerve to fly these babies, maybe fall out of the sky." He rapped a fuselage stringer sharply. "But it's the old infantry that holds the ground. Cold steel. Grenades. I mean you're looking right in the bastard's eyeballs—you don't get that in the air."

Maynard smiled coldly. "Sure, I've heard that one, too, both sides of it, if you want to start trading stories."

"Both sides?" Biggers swung to face him, frowning. "I don't get it."

"Infantry. The Legion was where I started, in '14."

"I'll be damned!" Biggers grinned warmly. "I seen some Legion guys skin and cook a *dog,* once."

"They ate rats at Artois," Maynard said. "Not bad—it was the idea that was hard to chew. Anyway, what's this all about?"

Durkin's grin had soured. "We ain't here to shoot the shit, ace. You fuckin *know* what it's all about."

"Give me a hint." Maynard was wishing his service pistol were closer to hand and not out there in the Jenny, and at the same time he felt a *click,* like a switch thrown in a quiet corner of his mind, telling him: *a few bottles of brandy*—this is not worth shooting somebody over.

Durkin's freckles went brown over his flush. "You've cut

yourself into something, walking in where you don't belong."

Maynard shrugged. "At the time, I didn't know you had any interest in it."

"You know it now, ace," Durkin said.

"It doesn't even amount to much," Maynard said reasonably, "and you weren't dealing in this kind of stuff anyway."

"None of that matters, who done what, who knows what," Biggers said. "You just tell us where it is, okay, and I mean all of it, and we decide do you get to keep any cut at all, see? There's ways we can work together, you and that airplane, me and the Durker. Here's your chance to give us a friendly show of interest, a little down money." Biggers was tapping the fuselage stringer again, getting a little beat into it, bouncing the rib.

"So far, I've got an investment there that I've got to get out, but, what the hell, I can see leaving the field open for you in the future," Maynard said. "I never meant for it to be my life's work."

Biggers' nostrils flared, made little puckers at the corners. "The future is *right now,* know what I mean?" He rapped sharply with the rib and his lips peeled away from his teeth. Durkin unhooked his thumbs from his vest and shambled forward, one hand fumbling, hooking something out of his pocket—leather, *blackjack!* Maynard's breathing had gone shallow; he took a deep breath, not sure of his next move. The Dragonfly's control stick, a stout billet of ash with a knob on one end, lay a few feet away, toward Durkin.

"Know what I mean?" Biggers said again, but now it was growled through his teeth and Maynard saw a big pulse throbbing in his throat. The whites of his eyes gleamed around the irises. *That's how he does it,* Maynard thought, *works himself up to it, like a Berserker*—and at that instant Biggers slashed down with the rib and shattered it on the Dragonfly, sending shards of spruce flying.

"Hey!" Maynard said. Biggers reached back for another rib and shattered it too, snapping a stringer on the Dragonfly's

back. He turned toward Maynard, and breath hissed audibly through his nose.

Maynard hurled himself toward Durkin, snatching up the stick of ash, rolling, as Durkin swung the blackjack at his face. Maynard caught it on his shoulder and rapped Durkin across a knee with the stick, and then when Durkin moaned and lifted the knee to cuddle it, Maynard hit him on the other shin. Durkin squeaked a shrill grunt and went down like an armful of kindling. Maynard whirled—directly into another Dragonfly rib, brought crashing down on his head with stunning force. On his knees, he saw the kick coming, Bigger's knee, and felt his nose go when it hit, like white light blowing up in his skull. And then Biggers hauled him to his feet and hit him with both hands, short punches to the ribs and then an elbow across the jaw, and Maynard was down with blood streaming from the cut on his head and from his nose. He couldn't move. There was a roaring in his head like a locomotive. Biggers, raging, picked up a spruce wing spar and clubbed it down onto stacked, assembled ribs that literally exploded under the blow. He turned and hacked down between the Dragonfly's frames, buckling the spine of stringers, and then slashed through the leading edge of the tall fin. The Dragonfly rocked over and crashed to the floor.

Biggers, glaring, wind hissing through his teeth, bent over Maynard and lifted him by the front of his shirt. "Tell me where the stuff is."

Maynard's tongue felt like a football stuffed in his mouth. "Not . . . here," he mumbled.

Biggers shook him. "So it's out at the old man's, right? *Right?*"

Maynard nodded. "'F you knew . . . that . . . why . . . all this?"

"Kill the son of a bitch!" he heard Durkin moan.

"Where?" Biggers slapped him, hard.

"Sh-shed," Maynard mumbled. "Kid and . . . old man . . . they don't know."

Biggers slammed him down like a sack of grain. Still clutching his spruce club, he took three steps to Durkin, heaved him to his feet, ignoring Durkin's gasps and moans of agony, got a shoulder under Durkin's arm and dragged him to the door, where he swung around, glaring wildly at Maynard.

"You hear what he said about them Legion people?" he hissed to Durkin through clenched teeth, spitting outrage. *"Fuckers eat rats!"*

Ed Lindquist, Deputy Chief of Police, listened to Lexie's story in the *Courier* office, with Woodie Craddock looking on. "Might've helped if you had called then, instead of waiting, what, almost an hour?" he said.

"The man skidded out of there fast," Lexie said, "so there was no danger to the people in the neighborhood and I didn't want to alarm Marietta . . . Mrs. Ricks. I still can't understand it. I had twelve dollars in my purse and he didn't take it."

"Did he . . ." Craddock started to say. "I mean, was he *fresh*? Some kind of masher?"

Lexie grimaced. "No. He was looking for some certain thing, it seemed to me."

"And didn't find it," Lindquist said. "You're lucky, is what I think."

After Lindquist left, Craddock said, "Let me run you home."

"No, I told Maynard I'd pick him up at the airport. We've got to get Jason . . . and I'm worried about Uncle Hector. This whole thing is such a mess! I'm afraid I've been very shortsighted, trying to look after an eleven-year-old boy."

Lexie found Maynard sitting on the hangar floor in the splintery wreckage of the Dragonfly. He was still groggy and he was bleeding copiously from a cut on his head and a broken nose. She found a towel in his tent, wet one end of it and cleaned up his face. Using the towel as a kind of compress, and mumbling through the folds of the towel, he told her about Durkin and Biggers.

"I don't think I've ever heard of them," she said, "but what on earth did they want?"

He grinned crookedly at her over the towel. "You'll love this—they want the brandy I flew in from Mexico. They're pretty burned up about the way I cut myself in, and this was to tell me they won't tolerate competition."

"What did you tell them?"

"I tried not to tell them anything, but that Biggers—he's half a regiment by himself, and he knocked me silly, so I blurted it out—told him the stuff was in the shed out at the old man's place. No, *wait*! He seemed to know it was there if I didn't have it here. I'm not just sure why or how he knew. Can't figure it out . . . but we'd better get out there."

He got up and tried to walk, but staggered against the work table and clung there mutely, blood flowing down his face again. Lexie said, "Stay right there." She got another towel and a clean shirt from his tent, came back and took his arm over her shoulder, saying, "Let's go—you need some patching up." They walked awkwardly out to her car. Maynard shook off her arm and staggered to the Jenny. He opened the locker cover and took out his service pistol, and then came back and sagged into the car, holding the gun in its scuffed holster. Lexie started to protest, but, seeing the look on his face, thought better of it.

Dr. Geary's wife, Rebecca, said, "Good grief!" when she opened the door of their Palladian-style stucco house on East Mabel Street. Lexie was apologizing for breaking into their supper, and the doctor, brushing crumbs from his mustache, said, "No, I got clear through the rhubarb pie tonight." Approaching, spectacled, he peered at Maynard's head, saying, "It appears we have some crocheting to do."

He hustled them into his examining room, where he gave Maynard a drink of brandy and stretched him out on the table.

He clipped away the hair and took a dozen stitches in Maynard's scalp, bandaged it, and then he set his nose, centering it with his fingers, causing grinding noises and an eruption of fireworks inside Maynard's head. When the nose refused to stop bleeding, he peered up inside, making *tic-tic* sounds with his tongue, and then he cauterized it with silver nitrate. He said, "Don't stick anything smaller than your elbow in there for a couple of days. It might be a good idea if you went home and went to bed for about twelve hours. I want you to take this—" He handed Maynard two pills and a paper cup of water.

Maynard swallowed the pills with difficulty. "Wha' was that?" he said.

"Something to help you get some rest—the twelve hours or so I was talking about."

"Hey! I've got . . . things t'do. . . ."

"I'm sure they'll keep." The doctor and Lexie peeled off the bloody shirt. He prodded Maynard's extremely tender ribs and put a broad band of tape on the left side. He nodded to Lexie to pull on the clean shirt. "That'll be four dollars, please, cash on the barrelhead or a lien on your car. If you want my advice, don't climb in the ring with the same guy again—you're way overmatched."

Othello Biggers let Red Durkin off at his hotel. "Them people aint going anyplace," he said. "Get some shut-eye and I'll pick you up at four-thirty"—he held up a hand to stop Durkin's muttering—"so's we can get out there by daybreak, see? And wear some old clothes. We may have to take that dump apart stick by stick."

Durkin hobbled into the Territorial, limping on both legs. Biggers went on to his own rooms next to the San Agustin. He was restless. He wished he had asked the ace a few more questions, for one thing. Biggers did his hundred push-ups and hundred sit-ups and did the one-armed push-ups, and he was still thinking about how he should have questioned the ace. Trouble was, he got himself stoked up and just about stiffed the guy. Felt good, too. And he was still stoked. Needed shut-eye, but his blood was hot. He brushed his dark suit and then slipped the trousers back on and pulled on a maroon silk smoking jacket. He went down the long corridor to a curtained doorway at the end. Bright light spilled around the curtain. Someone was playing "Bye-bye Blackbird" on the piano. He heard voices murmuring, a laugh, smelled cigarette smoke.

Biggers pulled back the curtain and leaned into the room. "Hey, Darlene, you busy?"

Maynard's walk was loose and shambling as Lexie led him from the doctor's house out to her car. He stumbled against the fender and had trouble getting the door open. When she opened it for him, he half fell onto the seat.

"Whatever he gave you," she said, "had a kick in it."

Maynard smiled, said *mm-hmm.* She said, "You can't go to Uncle Hector's. What am I going to do with you?" His hand fluttered. "Okay," she said, "you can't go back to that mess at the airport—you can have Jason's bed."

She drove the few blocks to her own place. The driveway allowed her to get the Star within six feet of her door. She got Maynard's right arm over her shoulder and staggered with him to the door—and rolled her eyes upward at the thought of what Mrs. Hazeltine, next door, would be saying if she were watching. She glanced hastily that way. Mrs. Hazeltine was indeed watching. Lexie rolled her eyes again. Inside, she got Maynard into Jason's room.

"Oh, no!" she said. She had forgotten that Jason's bed was of a size to take his four-feet-six very handily, but Maynard was a six-footer. Her sofa was a small, carved Victorian love seat that had been her mother's and grandmother's. She was holding Maynard against the wall, and he was starting to slide down. Again getting an arm over her shoulder, she maneuvered him to her own room and onto the bed. She unlaced and

pulled off the flying boots. His whipcord breeches were dirty and spotted with blood. With an effort, she unfastened them and pulled them off, and then she worked his shirt off, which drew a grunt of pain from him, probably because of the ribs. When at last she had him under the covers, she was mussed, tired and a little grumpy at the idea of giving up her bed.

She remembered she had promised to call Amanda Perrell back. "Of course it isn't too late," Amanda said when she answered. Lexie said she hardly knew where to start. She told her how Jason and Uncle Hector had gone to see Maynard that morning, and how he had been forced to disappoint them, and then she told her about what had happened to herself and Maynard.

"Do you want to bring him here?" Amanda said. "We have plenty of room."

"I've just gotten him undressed and into bed," Lexie said. "Does that sound dissolute? I'm blushing anyway—but I couldn't possibly move him again."

"All right, but when you get Jason back, please do bring him here," Amanda said. "Uncle Hector too, if you want."

Lexie said she would, and hung up. She squirmed on Jason's small bed for over an hour before she gave up. Muttering to herself, she stalked to her own bedroom and slipped into her own bed next to Maynard. "Move over, Lucian," she whispered.

III

Nemo me impune lacessit
[Lat.] No one attacks me with impunity.

C'est plus qu'un crime, c'est un faute
[F.] It is worse than a crime, it is a blunder.

En prise
[F.] *Chess*. Exposed to capture.

Con brio
[It.] With spirit.

20

LEXIE REMEMBERED Dr. Geary's words, telling her that what he had given Maynard would knock him out for the twelve hours of solid rest he needed, so that she carried in her mind the idea that she would get up early and just let him sleep. She would go on out to Uncle Hector's place and get Jason and see what she could do to calm the poor old soul. Leave Maynard a note, she thought, as she drifted off to sleep.

She was running along an elevated train platform, among a crowd of hurrying people. She was looking for a certain train, but she couldn't remember the place name that would identify the train and she was desperate to get to the hospital to see her husband, David. She ran until she was exhausted, reading all the signboards telling where the trains went. The trains pulled in and stopped and people poured off. She asked a man which train went to the hospital. He was in a hurry and told her, but so fast that she couldn't catch his words. She thought she would find her room and rest a while, but she looked in her purse and the key was gone. She couldn't remember the room number. The hotel looked so filthy—oh, *no*!, it can't be the right hotel. All her clothes were in that room, too. She looked for her money. It was gone. David had it, at the hospital. She stood on the corner by the filthy hotel with trains rumbling above, and she began to cry.

Lexie lay in despair in the darkness for an eternity, it seemed, before she realized at last that it was a dream and that she was in her own bed at home. She had the dream often. The trains and the hotel were Los Angeles, not exactly as she had known it in her two years there while David was in the hospital and she was working in Classified at the *Examiner,* but horrifyingly close. She had described her dreams to her friend Jessica, who liked to interpret dreams, had a book about them, talked with excitement about Jungian and Freudian dreams. Jessica said it was a guilt and horror dream because she felt in her subconscious that she had not done enough for David. *You've bottled it up inside,* Jessica told her. *Get it out in the open.* She didn't want it out in the open, that was it—she wanted it forgotten. A slight, muffled snoring sound startled her. It was Maynard, snoring a little through his broken nose, and she had forgotten him in her despair. *Crazy,* she thought, absolutely whacko crazy.

And she was worried about Maynard. He disturbed her, aroused feelings she kept smothered. Like thinking what it would be like to be loved by him, even if she didn't want to love him. She didn't like the bootlegging. It was something tainted. And the war—he went into it in August of 1914. That was over four years—had to leave scars in his mind. David was barely in it at all and it took three ghastly years for him to die. And Maynard with his Dragonfly, living in that hangar like a hobo—so improvident. Like Uncle Hector! Oh, Lord, she laughed to herself, drifting again, everybody's crazy.

Long after, in the dark, he stirred, mumbled something. She put her hand on his shoulder and whispered softly, "It's all right." His hand fumbled, found hers. He pulled it down to his chest, clinging to it, wouldn't give it up. He's beginning to wake up, she thought—I'll go back to Jason's bed. Her arm was numb. She tugged and Maynard rolled over, toward her, his arm on hers. She moved to extricate herself, but he drew her closer. The warmth was delicious. *I don't want to go,* she thought. *I'm letting this happen.* And then she thought, *is this me?—I'm making it happen!* A kiss, fumbling, tentative, dry. She felt a corner of the tape on his nose rasp her cheek and squirmed a little . . . better . . . and the cool, observing self within her watched with something like shock and amazement when she opened her lips to his, sought his tongue with her own. Funny, he wasn't supposed to wake up for hours! She waited for him to awaken fully. He slept on. *Lucian!* she thought, *you wretch*!

Hector Callard walked by the sea. It was December, and gray-bellied clouds scudded low against the shoreline and swallowed the tops of tall firs. Shreds of mist tore off the clouds and whipped past. Gray-green water pounded on rocks offshore and exploded in white spray.

A cliff of black rock loomed before him, its rough crags thrust into the heaving seas like claws. A column of spray shot out of the cliff face like cannon fire, and he heard a deep snoring sound, *oumm-mm-mm.* There was a cave in the cliff, and when a wave crashed upon it, as at that moment, it crushed a great volume of air into a tiny space within the cave, and as the water sank and drew back, the air blew out, blasting a thick jet of spray. *Oumm-mm-mm.*

Hector looked back. On high ground back from the beach where he had bade them stay, his three little boys, George, Tom Jefferson and Abe Lincoln Callard, heavy in dark winter coats, now capered and danced, waving at him and pointing out to sea. Hector turned and saw a vessel, a three-master, bearing down upon the coast at express-train speed, twin curling bow waves fanning out like white wings. But as the ship drew near, Hector saw that her yards were bare of sail. Nor did she spout smoke, like a steam packet. He heard no thrash and clank of paddle wheel. In ghostly silence she hissed across the foaming deep. And then he saw amidships the spinning blur of the Juggernaut's great drive wheel within the glittering brass-tendriled cage. The vessel drove her bow smartly up onto the beach. The captain smiled gravely down upon him and saluted. His three boys ran capering up the gangplank, and Hector sprinted after them. His boots were wet and heavy and, as he ran, the gangplank grew longer, the ship's deck higher. Higher. *Higher*. . . .

Hector awoke, the smell of sea spray in his nostrils, his throat aching with the thrill of what he had seen. *Where are my boys?* he thought. He returned slowly to his now aged self, sadly bereft, for the boys were long since gone. It was in '69, the year the railroad was completed, that Hector and Emma and Tom and Abe took the Union Pacific train all the way from Kansas City to Sacramento, a sternwheel steamer thence downriver to San Francisco Bay, and a steam packet called *Harfleur* north along the coast to the Columbia. He took up 160 acres a few miles from Oregon City in the Willamette Valley. Built a house of cedar logs, dug a well, fenced, cut timber, bucked cedar logs into great bolts and split shingles with maul and froe. Built himself a smithy, made tools for the farmers and loggers, shod horses, mules and oxen from the logging teams. Sheets of rain hung in the valley, gray, shimmering, endless. He stomped through the door, laughing, blowing bright beads of rain off his mustache to make the boys laugh, and hugged Emma, big then with little George.

After he buried poor Emma—not even 25!—he stood it alone for dark months. Heard the sound of weeping one night, woke up with his face wet. Next day he gave one of Emma's shawls to Maggie, the plump Indian girl who nursed little George along with her own baby. Maggie knew. Eyes like smoky dark cherries, lashes smudging her cheeks. She helped him. But the boys were growing. He needed a *wife*. Walked off and left the whole shebang, the house and 160 acres. Never set eyes on it again. Back to Missouri, down the clattering, shuddering tracks of time. . . .

Hector heaved himself upright, planted his feet on familiar tatters of rag carpet, pulled on his clothes. He picked up the box with the Juggernaut, took up his shotgun and went into the kitchen, where he struck a match and lighted the oil lamp. He left the wick turned low, barely a-glimmer. He went out onto the porch—*cold* out there!—and his hand, pulling at the quilt, found the hot little body of the boy. "Roll out, young sir," he said.

Speaking scarcely at all, they folded their bedding. While Jason carried their things to the car, the old man took the dim lamp and busied himself in his pump-house work shed. He taped two sticks of Red Cross Sixty Percent Straight dynamite together, primed and fused with three feet of Black Aztec fuse—which burned at the rate of one foot per half-minute. He buried the dynamite in one of his scrap boxes and then piled onto it all the rest of his cans and boxes full of scrap metal and discarded Juggernaut parts. He went back outside to the Ford.

"Spark up, gas down," he said to Jason, who moved the two levers on the steering-wheel mount. Hector cranked. The Ford fired right up for once, popping noisily until Jason advanced the spark. Hector let the Ford warm up. It was no longer dark. A band of rose-gray light washed the horizon to the east. The pump house and windmill were no longer merely black shapes looming against the sky. Jason could see the boards now and the cracks between them.

Hector reduced the throttle. He told Jason, "It's light enough to travel. We'll leave the sons of bitches a good-bye note." Jason, shivering in the Ford's open-sided cab, watched as the old man returned to his shop, where he knelt down in the doorway. Jason saw matchlight flare and a little squirt of sparks, and then the old man was up on his feet and legging it back to the Ford, climbing in with a grunt. He trod on the *go* pedal, and the Ford lunged and bucked its way out of the yard.

Othello Biggers spotted his old tracks in the light thrown by the headlamps of the Essex, and followed them to his familiar knoll. He took his binoculars and scrambled to the top, followed by Red Durkin. It was still black-dark, and the gulch before them appeared a bottomless void.

"What's the deal?" Durkin said. His teeth were chattering. "If I'd of knowed we was coming to the North Pole, I would've wore my sheepskin."

Biggers seated himself. He was wearing his woolen army breeches with wrapped puttees, an officer's khaki shirt with the ribbons of his decorations stitched above the left breast pocket, wool jacket and his campaign hat, with chin strap on the back of his head. "We can get a line on whatever is happening from here, see what the old geezer and the kid are up to before we go in there. See there?—the old boy must be up."

They watched as the dim glow of light moved from window to window, through the house. Biggers turned and saw the first faint gray light of day beyond the looming shoulder of the Catalinas. Durkin shook his arm.

"Now look. They're outside."

Biggers trained the binoculars on the lamp. Figures moved back and forth, causing the light to blink off and on, and then the lamp was taken across the yard to the pump house, where it sat for a few minutes, glowing in the window of the shed.

"They've put some junk in the Ford," Biggers said, "and now the old man is in the shed."

"He's getting the stuff," Durkin said. "They're fixin to leave!"

But Biggers was already halfway down the slope, running for the Essex. They jumped in and Biggers started the engine and ripped the car into a skidding turn, throwing up a wave of sand. Weaving and bouncing, he sped through creosote and cactus, clipping lobes of prickly pear and frosty arms of cholla. Lurching back onto the road, he shifted up to second with a crunch of gears and whipped down into the sandy gulch, the Essex fishtailing and bucking. Uphill on the far side, then, and Biggers sent the Essex churning into the yard in a spray of gravel. He swung to a stop in a broadside skid, between the house and the shed. The lamp still glowed inside the shed.

At that moment, the Ford stopped some three hundred yards away, having wheeled around the pump house and through the back gate onto a rutted track bearing away to the southwest. The old man, thinking of that Black Aztec fuse and counting seconds under his breath, got out of the car for a look back. He was saying, "Young sir, I want you to see—" as the Essex churned into the yard. *"Great jumping Jesus!"* the old man blurted.

At the house, Biggers and Durkin leaped out of the Essex. "They're still here—the lamp is on in the shed," Biggers said.

"Then where in hell is the car?" Durkin screeched. He turned toward the shed just as it blew up.

It erupted in a blastcone of weathered timber and a fiery rain of shrapnel and splinters. The shed and part of the pump house simply disintegrated, but the charge also shattered the two nearest timbered legs of the pump house and blew out all the cross-bracing. Unsupported on one side, the big redwood water tank hung in the air for a moment, and then toppled toward the Essex and the house.

Biggers and Durkin, both hurled off their feet by the blast, dazed by concussion and peppered by stinging shrapnel, were engulfed in a second explosion—this one as 1200 gallons of water caught them in a wave of surf and cannoned them across the yard on its crest, along with buckets, barrels, boxes and piles of trash, to fetch up against the house like two shot hogs. The Essex was skidded sideways with them, under a spiny shroud of splintered planks. It slammed a rear wheel against a stump, snapping two wooden spokes.

The water surged around them and then slowly subsided. Durkin crept out of a cocoon of trash and mud. Biggers did the same. Both men were deafened and cut and torn in a dozen places from the explosion of shrapnel. Durkin tried to shape words, gasped, tried again.

"Shee-it!" he choked.

21

THE SHINGLES did not merely burn—they exploded like gunpowder. Flames raced across the roof and curled under the eaves, crackling like small-arms fire. In seconds the whole top of the house was roaring, flaring yellow-orange against the cooler red of the dawn sky.

Othello Biggers mopped blood and muddy water from his face with a bandanna. Red Durkin, drenched to the skin, swore through chattering teeth and shook himself like a wet dog. "That crazy old coot! He seen us coming and tried to murder us!" Durkin's voice cracked into a plaintive bleat under the strain of his outrage.

"I was ready to reason with the old fart," Biggers said earnestly. "He could've lived out his last days taking his ease. This is going to cost him." He staggered out of the wreckage of the pump house and shed. He was almost deaf from the explosion. The roaring of the fire on the roof of the house mingled with the ringing in his ears. He stuck a finger in one ear and waggled it. Was that a backfire? He ran back to higher ground and cupped an ear—caught the faint clatter of an engine. And then he saw the dust boiling up, a moving cloud of it headed southwest.

Biggers ran back to the Essex, snarling at Durkin to get his ass moving. The door was dented and jammed from the explosion. Windows blown out. The whole side of the car looked as if it had been through the Battle of the Marne. Biggers was proud of his Essex, kept it polished, gleaming. Loved the elliptical rear window with the tasseled curtain. Pressed-glass bud vases on the doorposts—was that a *touch* or not? It *hurt* him to see this. Raging, he almost tore the door off getting in. He fired up the engine and wheeled out of the yard, through the back gate. The Essex seemed to slew wildly—*must be the sand,* he thought.

The Gulch road came to an end at the old man's homestead, but beyond that was the faint track leading cross-country, worn in past years by his taking off through the desert on this southwesterly course. Far out ahead of them now was the plume of dust.

"That old son of a bitch belongs in jail!" Durkin sputtered virtuously.

Othello Biggers floored the gas pedal. The Essex leaped ahead like a startled elk, spitting a rooster tail of sand behind. It shot along the vagrant course of the old track, threading between clumps of creosote and cactus. He swung wide around a huge saguaro—the rear end broke loose and took off on its own. The car whipped broadside and slammed into the saguaro, crumpling the door on Durkin's side and spraying him with cactus pulp.

Biggers kicked his own door open and climbed out. His face was pale and he was icy calm. Durkin had to climb over the shift stick, which, like something live, stabbed him treacherously. The two men examined the car. The trouble lay in the right rear wheel, the one that had been catapulted against the stump when the water tank burst. Because of the snapped spokes, the wheel was askew on the drum.

"Get the tools under the seat," Biggers said. "We've got to jack the bugger up and put on the spare. It won't take but a wink."

Durkin got out the jack, positioned it and levered away. The weight of the car drove the jack into the sand. Biggers went scouting, found a flat rock a hundred yards away that weighed about eighty pounds and carried it to the car. They finally got the wheel off, and then they took the spare wheel off the rack on the rear and bolted it into place. Gratefully, Durkin reversed the ratchet pawl in order to let the car down. Or attempted to—the little lever was stuck fast.

"I'll drive the son of a bitch off the jack!" Biggers growled. He got in, started the engine and drove forward. The Essex rocked off the jack with a satisfying *thunk.* He got out and saw Durkin staring at the wheel with a look bordering on desperation. There was no air in the spare tire.

Biggers' lips were drawn taut over his teeth. Speaking through his clenched teeth, he said, "Jack her up again. We'll take the tube out of the first tire and stick it in this one."

Now the axle, because of the flat tire, was too low for Durkin to get the jack under it. The axle was, in fact, resting on the rock. Durkin had to excavate under the rock with his fingers and a stick. He worked like a man fighting a nest of cobras. Sweat blinded him. His fingers were raw.

"Goddammit!" Biggers snarled. "Can't you dig a little faster?"

Sunlight streamed in the kitchen window. Lexie squeezed some orange juice and when Maynard walked in she sat him down at the table and gave him a glass. He was stiff and sore, his face battered looking beneath the bandages. They were somehow embarrassed, looking at each other, glancing away quickly. Lexie put eggs on to boil. "Five minutes okay?" she murmured. Had to look directly at him then, and an unbidden smile tugged at her lips, without mercy for her hidden feelings. He was smiling too, and then he tipped back his bandaged head and laughed aloud.

"Let me get something straight," he said. "Did you sleep with me last night?"

She nodded.

He reached for her, pulled her onto his lap and kissed her. "Did I behave?"

She nodded again. "Damn!" he said. "That doctor *owes* me!"

While they were eating, she suddenly remembered that she had not told him about her own adventure, of being robbed—or at least *accosted*—when she went to take Sibbie to Marietta. He was shocked and angered that he hadn't known, but agreed helplessly that he had been in no shape to do anything about it. Going out to the car, he complained of being stiff and sore. "You need more time in bed," she blurted, and then reddened, and they both burst out laughing. And sure enough, the head of her inquisitive neighbor Mrs. Hazeltine appeared at the window not ten feet away. Lexie bit her lip and struggled to stop laughing. Seeing Maynard's service pistol on the floor of the car sobered her.

Long before turning off the highway onto the Gulch road, they saw a column of smoke off to the west in the desert. They exchanged glances anxiously, neither wanting to say it. Lexie made the turn, her mouth now too dry to speak. A big dusty Reo truck came toward them. She pulled over to let it pass. It had *Papago Queen Mining Co.* lettered on it, and carried a big pumping tank and several rough-looking men in the back and on the running boards. The men wore work clothes and held shovels and looked sooty and smudged. Lexie wheeled the Star back onto the road. Gunned it.

It was almost ten o'clock in the morning when Lexie and Maynard reached the house. The last of the volunteers from the Papago Queen, called there by Ulysses Farney, had left. Farney himself was still there, looking dazed. There was nothing to save. The roof had fallen in on the house and continued to burn. It was still white-hot.

Lexie's first thought, in her terror, was that Jason and Uncle Hector had both perished. Thinking that, she sat rigid, clinging to the steering wheel of her car. Maynard tried to comfort her. Farney came and stood by the car.

"His Ford ain't here," he said. "Its tracks take off yonder. Thing is, they's another set of tracks on top of the Ford's—bigger tires."

Maynard walked out with him and examined the tire tracks. "Where could he be headed?"

"That's the track he used to take to his claim, if that's any help," Farney said. "But that's a hundred miles or more, way the hell out in Yuma County. Back door to hell."

"Why would anybody want to burn him out, an old man like that?" Maynard said.

Farney looked surprised. "Burn him out? I think the old boy done it hisself. Decided to clear out. Burned his bridges."

"What makes you think so?"

"This morning I run into my shop to grab a shovel when I heard the explosion. It was the blast that made me think about it—and Olive tellin me yestiddy that Heck had been to my place. To bring back a can of gas, is what he told her. So I looked around and, sure enough, he's took most of a case of dynamite and caps and fuse and such. He's also took some canned goods and some more gasoline, if I aint mistaken. So he *planned* to go, him and the little lad, together."

Lexie had left her car and now stood beside them. "But who would be following them?"

"Agents," Maynard said.

Farney laughed. "Yes, he's talked about them people, time to time. I never took him serious."

"Yes," Lexie said, "but those tire tracks are *real*, so the agents are real now. So who are they? Has that truant officer come around?"

"No," Farney said, "I called him myself and told him to stay away, even if Olive hollered on him to get out here. He said he would as soon walk over live coals as come here."

"It's pretty clear," Maynard said. "It must've been Biggers and Durkin, after that . . . *stuff*, the way I said." He shook his head very slightly to Lexie, flicking a sidelong glance at Farney. He didn't want to say anything about the cognac in front of Farney.

Lexie frowned and looked bleakly at Maynard. Farney said he had to get back to Olive—she would be half out of her mind with worry, he said. He got into his Chevy and left. Maynard put his arms around Lexie, but she kept her arms against his chest and her hands were clenched.

"You're thinking this is all because of that damned cognac, right?" he said. She nodded. He said, "I know how you feel about it, but are we in this together or not?"

After a pause, the stiffness drained out of her and she put her arms around his neck and kissed him. "The thing is," he said, "when I told them where it was, I said it was in the *shed*. I was groggy and not thinking straight. Biggers must not know about that old hut out there. This is the only shed he knew about. He must have figured that the old man was taking the cognac someplace. How do things like this get started?"

They heard the sound of another car engine. Seconds later, a light blue Buick touring car turned into the yard. Woodie Craddock was behind the wheel. He climbed out of the car and they stood together in the yard fanning away drifting smoke and ash.

"Some guy from the Papago Queen called the paper," he said. "Took me a few minutes to figure out it had to be *here*—Uncle Hector's." He listened while they told him what had happened—or at least what they thought had happened.

"What makes you so sure they're after your bootleg brandy?" he asked Maynard.

"It's the only thing it could be," Lexie said.

"I know they are," Maynard said. "They came to my hangar, told me I had cut myself in where I wasn't welcome and they wanted the stuff. Biggers . . . worked me over." Maynard indicated his bandaged head with a flick of his hand. "He just about destroyed my Dragonfly, too. I was punchy—told him where it was."

"You mean it was out here?"

Maynard looked uncomfortable. He nodded reluctantly.

"*Where* out here?" Craddock said.

"Do you have to know that?" Maynard said. "I don't want this on page one."

Craddock looked disgusted. "Let's try my original question again. Why are you so sure it's the liquor they want? Did they say it specifically? . . . You know, *booze,* liquor, brandy?"

"I don't remember exactly. Things were getting . . . ugly."

Lexie said, "You're following some kind of lead—something we don't know about, is that right?"

"Maybe I'm theorizing. Captain, how much is that liquor worth?"

"A lot more than I paid for it," Maynard said. "People in town will pay seventy-five dollars a bottle for it. It could come to, say, five thousand or more."

"Five grand is a pretty good piece of change, all right, but is it worth murder and arson?"

"It was worth a beating, but no one has been murdered yet," Lexie said.

"Could happen any minute, the way it's going. I don't see why it has to be the booze that they're after," Craddock said. "Another thing, Lexie—how much of that booze would you be carrying around in your purse?"

"*None* of it!" she flared. "What's this all about?"

Craddock squinted quizzically through curling cigarette smoke. "A guy roughed you up. Wanted *something*. Didn't take your money, right? Did he think you had a few cases of cognac in your purse?"

"But that had no connection with this or with what happened to Maynard!" Lexie said.

"How do you know? Both you and the captain attacked, or whatever you want to call it, within an hour. And now this."

"All right," Maynard said. "How do you read it?"

"It diagrams like this." Craddock drew lines in the dirt with a stick. "Lexie, here. Captain Gaylen, here. Uncle Hector. Jason. Biggers and Durkin. Who else?"

"Nobody else," Lexie said.

"There's a joker in the deck," Craddock said. "J. W. is the wild card."

"J. W. isn't even around," Lexie said. "He was just a lot of hot air, anyway."

"He scared you into hiding Jason out here with Uncle Hector. When he disappeared, Biggers and Durkin were after him—after something. Say they tried to get it from J. W. and failed. They must have figured he left it with his kid."

"Left *what*?" Lexie said.

"You're not going to tell me, are you, that they're after the treasure of Rodrigo Vega?" Maynard said. "Holy smoke!"

"What else?" Craddock said, grinning.

"We can't just stand here talking," Lexie said. "We've got to go after them."

"They've been gone for hours," Maynard said. "I'll go after them in the Jenny."

"What about the police?" Craddock said. "We'll have to tell them."

"Uncle Hector has his shotgun," Maynard said. "He will *know* the police are in the pay of the agents. He starts shooting, the cops will shoot back."

"What a mess," Lexie said. To Craddock, she said, "Do what you think is right. We'll try to find them."

"Durkin and Biggers have got a big stake in this now," Maynard said. "Short of shooting them, how are we going to get them to back off?"

"Deal them the wild card," Craddock said. "Maybe they need to talk to J. W."

Lexie and Maynard stared helplessly at him.

22

LEXIE PARKED her Durant Star in front of Maynard's hangar. Before she could open the door, she heard him say, *"Damn!"*

He got out and walked slowly to the Jenny. The splintered length of spruce Biggers had used for a club was sticking through the Jenny's lower port-side wing. She could see a crumpled rib through a gaping tear in the fabric.

"Biggers!" Maynard said, leaning down to peer into the hole. "He did this when they were leaving last night. He's a . . . *berserker.*" He gave it a broad French accent. "That's the way our *capitaine* said it—at Artois, in the morning, when the artillery began the shelling, he said to us, Today you will be *sauvages*, today I want you to be *berserker*. Howl and bite your shields!"—Maynard burlesqued the accent and the military stance of the French officer. "And the guy actually howled, and he got all those Algerian Legionnaires howling like a bunch of wolves!"

"How . . . dreadful."

"I guess so. He was dead an hour later. One of the first." He grimaced and shivered involuntarily. "No more of *that*! This will take a couple of hours at least, before we can fly. Why don't you go check with Woodie, see if he's come up with anything."

* * *

Maynard was sickened by the damage to the Jenny, further by the necessity of having to make hasty, crude repairs. And when he went into the hangar to pirate some pieces of spruce to use on the Jenny, and saw again the destruction wrought in those few seconds on his beautiful Dragonfly by that raging *berserker* Othello Biggers, his heart sagged. Over a year's work!

He tried to close his mind to it. He took glue, linen fishing line, knife, scissors, fabric, small clamps and various scraps of spruce out to the Jenny. He shaped splints for broken segments of the wing ribs with the knife, and then glued and clamped them. But knowing that the glue was slow-setting—more so on a day becoming rapidly colder—he wrapped the splints in place with whippings of fishing line. He placed a light bulb in a metal reflector trained on the glue for extra heat, and cut patches from the fabric and doped them into place, leaving a few small clamps inside. It was shabby and would all have to be done over again, but it would let him get into the air.

The morning's hazy high clouds had given way to banks of black-bellied cumulus. The bleak and ominous look of the sky was simply one more nasty thing to contend with. He wanted to be gone before Lexie could return.

First time he went this way, Hector told the boy, he walked, whacking his ornery burro every inch of the way with a stick. Looking for gold or silver in those days. Didn't know nothing about other metals, gold or silver would do the trick. Found some, too—yonder, in Mexico—but too damned far from water. None of it's any good, he said, if you can't get it out of the ground. Meant to go back there and sink a well, but got to doing other things instead and then twenty-odd years later, he did go back there, found a hell of a big mill in place, some cyaniding tanks, bunkhouses for the men, the works.

The Ford on its high skinny wheels grasshoppered along its old trail, the trail cut by this same Ford back when it was new—1910, that would have been. They crossed the railroad tracks within sight of the big water tank at Rillito—Hector getting out afoot and scouting ahead to be sure no one was about before making the dash across the tracks and the highway, ducking back into the brush on the other side, headed south and west.

"There's no one around here," Jason said. He was looking at miles of open desert.

"That's what Custer said one day on the Little Bighorn. Make no mistake, they'll have whole regiments of people out a-scouting for us. Heads have rolled today, bet on it." He caught Jason's shocked look. "When word reached headquarters that we had flew the coop, left them bastards empty-handed, the big boys at the top done more than wring their hands. You think they tolerate failure? Not on your tintype! They can't afford it. Way they look at it, not only do they aim to take the Juggernaut, they've got to crush us, stomp on us as you would an ant!"

Jason pictured a boot the size of a trolley car coming down on him, darkening the sky, himself looking up, seeing big hobnails in the heel. He shuddered.

They cut into a dirt road. "The way to the Zopilote mine," the old man said. "*Zopilote* means 'buzzard.'" And for a while traveled on that road at the considerable speed of eighteen or twenty miles an hour. Had their first puncture on that road. A nail in the right front. *How did that nail get way out here?* Jason wondered, but there it was. They jacked it up and Hector ripped the tire off and patched the nail hole, using the puncture kit. They wrestled the tire back onto the wheel again and then, taking turns, they pumped the tube full of air again and got the wheel mounted. Hector topped off the fuel tank with Farney's gasoline.

After a time, the Zopilote road veered south. Hector found his old trail and turned off to the west. "All Papago country in through here," he told Jason. "The Apaches left em alone.

There wasn't nothing to steal. You want to eat grasshoppers or snakes for supper, this is the place to live."

It was a country of low mountains, gullies and arroyos, cactus, all kinds of it. Wild and forbidding. They rounded a hump of red rock and came upon the great bony skeleton of a fallen saguaro lying across their trail. Taking turns with the ax, they hacked it apart and hauled it out of the way. Hector rested more, letting Jason do most of the cutting.

"You handle that ax like a Rogue River lumberjack!" he told Jason, who responded with a surge of pride and immediately redoubled his efforts. But when the trail was clear, the old man got out his coil of rope, tied it off to the rear axle and threw a timber hitch on the cactus trunk. He fired up the Ford and hauled the trunk around so the trail was blocked again. Untying the rope, he said to Jason, "Don't scorn to learn from thieves, young man."

"Learn what?" Jason was puzzled.

"Outlaws and thieves always watch their backtrail." Coiling the rope, he jerked his chin back the way they had come. Jason searched the horizon. There it was, a distant feather of dust. "I've had my eye on em since before we fixed the tire, and I hate to say it, but they're creepin up on us."

"Hreowan," Jason said. "Now will they rue the day?"

Craddock was on the telephone when Lexie walked in. He finished speaking and turned to her. "That's Costello, the railroad dick. When J. W. disappeared, I called Costello and said, you're a manhunter—how would you go about finding this guy? Now he's just called back, says he might have something."

They walked the few short blocks to Toole Street, which cut through town at an angle, parallel to the Southern Pacific tracks. Costello's office was in a building set among warehouses. There was a loading dock at one end and its sickly railroad-yellow paint was heavily sooted from forty years' proximity to the gushing smokestacks of locomotives.

Costello greeted Lexie with a little bow. "I have admired your articles, Miss Clark," he said. Thanking him, she saw that he was only a little taller than she was herself. A single word popped into her mind—*rawhide.*

She explained what had happened, or appeared to have happened. "We're afraid if we call in the police, and they don't understand my uncle's . . . motivations . . . the wrong people might get shot."

Costello's eyebrows lifted. "Including your uncle and maybe the boy, if the police get anxious. Well, it's the sheriff's jurisdiction, and he has to know about it—anything Red Durkin is involved in is a sure bet to spell trouble for someone. It might spill over into Yuma County, too. Thing is, that's open desert country and there's a lot of it. No roads atall, most of it. Could take forever to find anybody, unless they could pick up tracks some way."

"Captain Gaylen is going to search by airplane," Lexie said, "as soon as he makes some repairs. I think my uncle may be headed for his mining claim, somewhere out here . . ." She pointed to the wall map. "I've heard him say something about the Kinovari Mountains."

"Some of them places have got two or three names—Papago, Spanish, gringo . . ." Costello said. "What we can do is check the records for mining claims—"

Lexie shook her head. "My uncle didn't file the claim—he said that was the quickest way to let the big companies know where to dig. He was . . . *is* . . . well, suspicious."

Costello shrugged. "All right, we'd best tell the sheriff anyway. Meantime, you were asking about J. W. Whitlock."

"You've found him?" Craddock said.

"Not for sure. I telegraphed certain citizens, railroad people, bartenders, west to L.A. and east as far as El Paso and Socorro . . . and this morning a yardmaster in Lordsburg called me. His wife is an ex-army nurse who helps out in their little two-bed hospital. There's a man there with a busted jaw. He answers Whitlock's description, but he won't tell his name! Now, spose he's Whitlock—what good is this to you?"

"He'll have to be questioned, very carefully," Craddock said, "to see if the broken jaw is connected in any way to Biggers, Durkin, and Vega's packhorse." Somewhere in the back of Craddock's mind, a glimmer of an idea formed—he struggled to make it clear, something about the night at Kee's, yes, when they were in the can, kidding J. W. about his sockful of diamonds. *Who* was there? The thought drifted away.

"And if it is," Lexie said, "J. W. has to be somehow persuaded to tell Biggers and Durkin the truth about whatever really happened to Vega's packhorse, which he may be very reluctant to do."

"I have to travel that way myself," Costello said. "A matter of some freight-car thefts to look into, if anyone would like company. But first, I'd better have a talk with Sheriff Arnold."

Othello Biggers and Red Durkin crossed the highway at Rillito and found the Ford's tracks on the other side. Biggers swung back toward town a mile and filled the Essex at a little station near the big water tank. He bought a puncture kit, a desert water bag and two five-gallon cans of gas, which he tied onto the Essex's luggage rack in the rear. There was no food except for some dusty bags of peanuts and several cans of stewed prunes.

"You told me we was to be back at the Papago Queen having a steak by midday," Durkin said fretfully. "That was my expectation."

When they were driving again, Durkin opened a bag of peanuts. He took a mouthful and immediately spat them out. "Rancid!" he moaned. "I bet they been on the shelf since nineteen and five."

Biggers prided himself on accepting privations without whimpering. "Bitching aint going to fill your belly," he said.

"Call that bitching?" Durkin flared. "Hell, I done enough soldiering to know about going hungry. In Sonora, after Vega had to go and hit that train and the son of a bitch was full of *federales* with machine guns, we didn't eat nothing but our fuckin saddle strings for damn near a week! Thing is, if I'd of knowed there was the least chance of something like this, I would've had the Chinaman at the hotel fix us a picnic hamper . . . corned-beef sandwiches, jar of whiskey sours—"

"*Ne cede malis,*" Biggers snarled. "Yield not to misfortunes."

"Where do you get that shit?" moaned Durkin.

23

COSTELLO, as a railroad detective, was also deputized in the counties through which the railroad passed. His territory extended from El Paso to Los Angeles. He was on good terms with most local officers. After thirty years of hunting outlaws from Texas to Montana—not to mention Mexico, or even Argentina and Bolivia in the days of Butch Cassidy and Harry Longbaugh, the Sundance Kid—Costello's name evoked something akin to awe among police officers. But Costello's angle on a particular case did not always agree with a county sheriff's, especially a politically ambitious sheriff like Dave Arnold, who did not appreciate having to share credit with a legend.

Costello understood, but even so he was not fully prepared for Sheriff Arnold's response when he told him about the old man and the boy, and how they had left an explosive message behind them when they left. He told the sheriff that there was a certain confusion as to the motives of Biggers and Durkin. He did not mention Vega's packhorse because, to Costello, it was pure conjecture—and if it was to become public knowledge, could set off a stampede of historic proportions. So the sheriff, who had a symbiotic working arrangement with Othello Biggers, was willing to see Biggers' role as a benign one.

"What you're telling me is there's an old crackpot running loose with a shotgun and some dynamite, fixing to terrorize some citizens. My job is to disarm the old fool and take him into custody—so he don't hurt no one—and rescue that kid that's with him."

"The old gent is a citizen himself," Costello said, "and it does look more like he is the one being harassed. The kid is a relative. In this state, half the people you know sleep with a case of dynamite under the bed."

"Did you come to me to get me to do nothing?" the sheriff said.

Costello grinned. "No—even if doing nothing is sometimes the best kind of police work. But I wanted you to understand that this old citizen has reason to think someone is after him. He was pushed into that frame of mind by Red Durkin and Othello Biggers, one way or another. He aims to protect himself. If police officers attempt to subdue him, and he protects himself and some deputy shoots the kid, how is that going to look at election time?"

The sheriff sighed. He got up and looked at his wall map, which dated back to the Apache campaigns of 1885–86 and which had served several of his predecessors in office.

Costello indicated the general area where the old man's claim might be. Except for the mining town of Ajo, just north of the border, and Gila Bend, forty-odd miles farther to the north, and a few Papago villages, it was desolation itself.

"We'll have to send someone from this end to follow his trail from the beginning, but I'll call my deputy in Ajo, and then we'll give Luther Hightower a ring in *Healy* Bend"—old-time Arizonans always referred to Gila Bend as *Healy*. "They won't have near so far to go."

Costello winced. "Dave, this aint a *manhunt*. Both of those men . . . well, hell, it's like pinning a badge on a rattlesnake, either one."

The sheriff eyed him coldly. "Town like Ajo, all them

miners, you don't give them no sissy-pants deputy—they'd eat the bugger alive."

"I'm asking you then, please make it plenty clear that it aint a manhunt, that their business is to protect that old man and the boy."

"You want to handle it? You're a deputy." The sheriff's grin was icy.

"I've got business in Lordsburg first," Costello said, "but I'll be back."

"This aint even railroad business."

"It's close enough. If Red Durkin's got his feet in the trough, it could be anybody's business. The last thing he done that was in the public interest was to quit school in the third grade."

Luther Hightower was a railroad officer, or "bull," and Maricopa County deputy. Normally his chief duty was to patrol the trains and expel trespassers, meaning bums or hoboes, an end he pursued with singular dedication, for he sought to blend his own reputation with that of his predecessor, a malevolent railroad bull known far and wide in the fraternity of rambling men as Walapai Sam. Luther had even appropriated for his own use the polished ash pick handle that had belonged to Sam, and had heated a nail red-hot and burned his initials on the handle next to Sam's. And he wore on his hip the same .44 revolver found next to Sam's earthly remains in 1916, when Sam was, in the words of the poet, "gathered to his fathers" after an epic battle with an enraged bum.

Hightower received Sheriff Arnold's call in the stationmaster's office. A potbellied stove in the waiting room was at that hour of the day the center of masculine social life in *Healy*, and Hightower listened to the sheriff while trying not to miss the ending of a racy story being told by Leo Kohner, a fireman deadheading back to Yuma.

Anticipatory laughs were smothering Leo's voice, and the

sheriff's words over the wire were accompanied by a background noise that sounded like bacon popping on a hot griddle. ". . . so I want to make it clear," the sheriff was saying, "that this aint no ordinary manhunt, understand? But the old geezer is armed."

Laughter swelled. Leo slapped his thigh and whinnied. *Damn! What was it Leo seen her do?* Luther was missing the ending. "I getcha," he said. "The man is armed. Try to cut his sign where it crosses the Ajo road."

The line went dead. Luther hung up the receiver and strode across the room to a locker door marked *Employees Only.* He was frowning fiercely, annoyed both at having missed the end of the story, and because the sheriff's precise words, none too clear to begin with, were slipping away from him. He opened the locker and took out a jacket, a tarp-wrapped bedroll and a .30-.30 Winchester.

Leo, still wheezing, said, "Who's armed?"

"Guy tries to blow some people up, over near Tucson. Took off into the desert with a kid."

"You mean it's a *manhunt*?"

The sheriff's exact words about the manhunt were dancing away, just out of reach. Leo's suggestion nudged them back. Luther's jaw took on a grim set as he growled, "The sheriff says, by god, this is no ordinary manhunt!"

The men looked at one another. "How old is the kid?" one asked.

"Uh, he didn't say."

Henry Cagle, stationmaster, glared knowingly. "Hell, boys, how old does a kid have to be to pull the trigger? Billy the Kid started when he was a pup."

"Dammit, Luther," Leo blurted, "I aint letting you go down there alone! How bout you deppitize me?"

"Me too!" said a section foreman named Waddell Bates. "Henry can cover for me with the super if they miss me."

"Dammit," Henry said, "I caint leave my place of duty." He

leered and winked at Waddell. "Say the word and I'll cover for ye with your wife too, Waddell."

A short time later, the three men headed south on the Ajo road in Luther Hightower's dusty 1919 Maxwell touring car. The two new deputies were outfitted with borrowed bedrolls and weapons, and Leo had the foresight to pack two bottles of Indian Maid Gin—in case of snakebite, he averred.

Deputy Jackie Kid Argentos, in Ajo, had no way of knowing whether the fugitives would pass north or south of Ajo, which was about halfway between *Healy* and the Mexican border. Or indeed if they would even get that far. He interrupted a game of pool, deputized the two Grijalva brothers and sent them south toward Sonoita in their Chevy truck.

"Don't do no shooting, no matter what," he told them. If there was any shooting, Jackie wanted to be in on it. "You see anything, make a smoke. I'll do the same."

Jackie decided to cut northeast toward the lower tip of the Sauceda Mountains, and to go by horseback. He took with him a broken-down cowboy named Abe Cutter, who was either half drunk or half dry, depending how you looked at it.

Hanging from Jackie's saddle pommel was a huge Mauser pistol and a belt of ammunition clips. It had a boxy magazine under the breech and a wooden holster that became a gunstock when clipped onto the pistol butt, and it accepted 7.63 mm cartridges, ten to a clip. Jackie had won it from a sergeant in his outfit in France, betting on himself in the division boxing competition. He went clear to the AEF light-heavyweight finals before losing to a Marine named Tunney. That was also where he picked up the name Jackie Kid—his real name was Aristide, but Lieutenant Andrews of his field artillery battery entered him as "Jackie Kid Argentos, the Fighting Greek from Arizona." So far, he had only shot jackrabbits with the Mauser. He was aching to try it on something bigger.

24

MAYNARD took off in the Jenny at four in the afternoon. He climbed to barely five hundred feet, and soon spotted the plume of smoke that marked the wreckage of Hector Callard's house, and when it was off his right wingtip, he let down to two hundred feet. The track, when he intercepted it, showed up as a thin scar winding through the desert scrub. He dropped to fifty feet then, and could clearly see the two sets of tire tracks. He climbed back to five hundred again and followed the tracks west.

The two patched ribs showed up as ugly, puckered, lumpy scars on the Jenny's wing. Maynard's head ached fiercely beneath his helmet, which was too tight because of the bandage. The drug given him by Dr. Geary had left him depressed and dry-mouthed. Out ahead and off both wings he saw drifting curtains of rain hanging from black-bellied clouds. The Silver Bell mine passed beneath his right wing. He saw a coyote sniffing the tracks of the cars. It looked up curiously as he approached and then trotted away, looking back over its shoulder.

He saw where the Ford had turned onto the Zopilote road. He had landed several times on the road near the mine when he was delivering drill bits and blasting fuse and caps. From the air it was easy to see where the Ford left the road, heading almost due west. After a minute, he realized he was no longer seeing the tracks of the Essex. *Good, Biggers missed the turnoff.*

Rain rattled on his windscreen, and when he peered around it, his cheeks were pelted, his goggles spattered. It was dark and gloomy under the clouds, and the Jenny was pitching and bouncing in turbulent air. He saw brown water running in the creek beds now, cutting through the Ford's tracks. The rain became heavy, closing in around him like a shroud. The track was less distinct in the rain and deepening gloom. A butte of red rock flashed past his port wing, not fifty feet away. Maynard flinched and pulled up a few feet, his stomach knotting. Trouble was, any higher and he would be flying inside the cloud.

He saw blackness ahead, a solid wall of rain, and banked away to his left rather than slam into it. Wings vertical in the tight turn, he looked down. And saw the Ford.

Its rear wheels were in water in the creek bed. The old man was in the driver's seat, peering up at him from beneath the corrugated iron roof of the cab. Jason was in the water up to his knees doing something at the Ford's left rear wheel, and there was a rope stretched between the car and the far bank. Jason's face was pale under the red *kepi* and he was drenched. Maynard rolled out of the turn, headed back the way he had come. A flap of fabric peeled back from the patched wing. It clung there, snapping, and then whipped away. Rain swept in around him. He dodged the Jenny between red-black buttes. He didn't dare go back.

The Zopilote road was still a mile ahead of him when he saw the black Essex. It was back on the trail and heading west. It stopped, and Biggers opened the door to lean out and look up at him through slanting rain, and then he was gone as the Jenny roared over at sixty miles an hour. Too late, it dawned on Maynard—*he saw me turn off and follow the trail. I led him to it.*

* * *

When the rain closed in on them, Hector and Jason could no longer see the dust of the pursuing car. The washes they forded began to have rivulets of water in them, and then soon became running streams. The trail snaked through tortuous terrain, following washes a mile or two out of the way to get to a good place to ford.

"This road, she don't go where you want her to," the old man said. "She goes where she's by god *got* to go, and she cost me aplenty of shoveling to get her to do even that."

Jason grew arm-weary from clinging to the bucking seat and the side of the wooden cab. He was hungry, and the hunger was getting so fierce it nudged aside that lump of dread that was his constant companion. Not seeing the dust helped. It was harder to concentrate on fear when there was nothing to see. He could even tell himself that the agents had lost the trail, back there. When they left the Zopilote road, the old man had him get out and sweep their tracks with a branch of greasewood where they turned off onto the trail, and for a time Jason felt the trick had worked. He desperately *wanted* it to work.

Most of the washes were small, no more than ten or twenty feet across. But in late afternoon, with rain pelting down and Jason drenched clear down his right side because of the open cab, they pulled up to a—no, not a mere wash, this was a *river*. Jason felt his belly suck tight with despair.

"Damnation!" the old man said. "We've drawed the big casino. I've never saw her with this much water."

"Is that its name—Big Casino?"

"No, bless you, it aint. The Papagos call it Comobabi. And we've got to cross her."

"What if we can't?" Jason ventured.

"We'll be buzzard bait," the old man said.

Jason shuddered. In his mind he saw himself stretched out on the ground with a pack of huge buzzards tearing at his face and innards. The old man turned and took Jason by the shoulders.

"Young sir, I want you to swear me a mighty oath, an oath that's bound in iron and rawhide, an oath that caint be broke!" Jason nodded quickly, awed by the old man's ominous voice. "If the time should come that the bastards are upon us, you are to take the Juggernaut and skin out through the brush like a scared roadrunner. Pick yourself a place in the rocks and hide the Juggernaut, but make damned sure you remember where you put her, because someday it will be up to you to come back, even if it takes years and years, understand? You will be the only one who can give the Juggernaut to the People."

"I can't leave you!" Jason protested.

"Yes, you can. The Juggernaut comes before either one of us. This is a matter of honor, pure and simple, same as in battle. Just you remember that when the time comes." The old man spat in his palm. "You do the same, boy," he growled solemnly, and Jason did as he was told. The old man whacked his own palm with his left fist, and Jason did the same, and then Hector clasped their two hands together. "We'd seal her in blood, but there aint time—spit will have to do. Now let's get moving."

The old man wheeled the Ford around until its rear end was pointing toward the water, then he got out and took the coil of rope off the back of the truck. He hobbled down the bank and lurched into the water. Jason ran to help him. The old man stopped and leaned against the truck bed. He was breathing hard and trembling.

"I caint hack it," he said. "You'll have to do it. Take one end. Tie it yonder to that stump of mesquite. You know a bowline?—good. I'll pay it out from here and haul you back if you can't stand up. We can't wait—if the water gets any deeper, it will drownd the engine."

Jason tugged his *kepi* down over his ears and went into the icy water pulling the end of the stout rope—it was a hundred-foot coil of ¾-inch manila—and the weight of the rope, coupled with the drag of the water on his legs, made him gasp and heave as he scuttled ahead.

A rock rolled beneath his feet and Jason went under. The icy chill struck into his chest like huge talons. The current rolled him. He was bumping downstream along the bottom, but he clung to the rope, spraddled his legs to stop the rolling and lunged upright, sputtering, streaming sandy water from his nose. *Still had his kepi!*

Jason clawed his way up the bank to the mesquite and made the rope fast. Going back was much easier with the rope for a lifeline. Hector showed him how to throw two turns of rope around the drum bolted to the left rear wheel. The old man climbed into the cab and backed into the water.

A blasting roar of sound filled the air. Jason looked up and saw the Jenny roll into a vertical bank directly above him, saw Captain Gaylen's goggled face staring at him, and then the Jenny rocked out of the bank, threaded between two rocks and disappeared back the way it had come.

Jason was stunned for a moment. *Did it really happen?* He

heard Hector's strangled shout. Jason tightened the rope on the drum and waved the old man back toward the water.

The rope drew taut as it wound onto the drum. Shuddering and bumping, the Ford winched itself across. The drum filled and Jason had to cast off the rope and take a fresh turn. A tire lodged against a rock. Jason waved to the old man to pull forward and change course a little. The Ford crept on across and chattered up the far bank, shooting a spray of red mud from the drive wheels.

Jason cast off the rope and untied the other end from the mesquite. He staggered to the truck with the loose wet coils, but he was too weak to throw it aboard. His knees buckled and he sank into the tangle of coils. His teeth were chattering and he was shivering so hard his ribs hurt.

"Climb aboard!" the old man shouted. Jason looked at him helplessly, unable to move or to speak.

Hector set the hand brake, climbed down and helped the boy into the cab. He pulled a blanket out from under the tarp and pulled it over Jason's shoulders, then he heaved the rope aboard. He struggled back into the cab, where he clung to the wheel, his head spinning. *My tether is getting mighty short,* he thought.

He heard the sudden snore of another engine through the clatter of the idling Ford. A black car breasted a rise, back a quarter of a mile. He heard gears change and the car fishtailed toward the bank at reckless speed, as if the driver meant to hurdle the stream. At the last instant, the car's brakes squealed like a stuck shoat. It slewed broadside in a spray of red mud and stopped. Doors swung open and two men jumped out, stood there glaring at them through the rain.

Hector ground the Ford into a tight circle, trod on the *go* pedal, and the Ford lurched away through clumped cactus. Jason sagged against the old man, shivering violently. *Got to get this boy warmed up, or the little devil will slip away from me.*

* * *

Lexie and Costello rode out of Tucson on the Southern Pacific's crack mail and passenger train, the Sunset Limited, more popularly known as the Sunburn Limited. They shared a high-backed red plush coach seat and went to supper together in the dining car.

Costello commented again on her articles, and Lexie discovered that he actually had read them all. She said, "Maybe you'd let me do an article about some of the outlaws and detectives you've known."

"Kid Curry, Black Jack Ketchum, fellows like that? Sure, but, as for the detectives, anonymity is a detective's best friend. Now tell me about J. W. Whitlock."

After a while, Lexie realized that she had told Costello more about J. W. Whitlock and her sister Cynthia and herself and her family, and even her dreams and aspirations, than she had ever disclosed to anyone, except perhaps her friend Jessica—and all she knew about Costello was that anonymity was a detective's best friend.

They were in Lordsburg in just over four hours. While they were still on the platform, Lexie said, "I don't think I'll ever be ready for this."

"We'll do it together," Costello said.

"I thought you had business to attend to."

"I do, and this is it," Costello said with a slight smile. "If there was a train to Hell, I would buy Red Durkin a seat in the parlor car."

25

HECTOR CALLARD pulled the Ford in close to a rocky crag and stopped the engine. It was almost full dark and the acetylene headlamps had ceased to work years ago. He was no more than half a mile from where he had crossed the Comobabi wash, but he was certain that the agents would not be able to cross the flooded channel so long as it rained, and it looked as if it might rain forever, the way it was coming down.

Rock ledged out of the ground on both sides of the Ford's old trail. With rain pelting his ancient slicker and streaming off his hat, Hector scurried around gathering dry and near-dry twigs and dead branches he found beneath overhangs. He started a fire in the lee of the rock, and then he used the tarp to make a lean-to, stretching one side of it between the branches of a palo verde and the long arms of an organ-pipe cactus, and the far side to the bed of the truck, where he lashed it with baling twine.

He put his wooden case of dynamite in under cover, and then he got Jason tucked in close to the fire, wrapped in blankets, with the Juggernaut in its box next to him. He gathered more firewood and stacked it along the edge of the shelter. Hector let his coffeepot fill with water from a stream running off the tarp, and perched it on stones at the edge of the fire. He opened a large can of beef stew and set it close to the fire. He dug into the grub box and found the remains of Olive Farney's jar of milk, now gone sour. He greased his Dutch oven and put it next to the fire to heat. He poured flour onto a square of oilcloth, sprinkled baking powder and salt into it, spooned in a gob of lard and then added the sour milk and worked up some biscuit dough, and then spooned lumps of the dough into the hot Dutch oven and added a half a shovelful of coals to its lid. When the coffee boiled, he set it aside to let the grounds settle.

Jason slowly stopped shivering. He said, "I didn't know anyone could shiver so long or so hard. My ribs are sore."

Hector said, "You took to that water like a beaver, and I'm proud of the job you done. Now we've got to stoke your boiler," and poured him a cup of coffee, laced it with Eagle Brand.

Shortly the biscuits were done, and Hector served out plates of stew spooned over hot biscuits. He greased the still-hot Dutch oven again and put it back in the coals. He poured in a can of peaches and dusted it lightly with cinnamon, and then spooned the rest of the dough over it and once again covered the lid with coals. They ate their stew and biscuits slowly, savoring every bite. By the time they finished the stew, the peach cobbler was ready. Hector poured a little Eagle Brand condensed milk over each serving.

"If I got to Heaven and didn't get a plate of peach cobbler for dinner, I'd take my walkin papers and go to the other place for supper!" said Hector. He poured himself another cup of coffee.

"A drop of your restorative might taste good," Jason said. "I put it in the grub box."

"Bless you, young sir," Hector said. He rustled in the grub box, found the bottle of brandy and added a dash to his coffee. He paused a moment, cocking his head, and then poured a few drops, half a teaspoon, perhaps, into Jason's coffee.

Jason sniffed, wrinkling his nose at the pungent fumes. He

sipped experimentally. "Uncommon good, for man or beast," he said.

Othello Biggers barely restrained himself from plunging the Essex into the brown water of the Comobabi as the Ford wheeled around on the far bank and stuttered away. The whites of his eyes showed all the way around the pupils and his lips were drawn taut as rubber bands over his teeth. His stiff-brimmed campaign hat began to wilt in the drumming rain.

"Let's get under cover," he growled.

"What cover?" Red Durkin snarled. "I've got a dandy fly tent I bought to go fishin up at Mormon Lake, and if I'd've knowed we was going to be campin out, I would've brought the goddam thing—"

"Along with the fucking picnic hamper you also didn't bring?" Biggers snarled.

Both men climbed back into the Essex. Rain slanted in through the broken window onto Biggers' lap. He studied a rock formation near the bank, some forty yards distant.

"You see how that rock hangs over?" Biggers said. "We could build a fire under there and get warm."

"We could heat up a can of prunes," Durkin said. "They're real good that way."

Both men jumped out and ran to the jutting rock, picking up sticks of wood here and there on the way. Biggers knelt and got a small fire started, close in under the rock. Durkin returned with an armload of wood. Soon the fire was burning smartly. Durkin scuttled back to the Essex and returned with two cans of prunes. He opened them with his jackknife and set them next to the flames. The men huddled close to the fire, soaking up warmth, but the overhang was so shallow that there was barely room for the fire itself—rain continued to thrum down on their backs. Both wore woolen jackets, nothing to shed the rain.

Durkin squatted on his heels close to the fire with his back against the rock and hugged his knees. Steam wisped off his left side. "This aint too bad," he said. Seconds later, he flinched suddenly and slapped at his smoking arm. The smell of damp scorched wool wafted up. Moving away a little exposed him fully to the rain again. Durkin's teeth began to chatter.

The prunes began to steam. Durkin stabbed one out of the can with his knife and ate it. "Hey! That's *good*!" he said. The two men ate prunes greedily.

"Plenty of times," Biggers said, "I would've been damn glad to make a meal of these babies. Around Belleau Wood, we didn't get nothing hot for three days."

"We're lucky we got em when we did," Durkin agreed.

Biggers lifted his can and drank the juice gratefully. "I've got to say it. That makes a first-rate cocktail." He lifted the can again and sipped appreciatively. Suddenly he saw movement over the rim of the can—on the ground a few feet away. His eyes locked on it, staring. And *there,* just beyond it, *another*! And another. His bowels convulsed and a violent shudder racked him. *Tarantulas!* Huge, hairy—*dozens of them*!—lumbering out of the darkness toward him!

Durkin saw them at almost the same instant. His breath stopped. *Christ, I've saw plenty of tarantulas, but never like this! The rain must've drove them out of the ground!*

"Arr-rr-rgh!" A strangled scream ripped from Biggers' throat. He hurled the can away and sprinted for the Essex. Durkin had known Biggers since 1917, six years—gunsmoke, shot and shell, he had never seen him scared. Until now. Durkin slashed at the first tarantula with a stick. Missed. The spider sat back and wagged its hairy forelegs at him. His nerve broke. He ran for the Essex, leaped in. Sat shuddering, hugging his ribs.

The two men huddled in silent misery, shivering. Time passed. They may have dozed a little. Biggers stirred uncomfortably. Durkin squirmed, tried to ease himself. His belly rumbled noisily. At length a low moan escaped his lips. "Thel, goddammit, Thel, the goddam prunes is workin on me!"

"Me too," Biggers admitted through clenched teeth. "I've got to go so bad I can't hardly stand it. *But what are we gonna do?—the ground is covered with them fucking spiders!*"

Jason had the Juggernaut out of its box, sitting on the ground before him. Its brass openwork frame and the articulating knuckles of the wheel glittered and winked in the firelight. He leaned down to look at it closely, only inches away, and was filled again with a sense of its vast scale and awesome power. He did not see the tarantula amble up close to the base of the machine.

Hector Callard removed his pipe from his mouth and touched Jason's arm. "Don't take alarm, young sir, when I tell you we've got company." His voice was so mellow, so reassuring, that when Jason saw the first tarantula, he flinched a little, but that was all. But there were more. Many more.

"It's the rain," Hector said. "Drove em out of their nests."

"Same as us," Jason said.

"Yep. I've saw this before, same way. There's a stretch here, along the Comobabi, where the buggers are plentiful as ants." He stretched out his arm and let the tarantula crawl onto the back of his hand. He held it up for Jason's inspection. "Pet him if you want—he's soft as mouse fur."

Jason stroked the tarantula's velvety back. Hector put the creature back on the ground and it explored the base of the

Juggernaut, waggling its hairy legs. There were a dozen or more visible, out to the edge of the flickering ring of firelight. How many more out there in the dark?

Jason watched them curiously. He leaned close to the Juggernaut again, watching the tarantula squirm up onto the rim of the drive wheel. He laughed suddenly. He was beginning to feel sleepy, but he had a marvelous vision—he saw a broad avenue, and rumbling toward him on the cobblestones were Juggernauts, a fleet of them, all as big as huge trucks, with flags flying from their upper works. The Juggernauts were being driven by tarantulas, all bigger than gorillas, and people on the sidewalks waved and cheered and the tarantulas waved their hairy arms in return.

He told the old man about his vision. Hector slapped his knee and laughed. "You've hit on the perfect way to keep the politicians and the awl companies out of our hair. They couldn't *bribe* a tarantula, and they couldn't hire agents that would fight em."

"First we have to grow our tarantulas to the size of gorillas," Jason said. "Is that *possible*?"

"Why not? They say horses used to be the size of fox terriers."

"Maybe the tarantulas won't want to take orders from us—how about that?"

"You'd want to set up training farms," Hector said.

"I mean, maybe we would wind up working for the tarantulas," Jason said.

The old man laughed. "It could happen. I've worked for a few rattlesnakes in my time. Skunks, too. It might be a downright pleasure to work for a tarantula."

The whole idea tickled Jason's fancy, but something about it was disturbing, too. It was funny to think about having gorilla-size tarantulas driving huge Juggernauts, even if, right down at the bottom of it, he knew it really was only a joke. He could laugh and enjoy it, and in a way *believe* it could really happen, the way you believed any story. And know it was a joke. That was the disturbing part. If the gorilla-size tarantulas were a joke, how about the Juggernaut? A chill of apprehension threaded through Jason's innards. He thought again of the questions Captain Gaylen had asked, about the laws of motion and thermodynamics. He thought how it would be if Sir Isaac Newton or Sadi Carnot or Lord Kelvin could walk in right this minute and take a seat under the tarp and explain to him exactly how those laws affected the Juggernaut. What would Uncle Hector say? He would say that they were agents of the awl companies, part of the conspiracy to keep the yoke on the necks of the People. That led Jason to a further disturbing thought—those laws were written down a long time before there were any awl companies!

Jason pulled *Addison's First Book of Science* out of the grub box and, tilting the book toward the firelight, began to read again, the part about perpetual motion.

Hector was thinking along different lines. He was thinking that the agents had come to his place that morning not knowing that he, Heck Callard, and the boy were all packed and ready to travel. The agents had to follow them, but couldn't have with them much in the way of grub or anything else. Hector was betting the bastards would be mighty hungry. Cold and miserable and *hungry.*

Hector had an idea. He took a folded flour sack out of the grub box and shook it out. *Yes, sir, hungry enough to eat the moccasins off a snake.*

26

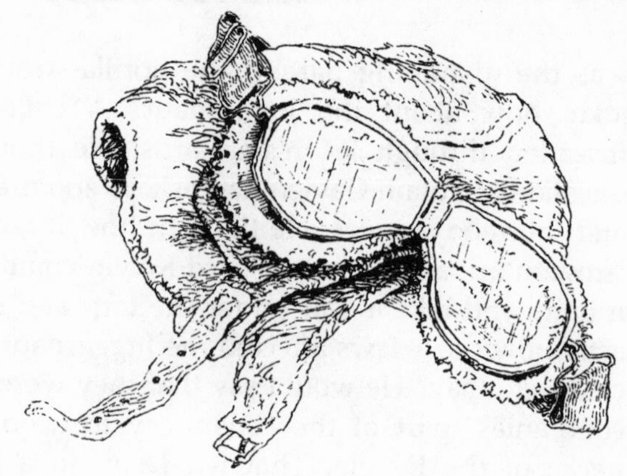

MAYNARD taxied the Jenny up to his hangar and switched off the engine. He had never been so grateful to get back on the ground, but when he stepped down his knees buckled. He clung to the fuselage for a minute and then staggered to the phone box at the corner of the hangar. He called the newspaper office and got Craddock.

"Lexie," Craddock told him, "has gone to Lordsburg, New Mexico, with the railroad dick, Costello, to see if J. W. Whitlock is holed up there, and if he is, to try to get him to come back with them."

"What the hell good will that do?" Maynard said.

"The idea is to get him to square this thing with Biggers and Durkin—get them to leave the kid and the old man alone."

"Even if he'd do that, which he won't, it may be all over by then," Maynard said. "They're out there *now*—I saw Biggers and Durkin right behind them. Somebody could be getting hurt this minute. We've got to get out there and put a stop to it even if it means shooting those two."

Craddock said, "The sheriff has sent teams of deputies out of Ajo and Gila Bend to intercept them, but hell, I'm as worried about the damned deputies as I am about Biggers and Durkin."

"The washes are all running water," Maynard said. "Nobody is going to help them tonight. I'm going to grab some sleep and go back out in the morning. If I can land anywhere near them, I'll do it. If you or anybody else decide to drive out there, you can save hours . . ." He told Craddock how to intercept the trail where the Zopilote mine road doglegged. "But you'd better be driving a high-wheeler or you'll never get through the washes."

Maynard went to his tent and fell onto his cot. He was asleep in seconds.

The Ajo road was unpaved, of course—it would be years before the idea of joining Ajo and *Healy* Bend with a paved road would take hold. The road dipped into and out of washes. Most could be driven through, but there was one—known as the Catfish—which was much deeper than the others. A quarter of a mile downstream from the road, the wash narrowed into a tight notch, and this notch became plugged with some old fence posts, mesquite branches and drifting brush. Water backed up until the Catfish was over four feet deep where the road crossed it.

Luther Hightower and his deputies, propelled by an urgent sense of mission and fortified with a couple of jolts of Indian Maid Gin, drove on, hoping to spot tracks crossing the road before darkness fell. The Catfish looked like all the other washes. Luther drove the Maxwell into it at about twenty miles an hour, sending out great white wings of water. The car settled to the bottom and stopped with water flowing two or three inches above what would have been its gunwales, had it been a boat.

Groaning and cursing and shivering, the men formed a line and passed their equipment ashore. Leo Kohner took a shovel and walked downstream until he found the dam. He levered out the key fence post and the dam burst, ripping away the rest of the obstruction. The water surged downstream with such force that it swept Luther's Maxwell along with it, driving it sideways, jarring and bumping, for some forty yards before the car rolled onto its side and stopped like a beached whale.

When the water subsided to a mere six inches, the four men heaved the car back onto its wheels. "No use tryin to start her," Leo said. "Her electrics is all grounded out."

"Well then," Luther said, "let's get a fire going and camp set up. A tasty meal and a cocktail will not go amiss."

Cocooned in clammy-wet clothing, the men were all shivering and muttering as they hiked in squelching boots, gathering sticks. In the near dark, Waddell Bates mistook an arm of cholla for a stick of wood and picked it up. Not for nothing was the insidious cholla known as jumping cactus. Needle-sharp spines bit into his hand. He screamed and tried to hurl it away, but the cholla merely broke apart, so one piece stayed stuck to his hand and fingers, and another foot-long segment rolled up his forearm. He slapped at it frantically with his left hand, and another piece broke off and clung like a hundred-fanged adder to his fingers. With a cry of anguish, he slapped at his thigh to dislodge the treacherous joint. Now his hand was firmly stuck to his thigh. He was immobilized, but not silenced. His screams rent the sky.

Leo had to hold Waddell, which he did very gingerly, while Luther, using two sticks as tongs, ripped away the segments of cholla. After the larger joints were dislodged, Leo, aided by the flickering light of a flashlight, attacked the remaining spines with a pair of pliers, to the accompaniment of a steady stream of moans and yelps.

"Goddammit, hold still, Waddell!" Leo said.

"Oh, shit, if you knew how it hurts!" blubbered Waddell.

Luther splashed a quart of gasoline from their five-gallon reserve onto the sand. "Trick my daddy taught me," he said. "Nothin starts wet wood a-burnin better'n gasarene." When he touched a match to the gasoline, it ignited with a *whoo-oom!* A red cloud roiled toward the black bellies of the clouds. Luther leaped back with a shrill cry, slapping at his scorched sleeve and singed hair.

They piled on wood and made a bonfire and then stretched wet blankets across clumps of brush to make a kind of saggy, porous yurt, under which they huddled, steam rising above in clouds as they passed a bottle of Indian Maid back and forth. Their crackers and sandwiches were mush, but Leo produced several links of fiery Mexican *chorizo,* which they chewed and washed down with gin.

After a time, Leo urged them to their feet and got them to help him push the Maxwell a few feet onto a bar. He draped a blanket over the front end and carried shovelsful of coals to the car, which he spread under the engine and tended diligently—in order, he said, "to warm up her electrics."

When it became clear to Jackie Kid Argentos that the rain was not merely a passing shower, he decided to make camp. He and his deputy, Abe Cutter, fed oats to their horses and then they made a lean-to with a bedroll tarp and built a little fire. They heated chili in a lard bucket and ate it from tin cups. Abe Cutter would have perished before going anyplace without what he called his "panther slobber." He had two bottles of tequila, which had cost him twenty-five cents each in Sonoita. He produced a tiny cribbage board and a deck of limp playing cards. He and Jackie Kid spent a companionable evening playing crib, drinking tequila and eating oatmeal cookies from a coffee can.

Lexie and Costello located the dispensary next to the Baptist Church. It was a small, weathered, false-fronted frame building that had once been a store. The front room had, behind a counter, shelves filled with homeopathic medicaments. The walls were decorated with posters—chromolithographs of the flayed human body and various organs in ghastly shades of pink and purple, with little boxes showing the proper remedies for various ailments.

Costello opened the door to the back room. It was a whitewashed, two-bed hospital lighted by a single bulb hanging

from the ceiling. There it stopped resembling a hospital. Costello and Lexie saw, through drifting layers of cigar smoke, J. W. Whitlock sitting up in bed sucking whiskey through a straw from a bottle cradled in the crook of his arm as he threw his hand of cards down faceup on the night table between the beds.

"Two pair, ten high," he growled in a slurred voice.

In the other bed was a man with his far leg hoisted in traction. Half-reclining next to him, in order to play his cards for him, was Lottie, a plump woman with bright orange ringlets. She was smoking a cigar, as was her companion, and she was wearing a black slip and black stockings knotted at the knee. The slip was hiked up about her large thighs. The top of the garment was a loose mesh of lace behind which bobbled generous bosoms. Large brown nipples peeked through the mesh, and when she turned suddenly, for she was first to notice the visitors, one leapt out of confinement to stare quivering but unwinking at the intruders.

"What the hell—" she started to say. Costello turned and gently steered Lexie back.

"If you would be so kind," he said, "we're going to need a couple of jugs of strong black coffee. Would you mind going across to the hotel for some? I'll tidy up here."

Lottie was gone when Lexie returned. J. W. was protesting to Costello, something about his rights, and Costello was smiling and nodding solicitously. The other man was muttering, his eyes glaring out of an unshaven face. The liquor bottles were across the room on a small table. When J. W. saw Lexie, he grinned crookedly, his mouth glittering with a network of wires. He had bandages on his neck beneath his left jaw, which was still puffed out like a squash, and his left eye was ringed with shades of black, purple and green.

"My li'l sis, come to visit," he slurred through wired teeth. One of his teeth had been removed to make room for a straw, and indeed a straw was sticking out of it, wagging as he talked. "Preciate y'coming, b'whass all about?"

"We have a problem," Lexie said. "It has to do with Jason and your friends Red Durkin and Othello Biggers."

Costello poured coffee into a large mug and pushed J. W.'s straw into it. "Start pullin on that," he said.

J. W. glared. "Spose I don't?" He swiveled back to Lexie. "Biggers, he done this to me." He pointed to his jaw. "There's no way inna world you're gone get me go back there."

"You know what a come-along is?" Costello smiled. "It makes lap dogs out of big ugly studs." He caught J. W.'s fingers suddenly in his own and whipped his own elbow over J. W.'s forearm. He tugged slightly on the fingers of the now bent hand and J. W. grunted sharply. He started to resist, but Costello merely twitched his hand and J. W. squirmed and cried out.

"Mr. Whitlock wants to freshen up," Costello said. "You would have plenty of time for, say, piece of pie, coffee, maybe a glance at the El Paso paper."

"I'll leave you gentlemen to it, then," Lexie said.

* * *

Just after midnight, they boarded a coach on a westbound mixed passenger-freight. A party of Indians took up the seats at one end. A slant-eyed, moon-faced baby with a red flannel headband regarded Lexie silently over its mother's shoulder. Steel grumbled beneath them, rail joints clicking, as the train sped west through the desert.

27

JASON AWOKE in the gray light of dawn, smelling coffee and fried bacon. He rolled over and looked out—it was no longer raining, although the clouds were still there, dark and threatening. Scarcely had he stirred when Hector handed him a steaming cup of coffee laced with Eagle Brand. Breakfast was bacon, eggs and biscuits, followed by warmed peach cobbler generously doused with Eagle Brand.

"I scouted back yonder at daybreak," Hector said. "They was curled up in their car, half froze, I spect. But the water is dropping fast. We'd best get moving."

Before Jason had finished eating, Hector had the skillet cleaned up, scoured with sand and put away, the tarp pulled down and folded and the truck reloaded. He left the Dutch oven half full of water on the fire, along with the coffeepot and a lard can almost full of bacon fat.

"It was mighty cold last night," Hector said. "A skim of ice in the coffeepot, and that makes this here engine hard of starting." He set spark and throttle and then cranked. Cranked again. The engine refused to start. "Just what I spected. The engine block is too cold for her to fire."

Hector jacked up the right rear wheel. When the wheel was clear of the ground, he opened the drain valve on the radiator and let most of the water drain out. Popping and sputtering noises sounded in the distance as the engine of the Essex was started.

"Better hurry," Jason said.

Hector pulled the Dutch oven out of the coals and poured steaming water into the Ford's radiator. He poured in the last of the coffee, grounds and all, and then he poured the hot bacon fat into the oil filler hole. Steam boiled out in clouds and they heard snapping and crackling noises from the engine block. The old man released the hand brake—which Jason understood engaged the gears—and then he beckoned to Jason and they cranked together. The jacked-up rear wheel turned. With the gears engaged, it became a kind of flywheel, adding its momentum to the cranking. The warmed engine suddenly blasted into life. They ran to let the rear end down. When the tire hit the ground the Ford began to creep forward. Jason jumped in and held it back with the hand brake until Hector could climb aboard. They started to pull away.

"Hist!" the old man said. He set the brake again and leaped out with astonishing agility. Jason watched the old man curiously. Hector took two of their cold biscuits and a flour sack half filled with something—Jason wasn't sure *what*—and he put the sack down not far from their campfire, with a stick of firewood across the neck, and then he put the two cold biscuits in the mouth of the sack as if they had just spilled out. Jason thought he heard the old man chuckling under his breath.

The devastatingly heavenly and seductive odor of frying bacon awoke Red Durkin from a hellish doze. He was shivering violently, exhausted from trying to hug himself warm while coiled on the front seat of the Essex. He kicked the door open and slid out, raking himself painfully on the gearshift and brake levers, moaning and grunting as he endeavored to straighten his contorted body. He saw Biggers a few feet away, feeding sticks to a tiny fire.

Sniffing, Durkin said, "I just had this crazy idea you was cooking bacon."

"It's coming from over there." Biggers pointed with a stick, and Durkin saw a wisp of smoke curling up above clumps of organ-pipe cactus and scrub, some distance away.

Durkin hunkered down and tried to get warmth from the meager, smoky fire. "Jesus, Thel, my ribs is wore out from shivering and my belly feels like it was run through a wringer. Them goddam prunes—I was up half the night."

"Don't tell me nothing about it!" Biggers snapped. Both men shared the memory of crawling out of the Essex time after time, taking turns guarding each other from, dammit, *regiments* of huge hairy tarantulas while they attended to the needs of nature. Biggers pointed with his stick. A can of prunes was tucked in among the sticks at the edge of the fire. Rage and frustration fought for supremacy in Durkin's breast. His voice cracked pitifully as he blurted, *"Shee-it!"*

But Biggers wasn't listening. "The water is dropping," he growled. "Another few minutes . . . no more . . . we've got to move out. The ace could come back anytime."

"He can't put the law on us—we aint done nothing. In fact, goddammit, we are the injured parties! What could he do?"

"Who knows? But we got to talk to the old geezer before the ace or anyone else butts in. After that, see, we just laugh. They don't have nothing on us. We're out here on a camping trip, that's all. The old fart is cracked—everybody knows that, and the kid, dammit, nobody is going to listen to no kid!"

They ate their austere breakfast of warmed prunes. From time to time, Biggers took a long curved stick and probed the depth of the water. When the water dropped below a foot, he started the Essex. It stalled repeatedly. When they were in the middle of the Comobabi, it stalled again and the battery was too low to start it. Durkin had to wade out and crank it.

"Hey!" Biggers said. "Hear that? We're getting the jump on em!" Over the rush of water, they heard the distant clatter of the Ford's engine.

Durkin cranked. He followed the car, lurching, slipping and swearing, cranking it every few feet until it reached the far bank, when he had to push, helping it slither up the slope in a spray of red mud. And less than five minutes later they reached the smoldering remains of a campfire.

"Holy shit!" Durkin said. "They forgot their grub sack!" He leaped out and lunged for the flour sack. Snatching up the two biscuits, he crammed one into his mouth.

"Well, goddammit! Give me some!" Biggers raged, holding out his hands. Durkin quailed before the fury in Biggers' face. He upended the flour sack. Biggers screamed. *Tarantulas, dozens of them, poured out of the sack onto his hands and forearms and began to crawl on him.*

The first attempt to start the Maxwell caused a sinister crackling noise and a curl of sharp-smelling smoke from the vicinity of her "electrics." After an hour of wiping plug wires, distributor cap, rotor and points, and taking turns cranking, Luther Hightower and his deputies finally got his Maxwell started. With Luther driving and gunning the engine and the other two men pushing, they ran the car onto the road. Exhausted from pushing, they loaded up their sodden gear and headed south again, the car bucking and jolting on the severely gullied road.

A few miles to the south, Jackie Kid Argentos and Abe Cutter swung into their saddles and rode to a high point of ground, where Jackie scanned the surrounding desert through binoculars. He spotted a wisp of smoke hanging in the still air two or three miles away to the north and east. They set a course considerably to the west, in order to intercept the fugitives.

The conductor on the westbound train, an old-timer, greeted Costello warmly, surreptitiously ogling J. W. Whitlock, who promptly grumbled through his wired teeth, "I want you to know, my man, that I am being took aboard this train against my will."

The conductor broke into wheezing laughter. He winked at Lexie and Costello. "Them are the exact words Black Jack Ketchum used in my presence in nineteen-and-twelve, would you agree, Mr. Costello?"

"Near enough, Mr. Purdy," Costello said.

"When they hung Black Jack"—the conductor's voice dropped to a doleful whisper—"he hit the end of the rope so hard it snapped his head off his shoulders! Just popped it right off! They took it away in a gunnysack!"

Lexie gasped. J. W. glared. Costello said, "Would you be good enough to ask the porter to drop around with some coffee, Mr. Purdy?" The conductor tapped the side of his nose, winked conspiratorially and left.

J. W. mumbled, "You've no right to snatch me away like this! I'm not a well man."

"Please, J. W., do listen now," Lexie said. "This is all about Jason. When you threatened to take him, I . . . felt I had to protect him—"

"*Protect* him?" J. W. reared back fiercely. "M'own boy?"

"—so I took him to stay with an old man, a great-uncle of my father's. And your friends Othello Biggers and Red Durkin got the idea that you had left . . . *something* of great value—you'd know what it is—with Jason."

J. W. turned to face her, frowning in startled amazement. Lexie went on to tell him what had happened, or what *apparently* had happened. "No one is really sure," she finished, "who caused it or why, but there was an explosion and the house burned up and they're out there in the desert now and Biggers and Durkin are after them."

"Wha' you expect?" J. W. snarled. "Messing around . . . a man's family affairs."

"So, the thing is, you have to talk to them—"

"Hell you say. Talk to no one. Those crazy bastards . . . kill me!"

"I'll be right there with you," Costello said.

"You're no different, goddammit! . . ."

The train pulled into the Tucson yards at 5:48. They walked directly to Costello's office. Costello sent a callboy from the telegrapher's office to get a tray of toast and scrambled eggs and a jug of coffee. Lexie telephoned Craddock, who answered sleepily.

"J. W. is here with us, mad enough to bite nails," she said, cupping her hand over the mouthpiece. "Have you heard from Maynard?"

"He saw them—knows about where they are. Says he's going back out there at daybreak. We ought to talk to him first. He gave me the number of the phone box at his hangar." Craddock read the number to her and said he would meet them at Costello's office.

Lexie gave the operator the number, let it ring. J. W. muttered something under his breath. Costello heard his audible hiss. J. W. was looking at the picture of the corpse of Rodrigo Vega sprawled on a rocky patch of ground that was littered with broken prickly pear.

"That crazy sumbitch Vega—so tha's how he ended up," J. W. mumbled through his wires.

Lexie was speaking to Maynard on the phone. She turned to Costello. "Captain Gaylen says he can find them from the air. He wants to know if you can get to Gila Bend in a hurry and head south on the Ajo road. You'll save hours that way."

Costello took the telephone from her and spoke briefly to Maynard. He said, "Right, one way or another, we'll see you there. Four hours, but I'm guessing. We'll look for you, Captain."

He clicked the fork on the telephone, got the operator and asked for the Division Superintendent. "This is Costello, sir . . . Indeed, I do know what time it is. I need a locomotive and a flatcar in a hurry, and a call from you will do the trick. . . . Railroad business? I'm thinking what it would look like if the railroad stood by and let a child get injured or possibly worse. . . . We need the equipment on account of the road will be washed out in at least the same dozen or so places it always gets washed out when it rains the way it did yesterday. . . . Yes, sir, twenty minutes, and thanks."

Costello called Jack Perrell and asked him to stoke up his Stanley Steamer mountain wagon. "Our old pal Red Durkin is out in the desert south of *Healy* and I need to get to him before somebody gets hurt. The roads are washed out. . . ." He hung up just as Craddock entered.

The callboy came with a huge tray of food from the railroaders' all-night restaurant across the street. Before they had finished eating, light flickered on the ceiling and they heard the slow *chuff-chuff* of a locomotive moving through the yards toward them, and then a soft exhalation of steam as it ground to a halt nearby.

"That's us," Costello said. He helped Lexie into a long yellow slicker, and then led the way to the loading dock at the end of the building. A big locomotive sat hissing quietly, a single flatcar coupled behind its tender. Costello ran ahead and talked urgently to the engineer.

Headlights flashed as an automobile turned into the street and sped toward them. Strangely it made no sound, except for a whisper of tires on pavement and a slight squeal of brakes as it drew near. The car—a *huge* car, or bus, Lexie saw now in the faint dawn light—rolled silently up the ramp, wheeled onto the flatcar and stopped. Lexie boarded the flatcar with the others and climbed into a seat in the big Stanley Mountain Wagon. In the half-dark, she bumped into someone.

"Amanda!" she blurted.

"What did you expect?" Amanda laughed. "If Red Durkin is going to have a knot tied in his tail, I mean to be there."

Costello waved to the engineer. There was a gasp of steam, a slight jolt, as she *chuffed* and took up slack and then the locomotive was under way, clicking across rail joints, faster and faster.

Icy wind whipped at Lexie's slicker. Light from the locomotive's headlamp picked out the tall, ghostly-pale shapes of saguaros ahead, shapes that melted back into darkness again as the light fled past them. And then gray light, moving imperceptibly, flooded the sky. Lexie examined the huge car curiously. She could see now that it was red, with red leather seats, open-sided like a buggy, decidedly antiquated by the fashions of 1923. There were two seats forward, followed by a space filled with what appeared to be camp gear, and then another seat in the rear, all covered by the canvas top, drawn drum-tight over varnished struts and bows.

"What d'you think of our steamer?" Amanda said. "She could outrun this train if the gullies weren't full of water and she had a road to run on."

"Then she would be going like the hounds of hell," Costello said. He had his watch in hand and was timing the train between mileposts. "We're doing eighty-five."

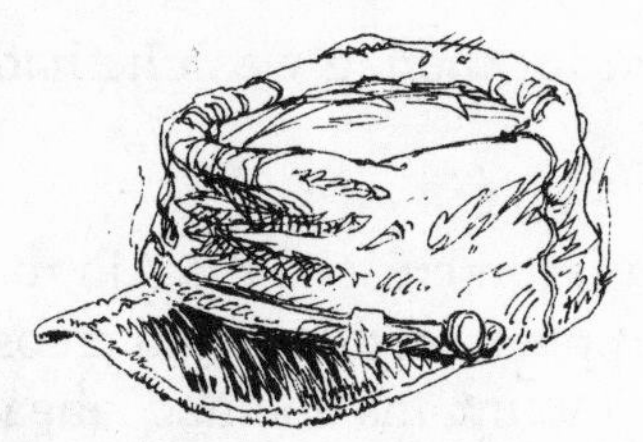

28

MAYNARD was pulling the propeller through to prime the cylinders with fuel when he heard the distant *chuff-chuff* of a locomotive. Except for the yapping of a dog, it was the only sound in the predawn air.

A faint wash of gray light glowed behind the mountains to the east. Maynard took off to the west in the near-dark with no horizon to guide him, leveling his wings with the help of scattered, distant pinpoints of light.

The locomotive's headlight was a white-hot brush stroke piercing the gloom. Maynard turned and chased it, but the beam of light stayed firmly ahead. He was at one thousand feet. He put the Jenny into a shallow dive, felt her speed build up as the wind plucked at the streamer on his helmet, gaining slowly now—he longed for a moment to feel the power of his sturdy Spad with its booming Hisso engine—and then, still in the dive, there was suddenly light enough to see the speeding locomotive and the single flatcar and the *immense* automobile on the car, Jack Perrell's Stanley Steamer Mountain Wagon. Maynard laughed and held the Jenny in the dive until she was alongside, just above the car and even with it. Startled faces turned to stare. He saw Lexie in the second seat, bundled in a yellow slicker. He waved and then pulled the stick back. The Jenny shot straight up. He laid her over on a wing and rolled out, headed for the big wash he had located on his chart. The Comobabi.

Hector and Jason crossed the Ajo road. For miles their trail cut across a flat plain studded with creosote and greasewood. Low red-tawny mountains loomed ahead. The ground broke up again into a tortured tangle of rocky crags and narrow arroyos. The Ford climbed slowly, tires spinning on slabbed rock, chattering, then catching, lunging ahead a few feet.

The engine overheated. "She's losing water," Hector said. He wrapped a gunnysack around his arm and loosened the cap—it shot up into the air, rising on a blossom of steam. When it stopped frothing, he took a handful of cornmeal from the grub box and poured it into the radiator, added more water and capped it off again.

Another hour passed. They were in a long chute, a spill of rocky ground running down between two great spiny fins of red rock. The engine coughed and spluttered. Hector turned the Ford around and backed up, sawing, skittering on steep pitches. Hector sent Jason toiling ahead, lugging one end of the hundred-foot rope, to tie it off around a knob of rock. And then, with Jason again manning the rope at the drum on the rear wheel, the Ford winched itself up until it crested out onto a kind of natural shelf that skinned along the flank of the mountain. Steam wisped from the radiator, then something let go and it spewed in a white gush.

"There's a leak corn mush won't stop," Hector said. "Fetch me the tape, young sir." He stopped the engine and slid off his seat—he stood trembling, clutching the side of the cab. Jason rummaged in the toolbox and found the roll of tape.

"Why do you back up the hill?" he asked the old man, who hobbled forward, wrapping his arm again in the gunnysack to loosen the radiator cap. Steam fountained, subsided.

"Bless you, young trooper, it goes back to your friend who dropped the apple. The gasarene moves to the engine by gravity from the tank, which is under our hunkers here, and when she sets up too steep, you see, the tank is lower than the engine." Hector wrapped the hose with tape.

"Ah-h," Jason said. The answer filled that gap or void in his knowledge so perfectly that hearing it was like eating a full and satisfying meal. His mind was charged suddenly with flashes of insight, of *comprehension*—that force of gravity so lucidly made clear, the bursting gush of steam—and he envisioned himself strolling through great domed caverns inside the snorting engine, observing the thunderous explosions that drove the pistons in their cylinders, with the little valves clicking open and closed and the drive shaft spinning to turn the wheels, all in perfect time. And beneath those spinning wheels, the earth itself turning, cogged somehow to the turns of the whole mighty universe—a great and endless Juggernaut. Jason's brain reeled with the blinding perfection of it.

Hector poured water from the water bag into the radiator and capped it. He mounted wearily to the driver's seat. "You'll have to crank her this time—I am just about too wore out to pull her through."

Before he could stop himself, Jason blurted his alarm, "Is your sand running out?"

The old man leaned on the steering wheel and laughed, wagging his head. "Damn close to it, young sir. Twist her tail now."

Jason pointed. "We've got a flat tire."

Hector looked back. Less than a mile behind them, hundreds of feet lower, the coffinlike Essex fishtailed on gravel. Jason cupped his ear, heard the thin snarl of the distant engine. Hector shook his head. "Never mind the tire. Crank."

Jason bent to it, using both hands, digging in with his feet and heaving. The engine came alive and he ran to his seat and jumped aboard as the old man trod on the *go* pedal. Leaning far over to the left, the Ford bucked along the ledge, the tire plopping and slapping. She rocked, hung there, rocked back.

Jason thought she was sure to roll over. He clung to the top and swung himself out as far as he could, to hold her down.

The Ford rounded a crag and turned in, away from the fearful pitch of the mountain's flank. It bumped into a saddle, a depression between the mountain's craggy humps, and Jason saw a long defile open before them, mounting between great pillars of rock toward a turreted summit.

It was like the approach to a mountain castle. Hector swung the Ford around and backed up the defile. The defile opened into the castle courtyard, as Jason immediately perceived it to be. The Ford gave a final agonized cough and stopped. Boiling water frothed out through the turns of tape. They were wrapped in sudden silence—or near-silence, for Jason now heard the soft, hollow sighing of breeze among the rocks, and heard the ticking and snapping of hot metal in the engine.

"We're here," Hector said. "This here is my claim."

The mouth of a mine tunnel yawned in the bank to Jason's left, as he faced it, and a long tongue of rubble spilled into the defile. There was an *arrastra,* a circular *trinchera,* or trench, where in past years Hector's pack animal, harnessed to a swing-beam, had pulled a flat stone to pulverize the ore taken from the tunnel. The beam had fallen from its mount and the *trinchera* was half full of blown sand. The remains of a tent lay in tatters around a pole standing on a level patch of ground. A scrap of canvas attached to the pole like a banner fluttered out in the breeze. Lettered on it in faded paint were the words: *THE HONEST CITIZEN.* Jason jumped down and faced the pole, tugged his *kepi* straight and saluted.

"Hurry now, trooper," Hector barked. "We must post our pickets and unlimber our fieldpieces."

Freight trains were limited by law in the state of Arizona to a speed of forty miles per hour. One November morning in 1923, a Southern Pacific 2-8-0 Consolidation locomotive hauling a single flatcar rocketed from Tucson to *Healy* Bend at an average speed of 86 miles per hour. Normal operating pressure on the steam gauge was 130 pounds, but Engineer Ernie Shutterbush that day "stuck the cork in her and run the needle plumb out of sight," as he put it.

Planks were laid down from the flatcar to the ground at *Healy*, and Jack Perrell drove the big Stanley Mountain Wagon off the car with a hiss of steam and sibilant whisper of tires and headed south on the gullied Ajo road.

Farther south on that same road, Luther Hightower and his deputies braked to a stop where car tracks trailed mud and sand across the road. A look at the marks showed two sets of tracks. Luther wheeled after them, the Maxwell sprouting twin plumes of red mud from beneath the rear fenders.

Jackie Kid Argentos and Abe Cutter, riding along a hogback and telling lies to each other about women they had known, saw Luther's car turn off from a distance of three miles. They angled farther west to cut off the fugitives. A jackrabbit sprinted out of a clump of organ pipe. Jackie Kid whipped up the Mauser pistol with its wooden buttstock clipped in place and tracked the bounding rabbit with half a clip of 7.63mm bullets. He hit it with the sixth shot and blew it into three pieces, one of which kicked for a full minute while the Kid timed it. Once they crossed the Ajo-*Healy* road—and could get occasional glimpses from high ground of two (or was it three?) vehicles churning the sand ahead—they stopped, and Jackie Kid built a fire and piled on green creosote and greasewood.

Jackie Kid's deputies, the Grijalva brothers, returning without sleep from a night of uninterrupted revelry in the border village of Sonoita, drove back to Ajo, where they attempted to subdue burgeoning headaches with coffee and brandy, eggs and *chile verde* in the Copper City Cafe. They also bragged about being in on a manhunt. Sobering a little, they began to worry about Jackie Kid Argentos, whose potential for devastating wrath was well known to them. They climbed back into their Chevy truck and headed north on the road to Gila Bend.

A few miles out of town they saw a white plume of smoke—Jackie Kid's signal. They cut off on a track to an abandoned mine in that general direction and Mateo Grijalva floored the Chevy's throttle.

What none of these participants realized was that, after Luther Hightower's departure from *Healy* the evening before, the stationmaster there, unable to contain his excitement, telephoned his colleague in Yuma, Harley Millard, and told him all about the manhunt. Harley had breakfast in the Valley Cafe, as always, and a veteran Yuma County deputy named Walt heard him telling about it. Walt sprinted to the sheriff's office and caught Sheriff Raybold just coming in.

"They're sayin this is no ordinary manhunt," Walt gasped. "It's the biggest goddam manhunt the state ever seen!"

"Goddammit!" Raybold exploded, "you mean to tell me them people are running a manhunt in *my* goddamned county?"

Raybold mustered three more deputies and told them to arm themselves and he commanded Walt to get the county's Dodge outfitted with food, a tent and extra cans of fuel on the racks, and aboard a flatcar on the 8:40 to Tucson. He could hear the huffing switch engine in the yards and the clash of steel couplings as the train was being made up. He called the yardmaster and asked him for the flatcar.

"I can put you aboard one with some army vehicles," he was told, "some armored cars headed for Fort Sill, Oklahoma."

"Goddammit!" said Raybold. "If you can find the officer in charge of them cars, I want to speak to him."

The officer was Captain Aaron Pope, and he had spent a long time in grade after the excitement of France. He loved the concept of armored vehicles—had a long-term game going with his friend George Patton, to see who could come up with the most outrageous and devilish tactical and technical tricks with their armored mounts—so Captain Pope leapt with unabashed glee at the chance to telegraph his commanding officer at Fort Sill that his unit had been "pressed into emergency manhunt service by civil authorities." *Wait till George hears about this!* was his thought.

Some of this caught the attention of a reporter for the New York *World* named Victor Van Meter, who was passing through, eastbound, after an alcoholic tour of coast cities from Seattle south. He put in a call to an old newspaper friend in Tucson named Woodie Craddock, and learned that Craddock was covering a manhunt in the desert. Van Meter gleefully abandoned the woman he had picked up on the train from Los Angeles, ran to a pool hall across the street from the station and had them put up a large thermos jug full of martinis and a package of sandwiches. He made it to the flatcar as the train was pulling out.

Sheriff Raybold rode in the cab of the locomotive with the engineer, Charlie Slocum, who was delighted to have a chance to pour the coal to the big locomotive. It was something over sixty miles to a siding at the bridge over the San Cristobal wash. Once they were past the Telegraph Mountains, trainmen cut the train into two sections for the long Mohawk grade, cutting it directly behind the flatcar, leaving the bigger half on a siding while the much lighter forward section sped on to the San Cristobal siding. A ramp was rigged, the armored vehicles and police car drove off and sped away toward the southeast spewing rooster tails of sand, leaving the engineer to throw his locomotive into reverse and go back for the rest of his train.

Nor had the citizens of Ajo been idle. The boasts of the Grijalva brothers reverberated through the town. Since it was Sunday, a lot of people were headed for church. They saw what amounted to a caravan of vehicles forming up. Thoughts of worship were abandoned. Parishioners sprinted to join the caravan. Women packed baskets of food. Men rushed to the back rooms of the Copper City Cafe and Ace Pool Hall, where stocks of snakebite remedy dwindled rapidly under the onslaught. Two cars were filled with ladies who, like the Grijalva brothers, were bleary-eyed from a night of revelry, but dead game for action. The undisciplined caravan straggled out of town in loose order and wormed northward.

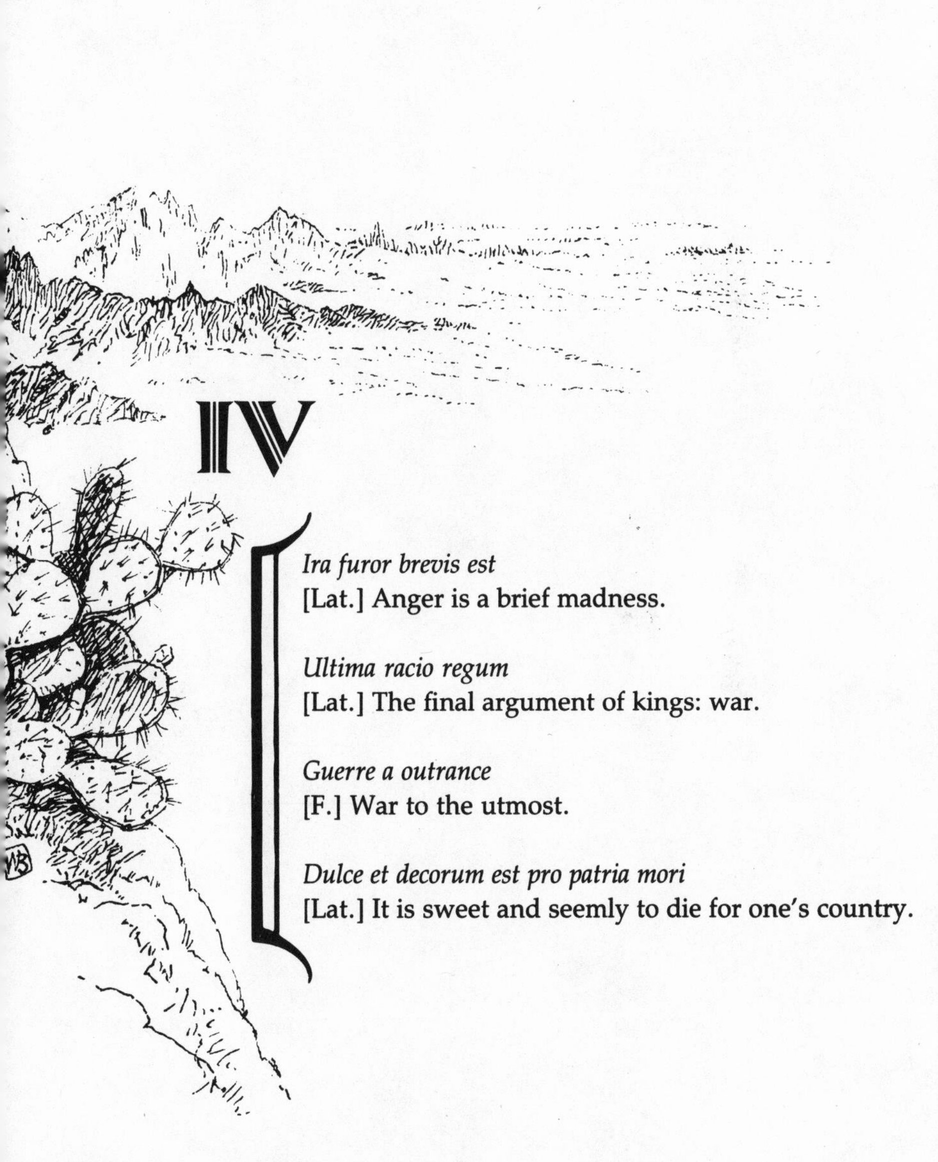

IV

Ira furor brevis est
[Lat.] Anger is a brief madness.

Ultima racio regum
[Lat.] The final argument of kings: war.

Guerre a outrance
[F.] War to the utmost.

Dulce et decorum est pro patria mori
[Lat.] It is sweet and seemly to die for one's country.

29

WET GROUND, gray light and numerous washouts made Hector Callard's old trail much harder to see from the air. Maynard picked it up briefly at the Comobabi, but lost it repeatedly. After almost three hours in the air, he landed on the straight stretch of road near the Zopilote Mine, woke up the foreman, who was sleeping in, and persuaded him to let him fill the Jenny's tank with company fuel. He pumped it himself from company drums and carried it in five-gallon cans a quarter-mile to the airplane where he climbed onto the tire and poured it in through a funnel lined with a chamois filter.

In the air again and flying west, Maynard feared he had overshot when he crossed the Ajo road, but after a time he saw a column of smoke off to his left. He banked over for a look at it, dropping to two hundred feet, and saw two men on horseback. They waved. One was holding what appeared to be a stubby carbine. *Hunters,* he thought, and then with a sudden chill he remembered what Craddock had said about deputies. He waved and turned north again, and almost immediately spotted the familiar boxy shape of the Essex, precariously clinging to the flank of a desert mountain.

And not far ahead of it, almost lost in a crag-walled chute below the pinnacled summit, was the old man's Ford truck. The mountain caused Maynard to think of a spiny desert horned toad, lifting its head for a look around while trailing a spiked tail. But this horned toad was of red-tawny rock and was a half-mile long and its head was almost five hundred feet above the desert floor.

Maynard throttled back as he approached. He saw the mine immediately, just above the truck—saw the tunnel opening, the dump below and the remains of a tent and odd scraps of trash and pieces of equipment, weathered boards and five-gallon tins, all cupped in a pinnacled fortress in the rocks with cliffs falling away to the desert floor on three sides. *It has to stop here,* he thought. No place left to go.

The Ford was turning around, backing, and Jason was running, trailing a rope. Maynard flew over him, slowing the Jenny, and as he passed he wagged his wings and waved. Banking away, he looked back and saw Jason's hesitant response. In the instant's look Maynard got of him, Jason's face looked drawn and pinched under the faded Legion *kepi.*

A pang shot through Maynard. Furious, he banked around steeply and put the Jenny into a dive, straight for the Essex. He held it to the last possible instant and just before he flashed over it, missing the roof by inches, the passenger door popped open and Red Durkin dived out into rocks and cactus.

Maynard suddenly spotted another vehicle bumping along up the twisting, spiky tail of the horned toad, an open touring car bearing three men—Luther Hightower's Maxwell, had he known. *More deputies!* he thought.

Maynard headed back toward the Ajo road, some thirty miles to the east. With the Jenny's speed in level flight holding at about seventy, it took him nearly a half-hour, but long before he reached it, he spotted Jack Perrell's huge red Mountain Wagon, last seen riding the flatcar from Tucson. He intercepted it, banking low and flew along in front of it until he saw a good stretch of ground.

He passed over the Mountain Wagon on his landing run and then he was down and rolling, but the flat light had not shown him the gullies cut in the sandy earth by the downpour. The Jenny's wheels dropped into a deep cut, she lurched, pitched up on her nose, and Maynard heard the sharp crack as the propeller shattered. He switched off the ignition, jumped down alongside the nose and ran to intercept the Stanley. Seconds later the big steam car wheeled up silently and Maynard jumped aboard next to Lexie. He planted a kiss on her lips before she could move, ignoring the startled look on Craddock's face. "They're up in those hills," Maynard said, pointing, "about thirty miles from here, and Durkin and Biggers and maybe some deputies are right behind them."

Only a few feet from where he could have followed the old man's Ford off the precarious ledge, Othello Biggers hung the front axle of the Essex on a knob of rock. And he must have cracked the oil pan back there someplace, because the needle on the pressure gauge had toppled over against the peg. The radiator gauge showed all red through the glass, and steam was roiling out of the seams of the engine hood. The engine stopped suddenly, but continued to rumble ominously. Just then, there was a sudden roar and the Jenny swept over, passing low above the crenelated pinnacle ahead. The Jenny wagged its wings, rolled into a tight bank and bore down on the Essex.

Red Durkin uttered a strangled screech, frantically kicked his door open and plunged headfirst into a clump of cactus and sharp rocks as the Jenny's landing gear swept over, a mouse whisker from tearing the roof off. Biggers climbed out. His nostrils were a little white and flaring slightly, but otherwise he was seemingly unperturbed.

"If you ain't too busy doing whatever you're doing down there, you could put some water in the raddiator," he told the recumbent Durkin, who was trying to pry a limb of buckhorn cactus off his arm.

"Goddammit, I was willing to give that old son of a bitch

the benefit of the doubt," Durkin raged. "Now he can strangle in his own guts, for all I care, and by god I'll tie the knot for him."

He struggled up and slapped the radiator cap ferociously to loosen it. The cap blew off with a pop and steam gushed around his hand. Durkin doubled up with agony. "Oh-h, gawd, she's *cooked*!" he cried, executing a crablike buck-and-wing while he caressed his parboiled hand.

After the steam subsided, Biggers grasped the projecting knuckle of the left front spring and heaved. The Essex shifted slightly and teetered outward. Biggers hastily caught the fender and steadied it. He looked up toward the pinnacle, hearing the insistent clatter of the Ford.

"We'll just park right here for now," he said. "Plenty of time to get unstuck after we've reasoned with that old party." Memory of last night's tarantulas popped into his mind. He looked around. "Hey! A man gets foolish, don't watch hisself, he could step on a fucking rattlesnake!"

Biggers reached into the car and lifted out his Springfield Model 1903 rifle. He snapped it to port arms and made the sling *pop* when he caught it in his left hand. "'Spec-*shun . . . harms*!" he barked, and whipped the bolt open. "Load and lock." He pulled a clip from a belt pouch, set it in the receiver slots and squashed bottle-necked .30-06 cartridges into the breech. "Ready on the firing line!"

"Ready, goddammit!" Durkin answered. He had his own .45 buckled on.

A black-headed Mexican buzzard made the mistake of gliding past the mountain. Biggers snapped the bolt closed, whipped the rifle to his shoulder and blew the buzzard out of the sky, all in one motion, and then levered the bolt again and hit the remains before they fell ten feet. Black feathers drifted down. He glared at Durkin, baring his teeth. *"Fortes fortuna juvat!"*

"What the hell—" Durkin mumbled disgustedly.

"Fortune favors the brave," Biggers said. "Let's go."

He pulled the Springfield's sling over his shoulder and moved forward toward the base of the pinnacle, with Durkin just behind him. He heard a peculiar whistling sound pass overhead and instinctively sprawled flat as the shell—or *whatever* it was!—exploded and showered the two of them with rock chips.

Biggers looked back. Smoke and dust curled off the rim of a crater thirty feet away. A stream of gravel rustled down past the Essex.

"Holy shit!" Durkin cried. "They've got *grenades*!"

Biggers scanned the pinnacle. "Hell they have. That's way over a hundred yards—it must be some kind of mortar."

He stared in disbelief at the battlements above. He could just see part of the Ford's front end, and he realized its engine was no longer running.

"They've stopped! We've run 'em into a hole! Now by god they'll have to talk."

He motioned to Durkin to follow him and scrambled forward, keeping his eyes on the Ford. As he moved, something—a shadow, *a spear, for Chrissake*?—lofted from the rocks and streaked upward, emitting an unearthly shriek as it flew. "Oh-h, *no*!" he heard Durkin moan. The shriek grew louder. It was terrifying. He heard a kind of whinny from Durkin. *BLA-A-MMM!* Shards of rock pelted them and fumes hung in the air. Glass broke in the Essex with a musical tinkling sound and the car rocked unsteadily, its outer door flapping like a broken wing.

"It's gotta be a mortar," Biggers snarled.

"Nah, there's no bang when she goes off. It's a fuckin rocket grenade!" Durkin said—and dove facedown again as another streak launched from the rocks. A warbling ululation filled the air, the cry of a berserk loon. *BLA-A-MMM!* It overshot, landing on the slope below the Essex. Boulders rolled, bounded away. The car's rear end slid downhill. Only the knob of rock under its front axle was holding it.

"We need *cover*!" Biggers said, pointing to a space between two big rocks. They lunged to their feet just as another missile wailed down upon them. It went through the roof of the Essex and blew up in an orange fireball. Coachwork sailed off the mountain. The chassis and engine tumbled down engulfed in burning gasoline.

Heedless of danger, Biggers ran to watch his beloved machine plummet down. "Who's going to pay for my Essex?" he cried. At that moment, a bullet spanged off the rocks close to him and whined away. Biggers ducked, stung by rock fragments, as bullets peppered the rocks around him and a rapid-fire string of gunshots sounded from below.

Jackie Kid Argentos and Abe Cutter, watching the two cars, heard two shots fired. A ricochet whined over their heads. Black feathers drifted out of the sky.

"Goddammit!" the Kid shouted, "they're taking us under fire!"

They whipped up their horses and reached the broken ground at the foot of the mountain just as the explosions started. A terrifying avalanche of leaping boulders bore down upon them. They galloped under a cliff overhang, their horses plunging and bucking while rocks, gravel and dust spilled past them. Both men leaped off their horses. More explosions boomed above. The Kid ran out for a look up, and dived again for cover when a blazing automobile chassis crashed next to him, splattering gobs of fire, chunks of metal, flaming upholstery and tires.

"The sonsabitches done that a-purpose!" the Kid screamed to Abe Cutter. He saw a figure on the skyline above and fired a warning shot from his Mauser. Flames crackled around him. He fired off the whole clip. Cutter moved out next to him, took a hefty pull from his tequila bottle and brought his .30-.30 into play.

The Grijalva brothers in their Chevy truck skidded to a stop forty yards back, leaped out and ran for cover from the pelting fragments of blazing bodywork. They heard powerful engines roaring down upon them from their left, beyond the column of smoke from the wrecked Essex.

"Thank God you've come!" Jackie Kid yelled. "We need reinforcements!" The Kid and Abe Cutter maintained fire on the gunmen above. Both Grijalva brothers opened up in the direction of the engine noise, unable yet to see that they were firing upon elements of motorized United States Cavalry.

A mile away, on the other side of the narrow mountain, just as the orange fireball blossomed off the mountain, Sheriff Raybold of Yuma County roared out of the San Cristobal wash leading a flotilla of six 1922 Dodge U.S. Army touring cars wearing sheets of quarter-inch armor plate painted olive drab. Raybold stopped and signaled the other cars to gather around for a hurried conference. He was somewhat shaken by the size of the fireball, but determined not to be intimidated.

"Captain, I suggest we sew up the perimeter with your armored vehicles while the peace officers move up to disarm the fugitives."

Captain Aaron Pope was unwilling to leave all the real action to the civil authorities, particularly since the New York *World* reporter, Van Meter, was riding with him in his vehicle. *Christ, if only Patton could see this!*

"They may try to bust out while you're going up there," he pointed out. "I may be *forced* to engage them."

A fusillade of rapid fire punctuated his words—shots fired by the deputies from Ajo, though he could not know it. Raybold nodded sagely. "I rely on your judgment, then."

"First, though," said the captain, "who the hell are we after? How will I know them?"

Raybold's face, already florid, purpled. "Goddammit, Captain, if the sons of bitches start shooting at you, that ought to tell you *something*!"

The captain flushed as more explosions boomed on the mountain. Without another word, he waved his cars into action—three wheeled away to the left and three to the right, souped-up heavy-duty engines roaring like aircraft. A steel post bearing a .30-caliber Browning machine gun jutted from each vehicle, and in the tonneau locker of each there reposed a Stokes mortar and two dozen rounds of ammunition.

Captain Pope and his three cars rounded the head of the mountain and proceeded along its far flank. A column of black smoke rose before them from terrain that was a confused tangle of rocks, mesquite and cactus. Clots of blazing wreckage clung here and there down the mountainside. Small-arms fire from the weapons of the deputies from Ajo chattered from the vicinity of the smoke ahead of them. He heard shouts. A bullet whined off his vehicle's armor.

"So be it! They're asking for it!" he said to Van Meter. He leaped into the back next to Corporal Hobbins and together they unstrapped the Stokes mortar and locked its tripod feet into mounting clips. It took thirty seconds to put the first shell into trajectory.

"Bracket the bastards," he told Hobbins. "One long, one short, and then blow the shit out of em!"

If the mountain resembled a great horned toad, Hector Callard and Jason were defending its head, protected there by a coronet of spines—their pinnacled redoubt—the Essex had just been blown off its left shoulder; Biggers and Durkin were clawing for cover among the rocky spines on its neck; Jackie Kid Argentos was down under the overhanging cliffs of its rib cage; and Luther Hightower's party was jolting up the curving, spiked tail.

Luther stopped his Maxwell short of taking the precarious ledge trail out along the horned toad's left flank. Heights bothered Luther, and he was fretting, anyway, over the damage to his Maxwell, so he got out, waving his deputies to follow, and he was proceeding on foot when Biggers' two rifle shots sounded ahead. They watched a buzzard explode into a messy puff of black feathers. They were within fifty yards of the Essex when the curve of the ledge along the horned toad's flank brought it into view. Just then the first missile exploded and they jumped for cover among the rocks. Moments later they were watching the flaming wreckage of the Essex spill down the mountain, and the uniformed figure of Othello Biggers appeared. *Soldiers?* thought Luther.

Bullets kicked up dirt around the solider and he ducked out of sight. The stunned deputies from *Healy* watched helplessly as successive explosions rained dirt and gravel onto them. And then armored cars came into view below. *Armored cars?*

"Luther," Leo Kohner said, "what the hell is the army doing here? I never counted on no fucking *war*!"

Captain Pope, for his part, was unable to see Jackie Kid Argentos and the Grijalva brothers, who were in good cover, but he saw the Maxwell above them and drew the obvious conclusion.

"Hobbins, this is our chance to cut off their retreat!" said Pope. They adjusted their Stokes, and moments later the dazed deputies from *Healy* watched Luther's Maxwell become the center of a bursting firestorm.

The cavalcade of automobiles from Ajo, snaking along like a giant sidewinder in the wake of the Grijalva brothers, crept to a halt at a respectful distance from the mountain where, it appeared, a battle was raging. An old-timer, a Confederate vet named Lucas Skaggs who had fought at Lookout Mountain, said that this reminded him of that engagement and was, if anything, a particle noisier. People sat in their cars to watch or took up seats on the sandy banks of the washes. Ladies spread cloths and set out baskets of food, just as had been done sixty-two years earlier at the first battle of Bull Run. Someone had thought to bring a tub of iced beer. Tequila and rum, a mere twenty-five cents a quart in Sonoita, were in better supply by far than water. Miles to the north, a similar cavalcade moved south from *Healy,* turning off to the west to follow the tracks of the Stanley mountain wagon's huge tires.

30

JASON SAW and heard the first two shots from the rifle of Othello Biggers, saw the buzzard blown into pieces. A terrible fear shot through him—it was as if every fiber of his body were suddenly encased in ice. He tried to cry out, but his voice was a dry croak. Inside the icy shell, he felt his heart pound. Its thunder filled his ears. Hector's voice sounded as if from afar, a distant shout—"*Man the fieldpiece!*"

Jason tried to move, to run, *anything*!, but felt himself sag to his knees next to the truck, where he crouched, his teeth chattering wildly.

A misty veil appeared to cloud his eyes. Hector's figure, dreamlike, towered over him. Dazedly, he watched the old man.

Hector mounted his springpole—that same twelve-foot-long springy ash pole that had helped him work the bellows at his forge all these years—back of the cab by wiring its butt to stakes set along the edges of the truck bed. The pole stuck out to the side like a casting rod. A light block and tackle was fastened to another stake on the rear of the truck bed. He clapped the free end of the tackle onto a thumblike iron hook fitted on the end of the pole, and with quick pulls on the tackle drew the tip of the pole back, back, back—until it quivered with tension.

"Pass me a Stinger!" the old man cried, his voice distant, faintly piercing Jason's shell of fear. Jason shivered, helpless. Dimly through the haze, he saw the old man reach to a bundle on the truck bed and take a long dart or arrow, which had a stick of dynamite and a willow whistle wired to its tip behind a hook of twisted wire. Hector hooked the dart's tip to a forged fitting on the end of the quivering springpole, and then he slapped a trigger that released the pole from the tackle. It shot forward like a great buggy whip, propelling the missile up and out. An eerie scream filled the air as it arced toward the position of the two awl company agents. Jason saw them dive for cover between huge rocks as the missile hit and exploded. Rock fragments whined, smoke drifted.

The old man laughed and shook his fist. He turned and pulled Jason to his feet. "You must help, young trooper, or we're goners." He rubbed Jason's paralyzed hands, slapped his cheeks gently, as if awakening him from a sound sleep. He put a dart in Jason's hands. He adjusted the pole tip upward, for more range, hauled it back with the tackle. *"Pass me a Stinger!"* Jason clapped the Stinger into place. The old man held Jason's hand on the trigger beneath his own.

"Fire!" he cried, and the missile screeched aloft—and with it, mysteriously, went Jason's fear. *Blam-mm-m,* the missile exploded below, and a ragged shout of exultation was torn from Jason's throat. And another missile was in the air screeching down before the dust settled. And another. He saw the Essex explode, heard with wonder and fierce delight a savage howl rip from his own throat.

Black smoke from burning gasoline, rubber and upholstery drifted through the battlements. Hector Callard looked down with satisfaction upon the fiery trail of the demolished Essex.

Jason now heard a hornetlike buzz, and in seconds it grew into the roaring of many engines. Captain Pope's motorized column charged out of the San Cristobal wash. Jason scrambled up among the rocks on the north side of the redoubt. He beckoned to Hector to join him. They had a clear view of terrain on both sides of the mountain. They saw a fleet of cars breaking formation, fanning out around the base of the mountain. Jason's keen eyes discerned the sinister tapering snouts and jutting machine guns of the armored vehicles.

To the northwest, they saw a large red vehicle approaching at high speed, its wheels spraying wings of mud, followed at a distance of two or three miles by a slower-moving column. Turning to the south they saw another long line of vehicles breaking their advancing column formation to swing out of line and stop. People dismounted and took up positions along a broad front.

"We're surrounded!" Jason said. "I counted eight cars—some with machine guns! And more reinforcements moving up!"

Hector Callard nodded serenely. "It don't surprise me none. I *expected* the sons of bitches to call in their mercenaries long before this. Let's man our fieldpiece."

They returned to the truck. Jason lifted the Stingers one by one from the bundle and passed them as the old man fitted them to the pole and fired. No two were exactly alike. Each had a light cane shaft some four feet long with a featherlike fin wired to the tail. On some, the fin was a piece of shingle, on others, a piece of flattened tin can. Fastened to the nose of each with baling wire was a willow whistle and an eight-ounce stick of Red Cross Extra Sixty Percent Dynamite, with a twelve-penny nail punched into its tip and a blasting detonator taped to the nail. The Stinger was a dart-borne percussion grenade, propelled by Hector's crude but serviceable *ballista* in strict accordance to the Newtonian principles governing propulsion and objects in flight. Weapons like it had leveled cities and castles in ages past.

Shouts and sounds of gunshots drifted up from below where the Essex had fallen. Hector swung a few degrees and lofted a Stinger down the mountainside. It dropped from sight and seconds later they heard the explosion. Smoke boiled up, followed by more shouts and gunfire as the Grijalva brothers joined the Ajo deputies in that sector of the fray.

The Stinger's springpole launcher was wired to two stakes in the bed of the truck. Hector could command another field of fire simply by moving one or the other of the two stakes to a different hole and by elevating or depressing the tip of the springpole. Hearing now the roar of engines from the armored vehicles encircling them from the north, he pivoted his entire rig and tackle and fired a string of Stingers up and over the pinnacle in the general direction of the snarling engines, allowing a little lead for the moving vehicles. Far below and out of sight, explosions flowered on the desert floor.

Othello Biggers and Red Durkin, pinned down by blasts from airborne grenades, heard a squeal of brakes from the armored vehicles below the cliff. A chatter of small-arms gunfire erupted from that sector, followed shortly by a distinctive *crump*. Biggers—seasoned infantryman that he was—instantly recognized the sound.

"Stokes mortars, for Chrissake!" he bellowed at Durkin. Both men tried to burrow deeper.

Hector swung his *ballista* with telling effect, lobbing Stingers onto both elements of Captain Pope's armored team, as well as onto the positions occupied by the awl company agents and, below them, Jackie Kid Argentos and his deputies, who now found themselves under a return barrage of mortar fire from the vehicles commanded by Captain Aaron Pope.

Pope's second-in-command, Sergeant Kryzwycki, dazed from the near misses of what he took to be mortar fire, decided that Pope had run into a trap. "Guide on me!" he shouted to the other cars. Another charge exploded next to him. He wheeled his bucking vehicle in a rain of blown sand and brush and raced around the base of the mountain to the aid of his captain, passing a dazed and confused Sheriff Raybold.

Kryzwycki caught sight of Pope's vehicles, a quarter-mile ahead, half-obscured by brush and smoke. At that moment, a

Stinger exploded in front of him. He flagged his three cars to a halt. It was perfectly clear to him what had taken place—Captain Pope's force had been swallowed up, massacred, and the enemy was turning the captain's guns upon Kryzwycki, himself.

"Those fuckers have overrun the captain! Break out the goddam Stokeses!" Tears of grief for his fallen captain streamed down his cheeks. He hauled back on the knob of the Browning's charging handle and fired a stream of .30-caliber lead toward the enemy. Soldiers leapt to the Stokes lockers, their well-rehearsed movements as precise and coordinated as those of musicians in a symphony orchestra, and in seconds the armored cars were thumping under the recoil of Stokes mortars.

The reporter, Van Meter, was huddled in a forward seat of Captain Pope's vehicle. He sank down until his head was below the armor. He pulled his portable typewriter onto his lap, opened it and fed in a sheet of paper. He uncorked his vacuum bottle and quaffed a slug of martini. All hell was breaking loose around him. His nostrils burned with the smell of cordite. Bullets stuttered off the armor. Shrapnel sang over his head. The car rocked as mortar rounds exploded. Van Meter began to type, punching the keys with two fingers. His title was ARMAGEDDON IN THE DESERT. He began: "This reporter is under fire as these words are written. The sinister forces of anarchy have been brought to bay in the Arizona desert by an outraged citizenry dedicated to freedom from wanton terror. . . ."

The fireball that rolled off the mountain when the Essex blew up was visible for miles. When Lexie saw it she covered her face with her hands. When she looked again, the whole mountain appeared to shudder as explosions rippled along its crest and one flank. She stared at Amanda, also speechless with shock and horror. Jack Perrell shoved the throttle lever almost to the stop on the notched quadrant. Broad web belts running the width of the seats held the passengers in. The big car bucked and soared, crunched through brush and cactus, its cleated tires churning sand.

Perrell struck the Ford's original trail and followed it up the twisting grade—the tail of the lizard. It swung out to the left, and for a moment they saw the field of action along that whole side of the mountain. Less than a hundred yards ahead and somewhat higher, Luther Hightower's Maxwell was being reduced to rubble by mortar fire. Beyond that, the fate of the Essex was clearly written in smoke and wreckage. A quarter-mile farther on, on flat ground below, a trio of armored cars was churning mad patterns in the sand as more explosions blossomed among them. The din was deafening.

All this disappeared from sight as Perrell followed the curve back in toward the spine of the mountain. He wheeled the Stanley into a narrow slot between great slabs of rock and stopped there.

"We'll have to go on foot from here," Perrell said.

"Right," Costello said. "We'll have cover that way."

"'S crazy!" J. W. growled through wired teeth. "'M not goin no goddam war!—get goddam head shot off!"

He came out of the car grunting and swearing, but with surprising agility under Costello's persuasive grip. They set off uphill through the rocks with Perrell. Craddock and the two women scrambled after them. Maynard started to follow, but then he saw an opening to his right and took off at a run. He broke out of the rocks onto open ledge low along the flank while the others followed the spine.

Maynard had the advantage of having seen the mountain from the air, if only for a few seconds, and he knew exactly where Jason and the old man were holding out. Having spent four years in the grimmest, most murderous war in history, where events had remained mired in insanity, he was appalled at the conflagration raging on and about the mountain, but not really surprised. It appeared to him that confusion was the principal architect of this firestorm. He thought that if he could get to Jason, he might actually nip out with him under cover of that confusion; but if order was restored, his chances would be slim indeed. Of all the people on the mountain, he was the only one who was able to put the hellish storm of fire to good use. Except, perhaps, for Jason and Hector Callard, who both now exulted in it.

Maynard ran along that steeply sloping north flank, dropping and scrambling forward on all fours to keep from sliding on down as the pitch steepened under him.

Below, Sheriff Raybold had left his car to attempt to climb up, but the cliff was too steep for a footing and, despite his explicit advice to Captain Pope, he himself didn't really know who, up there, ought to be wearing cuffs. There were just a hell of a lot of people running around that mountain, it seemed to him. When he saw a man running and scuttling along its flank two hundred feet above him, he yelled, "You there, halt! Police! Halt, goddammit! Halt! goddam you!" And then he started shooting. His deputies joined him in the fusillade, grateful for a target.

Bullets whined off the rocks. Maynard sprinted recklessly, leaped a crevice and gained the shelter of the lizard's shoulder. From there he crawled along a shallow fissure, angling up toward the critter's neck. Raybold and his men, unable to get a clear fix on him, ran along below, firing whenever they glimpsed the elusive fugitive.

Above, hearing fire from this sector, Jason and Hector swung their *ballista* and lobbed a couple of Stingers that rained gravel on Sheriff Raybold, who retreated through the smoke, waving his men to the relative safety of the car. By now, cars from the *Healy* cavalcade had pulled up, disgorging curious passengers. Later cars pulled up heedlessly in front of the early arrivals, eliciting hoots and name-calling. A fistfight started. Raybold's deputies busied themselves establishing order among the spectators.

Maynard found a chimneylike fold of rock beneath the lizard's chin and began working his way up. The cliff towered over him. He clung to handholds for a moment, resting.

Spread out below him and three or four hundred yards apart were two contingents of olive drab vehicles—*holy smoke! Armored cars? Mortars?* Through drifting smoke and blown dirt he watched the gunners methodically dropping missiles down the tubes of the mortars. Drivers gunned the snarling cars a few yards in violent evasive action and took up new positions as the old positions disappeared in smoke and flame. Maynard scrambled on, up and up.

Hector fumbled for the iron hook on the springpole. The tackle in his trembling hand weighed a ton. He hooked it, hauled back on the rope, stopped, his senses reeling. *You old buzzard! Don't quit on me now!* He hauled again. The rope slipped through his fingers, chirping in the pulley. Hector toppled against the truck bed and then slid to the ground as Jason leapt to help him. His eyelids fluttered. There was a roaring in his ears, a gray misty curtain before his eyes. The sharp fumes of explosives became suddenly the tangy salt-sea smell of blown spray on the Oregon shore. Hector walked out of himself, strolled on the sand, looked back and saw his little boys capering and waving. *No, don't let go . . .*

A white blur through the mist. The lad. *Ah-h, yes, young sir. I'm a little tired, to be sure, but lean close now, listen . . .*

Jason cradled the old man's head, saw his lips working, but no sound came. Tears flooded Jason's eyes. He brushed them away angrily, leaving smeared tracks on his dirty cheeks. A dry husk of sound came from the old man's lips. Jason bent down.

"Time for it now . . . you swore me a mighty oath. Matter of honor, understand? You take . . . Juggernaut . . . skin out of here and hide. Hide it. Let . . . sons of bitches find me, see? Nobody bother you . . . little kid. Damn good trooper, though. . . . Go on, *git!*"

Jason pulled the folded tarp over and pillowed Hector's head on it. The old man's face wore a serene smile. He fumbled his pipe and matches from a vest pocket. "Strike a light for my pipe," he whispered. Jason did so. Hector puffed. "Git, now."

Jason scrambled to the cab, reached in and pulled out the wooden dynamite box that held the Juggernaut. He turned to run and slammed into the hard belly of Othello Biggers.

31

THE COUNTY MAN! Jason knew him instantly, despite the uniform, the blackened face. Terror shot through him. His knees trembled. He backed against the rock crag, clutching the dynamite box. The county man's lips were skinned back over his teeth in a ghastly rubbery smile. The whites of his eyes gleamed, showing clear around the pupils. Behind him was a stringy, seedy, grinning, buck-toothed man. Both were sooty and scorched, with torn clothing and bloody scratches on their faces and hands.

"Ah-h," breathed the county man through clenched teeth, "still playing hooky, are we? There's a good lad now. Don't fret. Spose we take a look at what's in that there box." Still Jason did not move.

"Run, lad!" croaked Hector.

"Afraid of the gun, is that it?" Biggers went on warmly. "Don't be afraid, boy, the gun is for rattlesnakes—I have a mortal fear of the buggers."

He set his rifle aside and reached to put a hand on Jason's shoulder, but Jason scuttled back, staying just clear. "Kindly give me the box," the county man growled through his smile, "to avoid mischief, is the thing of it, understand, boy?"

"Belt the little bastard," the buck-toothed man said, sidling around the Ford to get on the up-side of him. "Just hand the whole thing over, kid. No one wants to hurt you."

Jason licked his lips. "All right," he whispered. "I'll do it."

Hector moaned in protest. "No-o, *no*, boy!"

Jason laid back a corner of the flour sack and thrust his hand down inside. The polished brass framework of the Juggernaut gleamed like gold. Smoke drifted past them. Salvos of mortar fire roared below and a machine gun chattered in the distance.

"Here!" Jason said, a twisted, haunted smile on his dirty face. He pulled wadded sacking out of the box, whipped it—tossed a squirming cluster of tarantulas at the county man—and then snatched the Juggernaut free of the box, ducking, running, as the county man screamed and pawed at the hairy spiders now crawling on his face and neck.

Jason ran up past the fallen tent, hearing the hoarse and desperate shrieks of the county man behind him. Cradling the Juggernaut, he darted among spiky pinnacles cresting the lizard's head—glancing back, he saw the other man running after him. Desperation seized him. For a moment he froze. His brain fumed with turmoil. Images flashed behind his eyelids—the chase, the thrill and horror of the bombardment. Below, the desert floor erupted with explosions, deadly yellow-red flowers.

Feet pounded on stone behind him. Jason squeezed between rocks and sprang out onto a ledge—the very tip of the reptile's nose. He heard the scuffling of shoe leather right behind him. Trapped! He drew back the Juggernaut to hurl it—he would never let the agents have it. *"No-o-o!"* he cried out, lunging to throw as his footing gave way beneath him.

Powerful hands snatched at him and pulled him down onto the ledge. Jason squirmed, kicking, tried to bite. His head was caught in an armlock. A man's voice spoke a single word in his ear.

"Mesquite!"

His password. Jason shivered. The fight drained out of him.

"Javelina!" he said.

They heard grunts, heavy breathing, scraping and rustling as Red Durkin squirmed between rocks to get to the ledge. Maynard pulled Jason out of the way, rose to his feet and set himself as Durkin leaped out onto the open ledge.

He hit Durkin just below his wishbone. "No extra charge, pal," Maynard said. "This one is on the house." He hit him again. Durkin sat down hard, gagging noises coming from his throat. The service pistol clattered out of his hand. Maynard picked it up and tucked it in his waistband.

"Do you want to discuss this further?" Maynard said. "Or have we reasoned enough?"

Durkin made feeble swimming gestures. His face had a greenish cast. His mouth opened and closed. He resembled a beached fish. Maynard hauled him to his feet. "How about we try for the dropkick record?" he asked Durkin, who, weaving on his feet, looked down almost five hundred feet to the desert floor and shook his head vigorously.

"Hey, look," Jason said. "They've stopped shooting."

It was true. Through the smoke they saw a bandanna being waved from one of the armored cars, a khaki shirt from another. The voice of Captain Aaron Pope rang out below, incredulous, quavering.

"For Christ's sake, Kryzwycki, is that *you*?"

Costello was impeded by having to hustle J. W. along. Lexie, Amanda and Jack Perrell scrambled ahead, up the chute, followed closely by Woodie Craddock. The old man's Ford was almost obscured by smoke. They burst through it. Othello Biggers was standing against a great slab of rock with his hands high in the air. Hector Callard was sitting up, leaning against the rear wheel of the Ford, smiling and puffing his pipe. He held a stick of dynamite with a very short fuse poised over the bowl of the smoking pipe, and on his lap was a wooden box half full of dynamite.

"I'm selling tickets to Kingdom Come," the old man said happily. "Who's buying?"

"Uncle Hector!" Lexie said. "There's no need of that now. We're here to help you. Where's Jason?"

"Gone. Got away, I hope. One of these bastards was after him." He nodded at Biggers.

"Can't you get him to put that thing down?" Biggers pleaded.

"*Please,* Uncle Hector."

"Nope. When the boat is loaded, we can all go together." The old man puffed vigorously. Sparks flew. His hand was trembling.

They heard footsteps. Red Durkin shambled into their midst. He seemed to be having trouble breathing and was clutching his middle. Behind him were Jason and Maynard. Jason was holding the Juggernaut in his arms. He knelt beside the old man.

"They didn't get it. We saved it. Look." He held out the Juggernaut.

A look of consternation twisted Biggers' face. "Get *what*?" He and Durkin stared at each other. *"What the hell is that thing?"*

"You know what it is," Hector said. "Now watch 'em try to squirm off the hook."

"What is it?" Biggers' voice was edged with horror.

"I told you they was slick, Lexie—slick as snot on a brass doorknob," the old man said. "The bastards are trained agents."

"Agents?" Biggers said helplessly. *"Agents?"* He saw J. W. Whitlock. "Where the hell have you been, Whitlock, and what the hell are you doing here?"

"You bassards tried . . . *kill me*!" J. W. raged. "Tried kill m'boy!"

"Agents?" Biggers said again, dazedly wagging his head.

* * *

The silence was eerie after the din of battle. The lawmen cautiously identified themselves and each other. They agreed that the mountain was in Raybold's county and it would be up to him to make the necessary arrests; but the others, as cooperating peace officers, went along to assist him in identifying the fugitives, who fortunately appeared to have been subdued.

When it was clear that the shooting was over, ranks of spectators surged forward, gathering silently by the armored cars to watch the procession come down the trail.

Captain Pope, red-faced, assembled his flotilla of battered vehicles near the tail of the lizard, where the trail came off the mountain, to assist the peace officers. Next to him, Van Meter swallowed a jolt of his now-tepid martini and started a new paragraph: *The cacophony of battle gives way to an expectant hush as grim-faced officers*—he glanced up at Captain Pope, standing next to him—*and troopers in khaki form ranks to apprehend the sinister*—Van Meter remembered he had already used *sinister* and made a mental note to change it later—*gang now brought to bay . . .*

A buzz of murmuring sounded as the teams of lawmen appeared. They were escorting a big Stanley Mountain Wagon. The top of the wagon was folded down. Behind the driver sat a small and very dirty boy, about a seventy-pounder, and next to him, supported by a young woman, was a frail old man with wild-looking, spiky white hair.

The murmuring grew louder. "Where are the goddam outlaws?" someone called.

"Took a hell of a lot of badges to bring in that little kid," a big shift boss from Ajo said.

Up on the car, Hector saw them gathered there—the People. His face cracked in a serene smile. He nudged Jason. "Show 'em the Juggernaut, boy. It belongs to them."

Jason held up the Juggernaut. Sunlight breaking through the clouds flashed off the polished brass.

"We saved the Juggernaut!" exulted Jason. "We saved it for the People!"

A ragged cheer rippled through the crowd. Hector waved. "Tell 'em, lad—it's Power, unlimited Power for the People! It will get their necks out from under the yoke forever!"

"Power for the People!" Jason cried, holding up the glinting Juggernaut.

People cheered, whistled and clapped. Hector waved again. His mind wandered a little, vaulting easily over threescore years of time—to a parade back in Bosworth, Missouri, May of '65, himself with gold sergeant's chevrons on his sleeves, astride Dan, his big bay charger. And Dan pranced and capered as Hector waved. "Hurrah, boys, for Union!" he cried.

"Hear that, men?" shouted the shift boss. "A union man!" More cheers rang out. The shift boss' wife handed him a soft tomato from her picnic hamper. A moment later, Sheriff Raybold's hat went sailing, knocked off in a splatter of tomato. Wild-eyed, he raised his shotgun and shook it at the shift boss, who peeled off his coat as he stepped out of the crowd.

"You badge-happy son of a bitch!" he bellowed. "D'you think you bastards can threaten working people and their families?"

An ominous roar rumbled through the crowd. Men were seen to push women and children to the rear. Some picked up rocks. Hats were tugged down, sleeves rolled up.

Othello Biggers stepped forward, stood at attention in front of Sheriff Raybold. *"Bat-tal-li-on-n-nn!"* he sang out, his voice that same thunderous trumpet that in November of 1918 had brought whole divisions to attention for review by General Pershing, Clemenceau, and Generals Joffre and Haig.

"Ba-tal-li-on-n-nn, a-tensh-hut!"

Miners, deputies, soldiers stood to attention, transfixed by the golden parade-ground voice. *"Pre-sen-n-nt, ha-arms!"* cried Biggers. His '03 Springfield leaped into his hands with a pop of the sling as it slapped his palm and then was smartly turned to the vertical, pausing there but an instant before Biggers whipped the piece into the spin, stop, spin and whirl of the Queen Anne salute—the humming rifle a hypnotic blur of precisely timed motion—Biggers a one-man drill team finishing on one knee before stomping back to attention and present arms. "*Pass in review!*" sang out Biggers, waving the Mountain Wagon forward.

Captain Pope and his soldiers saluted smartly. The people cheered and whistled. The deputies saluted raggedly. Woodie Craddock had not saluted in five years, but he saluted now—in his mind he was composing the lead to his own story: *Today, heroes came down from the mountain. . . .*

Hector Callard returned the salutes gravely. Jason stood holding the Juggernaut aloft with one hand, his *kepi* at a jaunty angle as he saluted palm out, in the manner of the French Foreign Legion.

32

THE BIG RED Mountain Wagon was escorted all the way to *Healy* by the cavalcade of vehicles, including Captain Pope's battered team of armored cars. Law officers were seen to remove their badges and slip them out of sight into pockets. The Mountain Wagon and armored vehicles were loaded back aboard flatcars, two of them, for the trip to Tucson.

Van Meter, the New York *World* reporter, managed a quick refill of his Martini jug at the hotel in *Healy*, and then caught a ride with Woodie Craddock on the flatcar. Van Meter had a head start, but Craddock was soon comfortably squiffed as well. He saw the corner of a piece of paper sticking out of Van Meter's typewriter case and insisted upon looking at it.

"*Great* title!" he said warmly. "Wish I'd thought of it first." Van Meter simpered. But then, as Craddock read on, his face grew livid. "What the hell kind of drivel is this?" he demanded. "'. . . sinister forces of anarchy'! Have you taken leave of your senses? That boy and the old gentleman are *heroes*, goddammit! You want a line for your goddam story, I'll give you one. How about starting with Tennyson? 'Far on the ringing plains of windy Troy.' No, never mind, I'll use that one myself."

"I've, uh, maybe got some rewriting to do," Van Meter said. "The picture kind of changed out there."

"Hell it did. You just didn't see it. Goddammit, this thing is a parable of how wars get started. Give me another belt of that stuff, Van Meter, and I'll help you write it."

Hector Callard, covered with blankets and with his head pillowed, slept next to Lexie and Jason in the second seat. Jason said to Lexie, "The house got blown up—where are we going to take Uncle Hector?"

"I thought at first he should go to a hospital," Lexie said, "but that might be hard for him to understand. I talked to a lady named Marietta—when? a day or two ago; it seems ages—and she said she was intending to have guests come into her home, old people like herself, for company, understand? There are some ladies with her now. And she said she would especially like to have a couple of gentlemen. Supposing you come with me and we decide together about that?"

Jason nodded. "I think the company would be good for him. Maybe it's company he needed all along."

Jack Perrell was studying the Juggernaut. He asked Jason if he could hold it. "Machinery is my game, and I have to tell you, I've never seen a prettier piece of work." He moved the little flywheel and the pivoting momentum arms. "I see the principle of it. Have you ever seen it work?"

Jason shook his head. "No. He hasn't dared to run it—he has to finish the brake first, to keep it from going too fast and burning itself up. When that's done, we're going to give it to the People."

"A brake," Perrell said, glancing at Maynard. "Neat idea."

"It will need a little motor to get it started," Jason said, "then when it reaches a certain speed, it will run by itself . . . forever."

"Maybe it needs something like the motors that run dentists' drills. I could help you with that," Perrell said. And then very carefully he said, "Have you studied, m-mm, the laws of mechanics, of physics, that is, regarding motion and friction, or, say, the idea of entropy?"

Maynard looked away uneasily. Jason frowned slightly. He looked over at the soundly sleeping old man, and then he looked back at Maynard and Perrell, his blue-gray eyes very level and steady—and *old,* thought Perrell. *The kid is older than I am.*

"You mean," Jason said, "the idea that perpetual motion is antithetical to entropy? And that the laws of motion and thermodynamics are, um, immutable?"

Maynard and Perrell stared at each other. Jason rummaged in the bundle at his feet and brought out a book. Perrell read the title. *Addison's First Book of Science.* Maynard was startled to see it.

"Captain Gaylen gave me this, and I've been studying it. Especially the parts you're talking about." Jason did not elaborate. After a pause, he said, "If you could help with the little electric motor, do you think you"—he glanced again at the old man—"could get *two* motors?"

"Sure, but why two?"

"I want him to see it working . . . before his sand runs out," Jason said. "We'll mount the Juggernaut on a box, and we'll use one of the motors, attached here, to get it started."

"I see—and the other one will be . . ."

"Out of sight," Jason said softly, warily. "And I don't want him"—he nodded at the old man—"ever to know anything about that."

Lexie and Maynard exchanged glances. Her eyes glistened. Amanda turned away, dabbing at her own eyes. Lexie tried to speak and couldn't.

Perrell sighed. "I think I see what you mean."

Jason was nodding. Soon he slept. He woke briefly a little later, looked up and saw Amanda Perrell's face above his own. She was spreading a blanket over him. He murmured something, frowning. She bent to hear him better, but his frown smoothed out and he slept again. She put her arm around his shoulders and pulled him close to her.

Craddock, sitting in the rear of the car with Van Meter, saw Biggers and Durkin talking animatedly with J. W. Whitlock, whose battered face was red and angry. They were sitting on some crates next to the Stanley, and they too had managed to pick up a bottle in *Healy*—it was tequila—and they were passing it back and forth. Van Meter had fallen asleep over his typewriter. Craddock slipped the jug of martinis out from under Van Meter's arm and stepped out to join the others. Perrell and Maynard and Costello had now joined them, too.

Craddock was just in time to see J. W. snarl at Biggers, "It hadda be you! I *seen* you, goddammit! You busted my jaw with a sap!"

Biggers said, "Dammit, I'm telling you again, I never used a sap in my life! And I know it wasn't the Durker, because him and me left Kee's place together."

Something rolled over in Craddock's memory, fell into place—*Kee's place*. . . . He saw them all at the pool table that night, the players and the watchers . . . sure, saw them back in the can, too, the little rancher laughing and saying to J. W., *a sockful of diamonds, right*?, and next to him this other guy, a drifter, with a face, what? Yes, reptilian, like a snapping turtle's, the more so at that sidelong angle, and he was looking J. W. up and down.

Craddock said, "The wild card! I always figured it was J. W. started all this, but the real wild card was the guy who clipped him! The person from Porlock."

"What the hell does that mean?" Biggers growled.

"It means, in a story, *deus ex machina*, a wild card, someone put into the action just to make the story move—otherwise he doesn't belong there. He's like a catalyst in chemistry."

"Who's the summabitch from Porlock!" J. W. said. "I've got something t' settle with that bassard."

"A poet named Coleridge was writing a terrific poem—this was a hundred years ago—he wakes up from an opium dream, see? . . . and the poem is complete and perfect in his mind, and he's writing it all down as fast as he can when a guy stops at the gate to ask directions." Craddock, enjoying himself, went on, "He gets back to his desk and the poem is gone, totally. Blooey! A random act by some guy nobody ever heard of—don't you see? That's how wars get started! A random act of violence—some sorehead shoots an archduke, and pretty soon ten million men are killing one another!"

"That don't tell me who busted m'jaw!" J. W. said.

"That night at Kee's, who was there? We were, all of us. Who else? The Kees were doing their figures at a table. There was a rancher—that little guy, Shorty Blaine, from Sonoita, just watching—and there was one other guy, a drifter, I guess, who was watching, too, and I remember how his ears pricked up when you were all talking about that sockful of diamonds from Vega's packhorse. And I remember how he was looking at J. W. back there in the can at Kee's. Sizing him up, right? And the guy was built something like Biggers."

"Summabitch from Porlock?" J. W. breathed. "Hadda be him—I 'member'm now." J. W. took a pull on the tequila bottle. His face contorted in a sly twisted grin, his wired teeth glinting. "You boys bit down on it, too, don' tell me different!" He began to laugh. Pain drove the laugh away. He put a hand to his jaw and took a deep breath—reached again for the tequila. He waved the bottle at Craddock, his voice slurred now by both tequila and the rat's nest of wires in his mouth. "Was *you* gimme the idea, Craddock. Got me started. You . . . made a believer outa the redhead. Biggers, too."

"Level with us, J. W.," Durkin blurted. "With *me*, goddammit! I seen you with Vega's packhorse. What did you do with the sumbitch? You owe me that much!"

"Don' owe you damn thing," J. W. said smugly. Yet the tequila was working on him. Jaw felt better. He took another slug. "'S a long time ago, right? Hell of a lot of noise . . ." He had the look of a man whose gaze was turning inward upon himself, as if to pin down and capture the fleeting and vagrant impressions of that hectic battle. His nostrils flared. He was smelling gunsmoke, hearing shouts, crazed screams of horses.

"Machine guns . . . that was it. When we go for the train . . . and I hear machine guns open up, thass when I resign from Legion. Betcherass. Screw Vega. And sure I'm right there with the goddam packhorse—always was, any fight or even skirmish . . . got his lead rope and skinned out . . . up little draw . . . brushy . . . horses crazy. . . ." His eyes peered at them through the haze of memory, roving, not focused. "Broke out on top, see, all rough ground, packhorse bucking . . . got a bullet burn acrost his rump . . . goddam pack slips under his belly . . . he's kick'n sumbitch to *pieces*! Stuff spills out . . . he gets a hind foot caught and throws 's self!"

Tears of anguish brimmed in J. W.'s eyes. He rocked, cuddling the tequila bottle. "I roll off m' horse . . . I'm down there with the packhorse . . . all Vega's *junk* . . . his goddam *candlesticks*, f' Chrissakes? I'm digging through all this shit, try'n' find, dammit, *something*!"

Durkin interrupted, a hoarse whisper. "You said there was a fuckin *sockful* of diamonds!"

J. W. reared back, outraged. He pointed the tequila bottle at Craddock. "*He said it, asshole!* I never said it! You bit for it, both . . . you." Craddock at that moment caught Maynard's eye—allowed one eyelid to droop in a gleeful wink.

"Didn't you get *nothing*? Not a damn thing?" Durkin too was almost in tears.

"By now there are a dozen *federales* on the rim of the draw, shooting at me . . . running . . . I grab this one thing . . . 's Vega's silver flask . . . you 'member, the one he always puts out next to his goddam candlesticks, whenever we camp?"

"But there was saddlebags full of gold coins!" Durkin insisted.

"If there was, the fuckin horse is on top of it," J. W. moaned. "All I could grab was the stupid flask—I'm in a shooting gallery, f' Chrissake! I'm trying . . . get on m'horse . . . sumbitch is bucking . . . and that's how I get outa there, hangin on saddle, half on, half off . . . I get one look at the *federales* . . . crazy bastards are down in the dirt fighting over Vega's fuckin candlesticks!"

J. W. sighed and wagged his head, took another jolt of tequila. "Rest of it, jussaway I told you. I get to Guaymas . . . there's boat there . . . Peruvian. Captain, damn him, he wants money, gold. I give him the flask."

"You mean, that's *all*?" cried Durkin.

"Not quite. We're coming in to port . . . Panama, see? Captain calls me in 's cabin, pours me a drink. Pulls Vega's flask outa drawer—he's got this shit-eating grin on 's face. He takes pair of . . . dividers, you know, off 's chart table . . . sticks 'em inna flask, pulls out, what? End of piece of cloth, silk . . . cloth keeps coming, keeps coming . . . and then the sumbitch tips up . . . flask and dumps these fuckin diamonds inna coffee cup! Vega has stashed the diamonds inna flask, with this silk hanky wadded up on em!" J. W.'s eyelids fluttered; tears streamed down his cheeks. "So we're in port in Panama . . . one hour later . . . *Sumbitch throws me off the boat!*"

Anguish spilling out, J. W. rocked back and forth. Horror and outrage were mingled on Durkin's face as he looked from one face to another, as if to find sympathy, a breath of hope for the lost treasure. He lifted his clenched fists over his head with a strangled cry. *"Shee-it!"* he bleated.

Costello tipped his head back and laughed aloud. He and Jack Perrell turned to each other and shook hands, laughing.

Biggers retained his composure, his expression approximating that of an anvil. "So," he rumbled, "no one got a damn thing out of it."

Craddock cackled suddenly, rubbed his hands together, and then took a hefty jolt from the jug of martinis. "Hell they didn't!" he cried, winking again at Maynard. "I got the story!"

33

WOODIE CRADDOCK covered the story for the *Courier*. For the news desk he wrote a two-column straightforward factual account: Who? What? When? Where? and Why? A model of reporting in which no significant detail was left out.

And then he also wrote an editorial, which he ran in a four-column box at the bottom center of page one, the balance continued on the editorial page. It was headed *From the Editor's Desk*, and was titled A TIME FOR HEROES. He gave the law officers credit for diligent pursuit of their duties under trying, even confusing, conditions. He wrote that Captain Pope's armored unit had displayed dash and initiative in what was perceived to be a civil emergency. And then he subtly turned to "the rights, indeed the duties of citizens under duress. . . ." He quoted Plato; the two Toms, Jefferson and Paine; Abraham Lincoln; and Walt Whitman. He wrote of "the rolling thunder of a People's outrage," and he defined who "The People" were in such a way that no man, woman or child could read it and not feel his or her heart swell with pride to be a member of such a splendid and devoted citizenry. "This event," he wrote, "is a lesson in how brutish forces spawned in swirling clouds of misperception will conspire to subdue a free people. It is a parable of how we are thrust into the madness of war.

Above all, it demonstrates that when a free people are confused, deluded, threatened, betrayed, heroes will appear—sometimes lonely, unrecognized, even abused by that very populace. Let us salute our heroes."

The editorial drew stacks of letters standing in praise of heroism, though there was no general agreement as to the identities of the heroes in the now celebrated event, for some still spoke of "outlaw fugitives." Fistfights broke out in Kee's and other saloons over this question. Combat spread to Mrs. Tatum's parlor, where Othello Biggers earned his season's ticket quelling a battle royal by subduing a platoon of combatants. "Convent Street Knee-Deep in Gore" was the title of Craddock's follow-up piece.

One solidly dissenting letter appeared, in which the writer stated that Craddock's editorial was a blatant "Handbook for Revolution."

In New York, the reporter Van Meter wrote a feature article. His title was still ARMAGEDDON IN THE DESERT. A lead line popped into his mind, which he used gleefully: "Far on the ringing plains of windy Troy, a beleaguered hero named Hector fought off the invading Greeks." He used phrases like "the sinister forces of oppression," and "embattled democracy." Another idea sprang full-blown to mind (how he chortled, congratulating himself, for this day he had to admit it, he was writing like a demon!). He wrote, "This is a parable of how wars are started. . . ." Liking the idea, he enlarged upon it. Before he was through, he saw that he had used the word *sinister* three times. He substituted *hooded* and *dark*. This article was to earn for him a national newspaper award for the year 1923 and a contract as a syndicated columnist. It earned for him also a blistering letter from Woodfin Craddock, who suggested that Van Meter was "worse than a common thief, because you have purloined *ideas*—more precious by far than jewels."

* * *

Maynard ordered a new propeller for the Jenny from San Diego, and it arrived two days later by Southern Pacific freight. That first weekend, he and Lexie, Jack and Amanda Perrell, and Jason went back out in the desert in the Stanley Mountain Wagon with the new propeller roped aboard.

The Jenny was just as they had left it, perched awkwardly on its nose. Car tracks and footprints showed that many people from the *Healy* Bend cavalcade had stopped to look at it. They pulled the tail down and Maynard tied tail and wings down to picket pins. He and Perrell removed the shattered prop and bolted the new one in place on the hub, and then they all got back into the Stanley and drove on to the mountain. They left the Stanley on the lizard's tail and walked up to the old man's claim, The Honest Citizen. It was sunny and warm, and a breeze made a moaning sound in the pinnacles.

Everything on the mountain was just as they had left it,

except that Luther Hightower's men had removed the dynamite. The grub box was there, with a few cans of peaches and Eagle Brand among other things, and Jason found the Dutch oven. Perrell unwired the springpole to take back with them, and in the clutter on the truck he found a Stinger, one that had not had dynamite taped to it. He told his wife, "I think I'll hang these up in the shop."

She seemed surprised. "Why?"

"Form follows function. It's pure design, like a windmill."

She laughed and kissed him. "If you say so."

There was nothing they could do with the Ford. "Someday, if you want," Perrell told Jason, "we could come and get it and haul it out of here, but it would be a lot easier, if you want a Model T, just to pick one up in town and fix it up the way you want."

Jason said he would think about that. Lexie opened her folding camera and took a picture of him wearing his *kepi* and standing next to the tent pole with its frayed banner fluttering out in the breeze, showing the faded lettering, THE HONEST CITIZEN. And then Maynard boosted him up the pole so he could retrieve the banner. He folded it carefully and tucked it inside his jacket.

They walked back down to the Stanley and drove the thirty miles back to the Jenny and made camp. Perrell pitched a tent for the ladies and the men spread their bedrolls in the open. Amanda had brought along a kettle of chili and the fixings for a salad. Jason made biscuits in the Dutch oven to go with the chili and, later, made peach cobbler, which they ate steaming hot with Eagle Brand poured over it.

After supper, Maynard and Lexie went for a walk. There was enough moon to make the desert bright. "You're preoccupied again," Maynard said. "Things haven't been the same between us since we stopped sleeping together."

She laughed. "Do you have to get back to that?"

"Yes, we do."

"I think I told you, I've got my life, you know, in order. I'm not going to mess it up again."

"You're like a miser—you're keeping all your money in the bank. Why not spend a little?"

"Go to bed with you, is that what you mean?"

"There's more to it than that, but that will do for a start." When she didn't answer, he said, "I guess I should tell you that Jack Perrell has put me in touch with some people on the coast, something to do with building airplanes. As soon as I get the Jenny in shape, I'm going over to talk to them. There . . . just isn't enough flying to do here, unless I go back to running booze." He laughed.

"Does it have to be flying?"

"Maybe not, but it has to be airplanes, one way or another. They're all I know. These people are planning to build an airplane with a closed cabin, for carrying passengers. I'd like to be in on that."

Later, in her blankets in the tent, Lexie talked to Amanda. She said, "I don't want my life to be a series of random accidents, like the things that have happened in my family. I want to be in control. I want to keep things in order. Does that sound crazy?"

Amanda said, "Say you're a juggler. You get ten oranges in the air at once. That's great juggling. Everything in perfect order, right? But what happens when you want to stop or change the pattern? Can you catch all ten oranges, or do you splatter a few on the floor?"

"I give up—what's the message?"

Amanda laughed merrily. "I don't know for sure, but you're going to drop a few. That's certain. Just when you least expect it. Look at me, now. I have a husband I'm crazy about. People buy my paintings. I have a ranch, money enough, but this year I'm turning forty and I'm . . . *desperate*."

"You? I can't believe that."

"It isn't just turning forty. It's turning forty without the baby we lost." She hesitated. "That's why I'm going to ask you if you will consider . . . just give it some thought . . . letting Jason come to live with us."

"I couldn't!"

"You could be his sister, you know. Not to say you couldn't be his mother too, but we're the right age for him, now. And we're settled."

"I'm settled, too."

"No, you're not. Not yet. All those oranges up in the air."

Lexie smiled. "Are you saying I'm about to splatter one of my oranges on the floor?"

"I'm saying, think about it. I'm short of oranges, myself. And now I think we've stretched that figure of speech about as far as it can go. Let's get some sleep."

Jason worked on the Juggernaut in Jack Perrell's shop every day after school. Perrell gave him a bicycle so he could go back and forth from school to shop to Lexie's house. Most days he stopped for a few minutes at Marietta's to visit with Hector before going on. Maynard and Perrell helped him with the design of the Juggernaut's brake and the mounting of the two motors, but Jason did almost all of the actual work. A few days after he started, Maynard and Lexie came by to take him to dinner. Jason cleaned up his workbench, put the tools away and washed up. He left the Juggernaut sitting out on the bench.

"Is it safe to leave the Juggernaut in plain sight that way?" Maynard said.

A slight smile worked at Jason's lips. "I think the awl companies have called off their agents, don't you?"

In the restaurant, while the waiter was taking Lexie's order, Maynard said to Jason, "How about you order for me too?" Jason ordered two hot roast-beef sandwiches, with mashed potatoes, dish of peas and two glasses of milk. Peach cobbler for dessert, if they had it.

While they were eating, Lexie said, "Jason, you know of course that your dad has gone to Dallas—says there's a deal there that can't wait."

"He told me," Jason said. "He said he thought I was better off the way things are, for now, anyway."

"Yes, well, Amanda Perrell has asked me if there is a possibility that you would go and live with them."

Jason kept his eyes on his food, a suggestion of dread in his face. After a moment, he said in a dry, husky voice, "Would I still get to see you?"

"Of course. You don't have to do it, understand—I'm not sure at all that I want you to, even. They're both very fond of you, though. You can take as long as you want to think about it."

"Think of it," Maynard said, "as a mission. You're the only man we can send. Your orders are to infiltrate, learn everything there is to know about their operation."

Jason took another bite of his roast beef, thinking it through. He looked at Maynard, then Lexie, his slow, grave smile working at his lips. "Javelina," he said.

Later, while Jason was intent on a large helping of peach cobbler, Maynard said to Lexie, "Excuse my saying so, but you seem, shall I say, a trifle distant."

Lexie smiled. "Maybe preoccupied is more like it. I'm trying to come up with some way to raise money. Marietta told me today that her house needs some substantial contributions if it's going to stay open. Eventually it will need a capital fund to draw income. Meanwhile, anything, just to keep going."

"Does it matter to you where the money comes from?"

Her smile returned. "I think I can guess what you're driving at, but why do you ask?"

"Because it seems to matter to you where *my* money comes from—I wonder if the same rules apply on money for Marietta."

"Not at all. In fact, I think we could accept money from the devil himself, for Marietta."

"Frankly, that's just what I had in mind," Maynard said.

* * *

The next morning, Maynard was cleaning up the wreckage of the Dragonfly in his hangar when Othello Biggers walked in. Maynard reached for the stout ash control stick and put it within easy reach.

"Speak of the devil," he said.

"At ease, ace." Biggers put his hands out, palms forward. "I unnerstand you wanted to see me." He was wearing his dark suit with razor creases, a wine-colored silk tie, pearl gray hat and gray spats over his burnished shoes. His face bore numerous nicks and scratches and a couple of pieces of adhesive tape. His eyes flicked, taking note of the destruction. He made a slight grimace. "I done that, right?"

"In about thirty seconds. Maybe less. You were—there's only one word—*berserk*."

Biggers stiffened. His eyes narrowed. "What the hell does that mean?"

"Old-time warriors who worked themselves into a rage. They howled and bit their shields. They were called *berserkers*."

"No shit?" Biggers relaxed. "I thought maybe it was something snotty, like once some son of a bitch told me I was named after a nigger."

"That could have been a mistake," Maynard said, allowing himself a slight smile.

"It sure as hell was, for him." Biggers paused. "Was he, you know—was Othello a nigger?"

"He was a Moor—from Morocco, see? North Africa. So he had to be a little dark, I would say . . . at least not lily-white. But he was a great soldier in the service of Venice. The greatest."

"I'll be damned," Biggers said, pleased. "I can live with that. My mom saw my name on a theayter marquee the week before I was born—she thought it sounded elegant. Look, tell me about the old man. Him and the kid."

"Why?" It was Maynard's turn to bristle a little.

"Because, goddammit, I know a first-class fighting man when I see one. Talk about *soldier*! The kid, too."

"They're both okay. There are about six old ladies fussing over the old gent." Maynard told him about Marietta and her house and the old people.

"Sounds great," Biggers said. His eyes swept the wreckage of the Dragonfly again. "I guess you want me to pay for this, right?"

"We can work something out if you're agreeable," Maynard said, "but what I really need is something else entirely."

"Shoot," Biggers growled.

"Marietta's place needs money. I've got a few dozen bottles of French cognac stashed away—you could get me a good price for it, couldn't you? I'm pretty much out of the business now, and anyway, your contacts are better than mine."

"I can get you a hunnerd fifty a jug," Biggers said.

Maynard's eyebrows lifted. "I thought seventy, seventy-five was tops."

"The price has just went up," Biggers said. "*Quantum sufficit.*"

"You lost me."

"As much as suffices."

34

ONE SATURDAY in early spring, Jason took the Juggernaut to Marietta's to show it to Hector Callard. Jack Perrell and Amanda drove Jason there in her splendidly restored Thomas Flyer, Amanda's birthday gift from her husband. Maynard flew in from the coast that morning, and Lexie met him at the airport and brought him to Marietta's in her Durant Star. Othello Biggers came by himself in a new Essex. Woodie Craddock came with Costello. The Farneys were there, as well.

The doll Sibbie sat on a cushion in a child's tall high chair. Maynard stopped to look at Sibbie, who was wearing new striped stockings and a new dress. Lexie touched his sleeve. She kept her eyes on the doll, a tremulous, uncertain smile on her lips, as if she had made a decision and wasn't sure how it would go.

"Will you have time to take me out to the old Atascadero stage station? I want to go back to the place where we found Sibbie."

"Sure I will, but I thought you finished that story."

Lexie wrenched her eyes away from Sibbie. She reached up and touched his cheek. "No. Only the first part. There's a lot more to come."

Maynard leaned close. His lips brushed her forehead. "You

realize, don't you," he said, "that if we go there, I'll be almost certain to get stuck again?"

She laughed. "Unavoidable, I would think. And this time you might remember to bring the coffeepot, all right?" She realized suddenly that Craddock was watching them from across the room. Seeing her eyes upon him, he approached them, frowning. Lexie caught his hand and kissed his cheek. "I guess you can tell—about Maynard and me?"

He gave them a wintry smile. "My dear girl, I could tell that a long time ago. But did you see"—his frown returned as he pulled a folded New York *World* clipping from his pocket—"what happened to that damned fool Van Meter? The bastard *stole* my story, and the Press Club has given him a silver plaque!"

Jason had set up the Juggernaut on a table in the sun parlor and had an electric cord plugged into a receptacle. He went to Hector's room and escorted him down. Altogether, there were twelve old people there, including three other gentlemen. Hector was barbered and shaved, wearing a blue suit. To Maynard, he seemed much smaller than the tall old buzzard who had accosted him with a shotgun—or perhaps Jason was taller. And the old man was a little vague when Maynard shook hands with him, as if he wasn't quite sure who Maynard was.

When they were seated, Jason showed the old man how he had mounted the Juggernaut on a sturdy oak base, with dovetailed corners—showed him a little hesitantly, as if apologizing for altering his original design, "It needs a place for the little motor, and the weight of the box helps to keep it from just flying right on out the window, once it gets going."

"It's all in your hands, young sir," Hector Callard whispered graciously, smiling and nodding, his hands before him, supported on a stick. The other old people smiled and nodded as well. Sunlight streamed in through tall windows, backlighting, setting clouds of white hair aglow. The scent of tea, baked apples, cinnamon toast and lavender sachet was in the air.

Jason touched a switch on the side of the box. The small electric motor connected to the Juggernaut hummed. The flywheel began to turn. Momentum arms, each in turn, reached the top and flipped forward with a little click, blurring them as the speed increased, the clicks merging with the hum until the flywheel was a glistening golden disc within the larger orbit of the momentum arms.

Jason held up a hand, like a magician about to pull a card out of the air, and then disengaged the electric motor by sliding it back from the Juggernaut on a track. He flipped a switch on the motor, which wound down and stopped. But the Juggernaut continued to spin. Its hum filled the room. *Oummmm-mm,* it sang.

"Power!" Hector Callard whispered. "Unlimited power. Now she belongs to the People." He turned and gestured to the old folks that it belonged to them. They were the People. It's for your trolleys," Hector said, "your trolleys and trains and dray wagons. *Power!"* They smiled and nodded and gazed fixedly at the whirring Juggernaut, white heads glowing in the streaming sunlight. "It will run the dray wagons," one old lady said loudly to her companion, who was hard of hearing. Pleased, the other lady nodded and smiled.

Jason demonstrated the brake, slowing it somewhat, and then let it speed up again, a silken blur of motion. . . . Of *power.* And then at last, Jason applied the brake, held the lever down until the Juggernaut clicked to a stop. No one saw him switch off the second motor, the one inside the box. Applause and excited murmuring erupted from guests and old people alike.

Othello Biggers poured a little tot of fine French brandy for those who wanted it, and hardly anyone refused. Holding his glass and a wedge of cinnamon toast, he said to Hector Callard, "That was a bang-up job you and the boy done."

"Yes," the old man said, "it's bully, but to tell the truth, I'm glad it's out of my hands now, so's I can attend to other matters. I'm just damn near wore out from work."

"What kind of work?" Biggers said.

"There's a carload of iron settin before my shop this minute, a-waitin for me to get to it—I've contracted to make chain for the log booms on the river. Links this big." He showed Biggers with his two hands how big the links were.

Perrell, overhearing, said, "Now that's my kind of work. My dad was a blacksmith."

The old man looked him up and down, measuring. "Can ye forge-weld?"

"Sure I can," said Perrell.

"Then look me up in the spring," the old man said, "for that's when I'll be hiring. Top wages for top men."

Biggers was frowning. He said to Jason, "What river? What logs?"

"He's in Oregon," Jason said, "and it's a long time ago."

"Ah-h," said the county man. "I see."

They buried him in uniform, blue blouse with sergeant's stripes on the sleeves, trousers with the yellow stripes of the United States Cavalry, all made by the ladies at Marietta's. The pattern had come from Marietta's attic, where she had gone with Lexie and found there in a steamer trunk the uniform once worn by her first husband, Lucian.

That morning, the open casket was on view at Marietta's, in the parlor. Maynard and Biggers had arranged with the commanding officer of the National Guard unit for a six-man detail to act as honor guard. "No kids," Biggers told the colonel. "I want veterans for this."

Lexie and Jason had entered and stood next to the casket. Marietta took a red rose from a cut-glass vase and approached them. While they watched, she tucked the stem of the rose into his blouse. With a ghost of a smile, she said, "I gave Lucian a rose to take with him, too."

Maynard, who was wearing his old uniform, was at the door looking out when a very shiny new Essex drew up in front. He said, "Lexie, come and take a look at this!" She hurried to the door, Jason beside her, and saw Othello Biggers and Red Durkin marching up the walk between the giant palms. Biggers wore a smartly creased dress uniform with the chevrons of a master sergeant, beribboned medals chinking on his chest. Durkin wore an ill-fitting olive drab private's uniform, wrinkled and moth-eaten, with no medals.

"They've got nerve! Bringing that Durkin here is . . . disgusting!" Lexie blazed softly. She moved to stand in the open doorway, blocking it. Biggers came to a halt directly before her, hands down the seams of his trousers, eyes staring straight ahead over her shoulder. Durkin slouched uneasily behind him.

"If you please, ma'am," Biggers growled. His face was very pale.

Lexie looked uncertainly at Maynard, who nodded. She stepped aside and Biggers entered, followed by Durkin. They marched to the casket, where Biggers stood looking down at the old man for some time. Maynard came and stood next to him. "What are you thinking?" he said.

"I'll tell you this," Biggers said, "I know a soldier when I see one." He unpinned the Silver Star from his own blouse, bent down and pinned it onto Hector Callard's blouse, then stood to attention and saluted.

Later, at the graveside, Woodie Craddock spoke a few words. He said, "I see we are an unlikely company here, those of us who have come to say good-bye to this gentleman. There aren't many of us, for he has outlived his own time; but we are here because we share a single thought: we know that when we speak of this gentleman, this soldier, we speak of honor . . . and of heroes."

Sergeant Biggers brought the honor guard to attention and directed them in the firing of the salute. A bugler blew "Taps." Maynard and Biggers and the other men in uniform, including Craddock, saluted. Jason, wearing Maynard's red *kepi,* saluted also—holding his hand palm out, in the manner of the French Foreign Legion. After that he took his *kepi* off and never wore it again.

But he never threw it away, either.

Non omnis moriar
[Lat.] I shall not wholly die.